Comprehending Care

Comprehending Care

Problems and Possibilities in
The Ethics of Care

Tove Pettersen

LEXINGTON BOOKS

A DIVISION OF
ROWMAN & LITTLEFIELD PUBLISHERS, INC.
Lanham • Boulder • New York • Toronto • Plymouth, UK

LEXINGTON BOOKS

A division of Rowman & Littlefield Publishers, Inc.
A wholly owned subsidiary of The Rowman & Littlefield Publishing Group, Inc.
4501 Forbes Boulevard, Suite 200
Lanham, MD 20706

Estover Road
Plymouth PL6 7PY
United Kingdom

British Library Cataloguing in Publication Information Available

Library of Congress Cataloging-in-Publication Data

Pettersen, Tove, 1973–
  Comprehending care : problems and possibilities in the ethics of care / Tove Pettersen.
    p. cm.
  Includes bibliographical references and index.
  ISBN-13: 978-0-7391-2615-8 (cloth : alk. paper)
  ISBN-10: 0-7391-2615-6 (cloth : alk. paper)
  ISBN-13: 978-0-7391-2616-5 (pbk. : alk. paper)
  ISBN-10: 0-7391-2616-4 (pbk. : alk. paper)
  1. Women—Psychology. 2. Women—Mental health. 3. Women—Care of. 4. Moral
development. 5. Developmental psychology. 6. Feminist psychology. 7. Gilligan,
Carol, 1936—Criticism and interpretation. I. Title.
  HQ1206.P439 2008
  177'.7—dc22
                                                            2007045645
Printed in the United States of America

∞™ The paper used in this publication meets the minimum requirements of
American National Standard for Information Sciences—Permanence of Paper
for Printed Library Materials, ANSI/NISO Z39.48-1992.

Contents

Acknowledgments		vii
Introduction		ix
Chapter 1	The Perspective of Care	1
Chapter 2	Gender Issues and Criticism	17
Chapter 3	Normative Foundations and Formal Features	31
Chapter 4	Care, Cognition, and Emotions	51
Chapter 5	Care and Traditional Moral Theory	65
Chapter 6	Care and Justice	85
Chapter 7	Distributing Mature Care	113
Chapter 8	Conditional Care	135
Chapter 9	Why Care? Ethical Justification of Thick Care	151
Chapter 10	The Circles of Care	171
Bibliography		185
Index		197

~

Acknowledgments

I am grateful to The University of Oslo, in particular their initiatives to promote gender equality, for granting me a free term to complete this book. I would also like to thank The Research Council of Norway for their financial support. Also, without the help, support and encouragements of many people this book would never have been finished. In particular I would like to thank Thomas Pogge, Arne Johan Vetlesen, Else Wiestad, Per Ariansen, Olav Gjelsvik, Inga Bostad, Joan Tronto, Chris Saunders, Grethe Netland, and Bjørn Ramberg. They have all given wise advice on various occasions. Special thanks to my family: My grandmother Thora and my grandfather Noralv, my parents Marit and Jan Kjell, and my children Viktor and Vilde.

Oslo, November 2007
Tove Pettersen

~

Introduction

In this book the ethics of care is subjected to a moral–philosophical examination. I aim to extract the philosophical foundation of this ethics, and probe its possible implications for moral (and political) theories of a more traditional stamp. In *Comprehending Care* I attempt to explore some of the normative problems and possibilities of the ethics of care, and to demonstrate its remarkable progress during less than three decades. The point of departure is the ethics of care as advanced by the moral psychologist Carol Gilligan in her book *In a Different Voice* from 1982.

Why do I find that Gilligan's twenty–five year old book deserves a revisit when aiming to investigate the philosophical foundation of the ethics of care? First, because of the connection I believe obtains between moral psychology and moral philosophy. As moral theories are concerned with justifying what morally ought to be done, the moral philosopher needs to attend to research on human capacities and development if recommendations found therein concerning how we should live our lives are to be taken seriously. Gilligan listened to the experiences, concerns and deliberations and observed the development of ordinary women facing real life challenges. On the basis of what she heard, she articulated a moral perspective hitherto ignored by traditional ethics and moral philosophy. Her perspective is not a full–blown ethical theory.[1] She never intended for it to be either. Her subject is psychology—more precisely moral developmental psychology—not moral philosophy. Her works are not written in the traditional style of academic moral philosophy; empirical findings alternate with interpretation and reflection, references to literature, poetics, myths and metaphors. As philosophers we should not allow ourselves to ignore her texts simply because they are not written in the traditional style of academic moral philosophy, nor because they defy certain philosophical distinctions. On the contrary, the absence of philosophical conventionality and the extraordinary amount of attention Gilligan's work has attracted, at least outside traditional academic philosophy, should rather inspire rigorous moral–philosophical scrutiny.

The second reason for returning to Gilligan is due to the fact that even if her research is an important source for the development of a modern ethics of care, the philosophical implications rendered in her works are still not fully explored. In addition to her own discipline, Gilligan challenged traditional moral philosophy and ethics. She holds that the dominant ethical theories, with their gender–blindness and emphasis on rights and justice, fail to see how care is an indispensable part of moral life. This failure weakens their credibility as adequate, universal ethical theories. Applying the perspective of an ethics of care to the challenge of moral life would, according to Gilligan, challenge the authority of the existing normative theories and result in a new mapping of the moral domain. Traditional moral philosophy, in my view, has failed to take up the challenge of Gilligan's findings and claims.[2] Mainstream moral discussions continue to ignore the importance of care, and to prolong centuries of insensitivity toward gender.

Within feminist ethics, however, the ethics of care have been discussed, developed, refined and applied in multiple ways. Recently, many care ethicists' focus has been on the political implication of the ethics of care in relation to social politics as well as to global ethical challenges. The ethics of care has important contribution to offer these fields; it brings ethical aspects otherwise neglected to the forefront of our attention, and suggests new and promising perspectives on well known and unresolved ethical issues. On the public and global arena, the ethics of care now encounter traditional theories such as utilitarianism, and theories based on rights and justice. These theories have been refined and sustained by philosophers for more than two hundreds years, while the ethics of care only for less than three decades. In order to further develop the political implication of the ethics of care, as well as to obtain its rightful place among other ethical theories, the endeavor of sustaining and developing the ethics of care with a sound philosophical fundament must continue.

In my opinion, there is still a need for a philosophically more cogent depiction of the ethics of care. In particular, there is a need to shed a more telling light on the ethics of care within a particular subfield of moral philosophy, namely moral theory. The formal structure of the ethics of care, its philosophical content, implicit premises, the soundness of its arguments and its significance for more traditional moral theory are far from exhausted. For instance, how does one get from *ought* to *is* in this ethics of care? What is the scope of this theory? Does it jeopardize a broader moral commitment? Is it a teleological or a deontological theory—or something else? Is it reasonable to assert, as Gilligan herself does, that the ethics of care challenges the authority of existing normative theories?[3] Answers to such questions are sought through an exegesis of Gilligan's texts, as well as discussed in relation to other care ethicists such as Nel Nodding, Joan Tronto, Virginia Held and Fiona Robinson and traditional ethical theories such as deontology, utilitarianism and virtue ethics.

Let me enlarge on my approach to Gilligan. I revisit the works of Gilligan on three levels: (1) a textual analysis of Gilligan's works; (2) a constructive approach; and (3) an evaluative discussion. Some *methodological reflections* on this tripartite approach are necessary. Level (1), the textual analysis, is inspired by the philosophical hermeneutics of Hans–Georg Gadamer, as presented in *Truth and Method* (1960). I examine the texts of Gilligan in order to suggest a philosophically consistent interpretation of the ethics of care. My interpretations are also conditioned by my own horizon of course—which means obviously that others might interpret these texts differently. As Gilligan did not follow up on the normative suggestion put forward in the 1980s, her later psychological works are relevant to the current interpretation. Her ethics of care evolved from elements of her psychological theories and empirical research, which, in her later work, she develops and refines.[4]

Now, even if her complete output is taken into consideration, her normative theory is far from fully developed: her suggestions are often not underpinned by arguments, central concepts are not defined, the links between her suggestions are often inexplicit, and their implications not fully pursued. Profiting from her psychological research, she points to apparent inadequacies of traditional moral theories and indicates remedial steps. This is what calls for strategy (2), the second level of my methodological approach. In order to make her normative theory clearer, I set out arguments and presuppositions on which her normative suggestions could be founded, as well as elaborate on possible implications. Wolfgang Iser's *The Act of Reading: A Theory of Aesthetic Response* (1979) has inspired this approach. Iser argues that a text always contains "blanks" which only the reader can fill through an act of interpretation. The reader may resolve contradictions between various viewpoints that emerge from the text, or fill the "gaps" between the viewpoints by taking the text into her own consciousness and making it her own experience. Particularly relevant to my "own consciousness" is feminist philosophy. I would not have found a way of "filling the gaps" without the texts of Simone de Beauvoir, Sandra Harding, Susan Okin, Annette Baier, Seyla Benhabib, Margaret Urban Walker, Joan Tronto, Virginia Held and others that populate my particular "horizon". Nor would I have been able to do without the virtue ethics of Aristotle, or the theories of Julia Annas, Lawrence Blum, Robert Goodin, John Rawls and Thomas Pogge. To separate the two levels of interpretation, I have made a terminological distinction between "Gilligan's ethics of care" and "Gilligan's normative theory" on the one hand, which refer to level (1) and, a "Gilliganian ethics of care", on the other, which refers to level (2). The latter term indicates that I have added more to the theory than there is concrete textual evidence for. The Gilliganian ethics of care nevertheless represents a tentative understanding of this particular ethics of care, based on a charitable, but also critical, reading.

Level (3) in this methodological approach explores the contribution the ethics of care can make to other normative theories and moral theory. The answer will depend, among other things, on how one defines and understands what passes for ethical theory and, of course, moral theory. Since Gilligan challenges the current "moral paradigm", this constitutes a methodological impediment: using traditional criteria and definitions would be at odds with Gilligan's assignment, while abandoning them would treat her normative suggestions as an anti–theoretical approach—which they are not. I have tried to solve the methodological problem of evaluating Gilligan's contributions to ethical theories and moral theory, which occurs because she challenges traditional definitions and demarcations, by following a middle course. Some aspects of moral philosophy are considered open for revision while others are regarded as unalterable. I advance this particular ethics of care with the view that an ethical theory should be a consistent system of recommendations and/or requirements, based on and justified by reasonable arguments, but so that the abstract structures of certain categories and a system of classification and evaluation are left open for revision. I also take the view that moral philosophy cannot be disconnected from historical, cultural, and political factors, nor from what has been accomplished in other fields of study such as psychology, epistemology, or political theory. Submitting Gilligan's theory to a moral–philosophical reasoning it becomes evident why and how the ethics of care challenges traditional ethical theory and moral philosophy in several ways: It draws attention to inadequacies in traditional ethical thinking, and it reveals a neglected realm of moral values and practices. Also it contributes to conventional moral theory by revealing inexplicit assumptions, unforeseen implications and deficient moral categories. Gilligan's research lays the foundation for a conceptual moral framework which generates alternative ways of framing, as well as solving moral challenges.

Since theories, philosophical as much as psychological, originate in certain contexts, in the first chapter I provide the reader with some contextual information relevant to the ensuing philosophical discussion. I give an account of Gilligan's critique of Lawrence Kohlberg, and her "perspective of care and justice". The perspective of justice is the type of response she and her co–workers most frequently found in male informants, while the care perspective was more likely to be expressed by her female informants. Her psychological explanation for this divergence centers on early childhood experiences of attachment and detachment. I highlight therefore certain illuminating aspects of her psychological theory and empirical research. I also demonstrate how it is possible to extract from her work three distinct types of care, which is termed *selfish care, altruistic care* and *mature care.* These concepts, especially mature care where concern for self and others are balanced, will become central in my discussion on how to comprehend care, caring and how to advance an ethical theory based on care.

In Chapter 2 I go on to consider some of the criticisms towards Gilligan's work, and also the controversies it has stirred up, in particular with regard to gender. Not only does Gilligan postulate a statistically significant correlation between women and care, she takes her findings to the normative level, where she embraces the value of care, and gives it ethical relevance. In fact, it is the value she finds empirically correlated with women which she places at the core of her normative ethics of care. This praise of care is one of the causes of the intense debate among feminists, where some maintain that her ethics of care could bring an end to gender oppression, and others that it sustains and even reinforces traditional constraints. I present some feminist views on Gilligan's ethics of care, and enter the debate on whether it is to be considered a feminine or a feminist ethics. Also, I address how the correlation between gender and moral orientation is to be understood, and I discuss Gilligan's ambiguity on this issue and her way of applying the distinction between gender and sex.

The third chapter proceeds by elaborating how and why these empirical findings have normative relevance. I discuss the formal structure of the theory—its basic principles and requirements. Gilligan does not conflate the "is–ought" distinction I argue, and suggest a strategy for ethical justification which is related to what I term "the expanded principle of not hurting". The ethics of care addresses a particular type of harm caused by the nonattendance of care in relationships, and it is the prevention of harm that explains why care carries ethical relevance. The ethics of care is concerned with non–violence, in particular emotional and psychological non–violence, in relationship—a moral issue frequently underestimated or avoided all together in other moral theories. Drawing ethical attention to this neglected domain is one of the ethics of care's major contribution to moral philosophy.

In the fourth chapter I investigate the concept of care. In particular I focus on the role of emotion, cognition, co–feeling and moral autonomy. Care is often associated with emotion as opposed to rationality, but as will be discussed there is interplay between emotion, rationality and cognition. This complex interaction has implications for, among other things, the understanding of moral autonomy as well as for moral motivation. A refinement of traditional moral concepts and categories is required, a refinement which in turn disputes traditional ethical theories and moral theory.

In Chapter 5 I discuss the challenge of the ethics of care to the "traditional moral point of view", in particular it's questioning of the ontological and epistemological assumptions of mainstream theory. I show the difference between the anthropology on which the ethics of care rests, and deontological, liberal and utilitarian views of human life. The ethics of care advises against seeing people as atomistic, isolated and independent individuals. It engenders instead a particular awareness of human vulnerability and of our embeddedness in complex relational networks. This has several theoretical implications, among them how we perceive the relation between care and justice.

In Chapter 6, I discuss the conflict between care and justice. I criticize readings of Gilligan on this particular topic that posit an irreconcilable gap between care and justice in her theory, and suggest as an alternative interpretation a "third way", that relieves some of the antagonism. The concept of mature care is significant here as it concerns the ability to harmonize care of one–self with care of the other, to find the mean between selfishness and selflessness. The theory of care I advance then is not agapistic. It inhabits the mean. Mature care requires a particular epistemological capacity for perspective substitution—i.e. substituting the perspective of care for that of justice. The point, I assert, is not to choose between them, but to find a "third way". It is an approach that requires us to adopt elements inherent in the morality of care and of justice. However, not all conflicts between care and justice can or should be solved in this way. Nor is the point to fuse care and justice, as some philosophers have attempted. A complete fusion of the two would impede the valuable ability to shift between perspectives, a capacity most needed in the search for solutions to real life moral problems. Drawing attention to a way of handling real life problems is one of this theory's strengths. As we shall see later, this particular moral epistemology and ontology provides the ethics of care with theoretical recourses required for addressing ethical and political questions such as child custody, gay marriages, health politics as well as global matters in a novel and promising way.

In the seventh chapter, I consider to whom, and how, we are supposed to proportionate care. As the ethics of care focuses on relationship, I ask whom the carer is to regard being related to, and whom the recipients of her moral concerns are. I develop and apply the distinction between *thick* and *thin care*. Thick care is carried out towards those we have concrete and established relationships with, such as family and friends—our related others. Thin care is performed when there are no established connection between the carer and the cared for, and the carer possesses only generalized knowledge of the other. We shall also see that to some extent the ethics of care allows us to prioritize responsibility for the related others. This demarks the ethics of care from theories where the main focus is on our responsibility towards the generalized other as found in most versions of deontology and utilitarianism—and John Rawls' liberal theory too. It also sets the ethics of care from theories that underscores our responsibility for the concrete anonymous other as advanced by Knud Løstrup and Emmanuel Levinas. This does not mean that concern for remote and anonymous others, what I call *thin care*, are disregarded, only that these potential recipients of care do not necessarily trump when the carer has to prioritize how to distribute mature care. Mature care implies the ability to balance between different groups of potential recipients as well as between the interests of self and others. Hence, the concept of mature care defies those care theories based on an altruistic conception of care. I discuss these two comprehensions of care in relation to professional care–work.

As professional care often involves caring in asymmetric relationship I draw upon Aristotle's virtue of friendship, as Aristotle here explains how reciprocity in relationships is possible also when the parties appear to be unequal. From this discussion I make a distinction between *symmetric* and *asymmetric care*. Comprehending care as mature care allows also for asymmetric care, as the carer's maturity enables her to see, acknowledge and pay attention to variation when acting. Mature care includes a balancing between interests, hence it protects against paternalism as well as self–sacrifice.

In Chapter 8 I elaborate further on the implication of this comprehension of care. Moral responsibility is not equivalent to taking upon ourselves responsibility "for the naked face of the first individual to come along", to quote Levinas. Nor does moral responsibility first and foremost consist of commitments to obligation. Therefore, the story of the Good Samaritan cannot, contrary to what other care ethicists assert, function as a paradigmatic example for the ethics of care. Comprehending care as mature care also has implications for the way a carer reacts towards, say, the medias' exposing of the heartbreaking faith of a particular individual, as well as towards the idea of going beyond duty. The relational and material situation of the carer must also be taken into account. Now one could certainly ask if this focus on related others is a desirable feature of ethical theory. A theory that emphasizes its moral attention to one–self and related others might be seen as ethically daring as it might ignore the interests of those outside the carer's emotional neighborhood. I investigate, in the ninth chapter, whether it can be given an ethical justification. Some contemporary pros and cons of the matter are discussed. I show that the ethical attention paid to the related other can be understood not as transpiring from an inclination to privilege one's nearest and dearest at the expense of remote others, but from an awareness of a particular type of harm inflicted in relationships. Now, even if we deny the chauvinistic origin of concern for those near and dear to us, it is nonetheless important to avoid ethical parochialism. Drawing attention to the ethical significance of care in close relationships is one of Gilligan's significant contributions, but her ethics also contains the potential to be developed and extended further. In recent years, the scope of the ethics of care has expanded: From being considered an expression of women's voice in private matters, it has been developed and applied as an approach to social policy as well as global issues. Therefore, in the tenth chapter, I consider how some care ethicists—Joan Tronto, Virginia Held and Fiona Robinson in particular—have extended the ethics of care to include the remote others. I examine the arguments for making the ethics of care an approach not only for individuals with regard to private decisions, but also for politicians, organizations and governments. The fount of the political implications now entailed from the ethics of care is, I argue, built on the philosophical advancements inspired and achieved by listening to ordinary women's reasoning on actual moral challenges.

Notes

1. Since I do not claim that Gilligan's texts comprise a full–blown ethical theory, it might seem inappropriate to use the term "theory" of her thinking. "Thinking", "ethical suggestions", or "ideas" might appear more suitable. However, the selection of words here depends on what one takes as constituting "ethical theory". As Gilligan is concerned precisely to undermine "traditional ethical theory", her thinking differs in regard to content and formal structure from other ethical theories. Whether these differences are regarded as theoretical deficiencies, or as necessary to the task is a major concern of this study. If I were to start the discussion of Gilligan's writings by refusing to use the term "ethical theory", I would be drawing a conclusion in ad-

vance on this particular issue. I will therefore use the term "ethical theory". By asserting that it is not a "full–blown ethical theory", I mean that it contains a higher degree of unsolved problems and indistinctiveness than does many other ethical theories. See also Chapter 5 for a further discussion on moral and ethical theories.

2. One may distinguish between "moral" and "ethical", where the former refers to individual and collective moral beliefs and practices, the latter is considered an explicit, systematic philosophical reflection on moral beliefs and practices. As their applications is evaluative precisely in relation to some important issues to be discussed and analyzed in this study, e.g., Gilligan's reports and systematic treatment of certain moral beliefs and actions, I will not fully apply the distinction.

3. Interpretation of Gilligan's thinking from the early 1980s to the present has varied greatly. For instance, it is called a "feminist" ethics (Lovibond et al. 1992), a "feminine" ethic (Tong 1993); it is considered to be a particularistic theory expressed through virtues (O'Neill 1996:74); others hold that it can be understood in terms of principles (Kittay and Meyers 1989:11), or that it contains one universal principle which is qualitatively different from the principles in traditional ethics. It is also understood as a variant of utilitarianism (Kuhse 1997:136–137), as a challenge to deontology (Sedgwick 1990:177); a version of deontology (Miller 2005:160–180), a kind of virtue ethics (Pettersen 2004:205–231; Sander–Staudt 2006: 21–39) as bearing resemblance to Confucianism (Li 1994), critical theory and Christian agapism (Puka 1990:194). Some readers view Gilligan's approach to care as a response to personal dilemmas and assert that it is already subsumed or presupposed by general obligations of respect, fairness and contract (Kohlberg 1981:349–350). Others claim that care is of the first importance to moral philosophy (Blum 1993). It is asserted that neglecting the ethics of care will severely impede equality, freedom and fairness (Kittay 1997, Dalmiya 2002), while others have characterized her work as "politics dressed up as science" (Sommers 2000). Gilligan herself has not advanced the ethics of care she began to develop in her early works, but instead focused on psychology (Bernstein and Gilligan 1990; Gilligan, Lyons and Hanmer 1990a; Gilligan 1990b; Gilligan, Rogers and Tolman 1991; Brown and Gilligan 1992, Gilligan, Sullivan and Taylor 1995, Gilligan 2002).

4. Gilligan's works also show her evolution in relation to central topics, such as moral maturity, gender and relationships, and reflects the changes in the political, social and psychological thought in which her normative theory is embedded. For instance, while her writings in the late 1970s and 1980s bear signs of those decades' discussions of feminism, ethics and psychology in their primary focus on females and the concept of womanhood, her book, *The Birth of Pleasure. A new Map of Love* (2002) puts the emphasis on boys, men, and the concept of manhood. Summers article was first published in *The Atlantic Monthly* in May 2000, and then in June 2000 in *The War Against Boys: How Misguided Feminism Is Harming Our Young Men*, New York: Simon and Schuster.

CHAPTER ONE

~

The Perspective of Care

In 1982, Carol Gilligan published a study called *In a Different Voice: Psychological Theory and Women's Development*. In this book Gilligan exhibits that what had been missing by leaving girls and women out of research in developmental moral psychology and from ethics was a different idea of the self and a different ethical perspective (Gilligan 1993:208). Gilligan's book can be understood as an assault on male–centered learning in psychology in general, and the moral developmental psychology of her mentor Lawrence Kohlberg in particular. Kohlberg developed a hierarchical stage model that was meant to measure moral development and moral maturity. What fired Gilligan's interest was the fact that women tended to score consistently lower than men in Kohlberg's empirical studies of moral development. According to Kohlberg's model, women are simply less morally developed than men.

Gilligan rejected the insinuation that women were moral midgets and therefore initiated an independent research program. As a result of her findings, she argued that women were not inferior in either cognitive or moral development, but that they were *different*. Women's development basically involved a stronger *connectedness* with other people—as opposed to separation from them, and a focus on the value of care—rather than the value of justice, which prevails in men's development. Gilligan holds furthermore that because traditional theories of justice ignore and neglect the moral relevance of care their credibility as adequate, universal ethical theories is severely compromised. The perspective of care would, according to Gilligan,

1

change traditional moral reasoning, and enhance the authority of existing normative theories (Gilligan et al. 1988:x,v,155).

Gilligan's work has been praised and criticized. In particular, it attracted the attention of feminists, inspiring some while infuriating others. There are now a variety of feminist responses to Gilligan's ethics of care, and today it is practically impossible to address questions related to the ethics of care without referring or dealing with her claims. Before entering the philosophical discussion on the ethics of care, I will in this chapter present the relevant aspects of Gilligan's work.

In a Different Voice

In a Different Voice had a quite extraordinary impact. It was subsequently translated into 17 languages, sold approximately 800,000 copies, and has given rise to considerable controversy and interdisciplinary debate. Some years after its appearance, the philosopher Bill Puka said: "Giving how much is missing from Gilligan's original account of moral development it is remarkable that the Kohlberg–Gilligan debate is still taken seriously" (Puka 1990:199). The discussion is still raging. In 2000, Cristina Hoff Sommers published the article "The War Against Boys", where she claims that boys, not girls, are the second sex in American schools.[1] She asks how we came to believe in a picture of American boys and girls that is the opposite of the truth, and why that belief has been enshrined in law, encoded in governmental and school politics. Attempting to answer her own question, Sommers refers to what she calls one of the American academy's most celebrated women, namely Carol Gilligan, and her book In a Different Voice (Sommers 2000). Sommers' article provoked extensive correspondence, including a reply from Gilligan (2000). Another example of In a Different Voice's continuing ability to foment controversy is its use by a columnist in the December 2006 issue of Time Magazine to smear gay families and same–sex marriage. Gilligan, in an open letter, demanded an apology from the writer for misrepresenting her work, and that both he and his organization should desist from quoting her.[2] So despite Bill Puka's wonder, warranted or not, twenty–five years after its first appearance, Gilligan's work is still taken seriously, still debated, still acclaimed and still disapproved of. The psychologist Chuck Huff, for instance, says, "if there is such a thing as a current classic, this is one of them" (Huff 2002). Lawrence Hinman, professor of philosophy, presents Gilligan as a contributor of a new moral concept: "The Ethics of Care" (Hinman 1997), and professor of bioethics Warren Thomas Reich asserts that before Gilligan's book in 1982 an ethics of care was nonexistent (Reich 1995:319). As this influential book originates as a response to a particular tradition in developmental psychology, we shall proceed by tracing this back-ground.

Kohlberg's Position

In the 1960s and 1970s Lawrence Kohlberg, a moral psychologist at Harvard Graduate School of Education, was in the process of publishing the results of his research on moral development. Particularly relevant in this context is his *stage theory of moral development*, a revision and extension of Jean Piaget's theory on moral development, based on empirical and conceptual studies (Kohlberg 1981:xvii). In the early 1970s Carol Gilligan was working with Kohlberg as a research assistant, and although she found his arguments "very powerful", she was nevertheless critical to his position (Gilligan 1982:xvii–xviii). Many of Kohlberg's conclusions on moral judgments were based on hypothetical dilemmas, and when Gilligan started her disserta-tional research on moral reasoning with real–life dilemmas, what she found caused her to dispute the model presented by her mentor (Larrabee 1993:3–4). To appreciate her objections, a short account of Kohlberg's stage theory is needed.

Kohlberg's theory of moral development was based on extensive studies. He and his students interviewed children and adults on their responses to hy-pothetical moral dilemmas. Kohlberg postulated six stages in moral develop-ment (Kohlberg 1981; 1984; Colby and Kohlberg 1987; Kohlberg, Levine and Hewer 1983). The first two stages form, according to Kohlberg, the "pre–conventional stage and are mostly observed in children under 9 years old.[3] At *stage one* the right thing to do is to avoid breaking rules and inflict physical damage on persons and property. "Right" is defined as obedience to authorities, and the reason for doing right is the avoidance of punishment and the superior power of authority. Kohlberg terms the morality of this stage "heteronomous". He also considers what he terms the "socio–moral perspec-tive" of each stage. The socio–moral perspective at stage one appears through the agent's applications of an egocentric point of view, and characterized by not considering the interests of others or recognizing that they might differ from one's own. Actions are thought of as physical entities rather than re-flecting the psychological interests of others. The standpoint of authority is confused with one's own. *Stage two* embodies an attitude of simple exchange: "If you scratch my back, I'll scratch yours". Rights are understood as promot-ing one's own interests—and letting others do the same. Morality is "instru-mental". The reason for doing right is to serve one's own needs or interests, in addition to recognizing that others have their interests too. The socio–moral perspective is concrete and individualistic: The agent is aware that others have their interests to pursue, and that they might conflict with one's own.

Stages three and *four* constitute the "conventional stage", the stage, according to Kohlberg of most adolescents and adults in most societies. *Stage three* is characterized by the "good boy/nice girl" orientation. This morality is termed "interpersonally normative morality". The right thing to do is to live up to what is expected of you, and the reason for doing right is the need to be a good person in own eyes as well as in others. Caring for the other, belief in the Golden Rule and the desire to maintain rules and authority that support "good behavior" may also be reasons for acting right. The socio–moral perspective is that of the individual–in–relationships, and the concern is for shared feelings. Expectations and agreements take primacy over individual interests. *Stage four* is characterized by a "law and order" attitude, a "social system morality". The right thing to do is to fulfill duties which you have accepted, and to uphold laws—except in extreme situations. The reason for doing right lies in the maintenance of social order and welfare of a group or society. The agent is able to differentiate between a societal point of view and interpersonal agreements and motives.

The highest stage in Kohlberg's theory on moral development, named the "post–conventional stage", covers *stages five* and *six*. This stage is reached only by a minority of adults, and usually only after the age of 20–25. Kohlberg calls the morality of *stage five* "Human Rights and Social Welfare Morality", where the validity of prevailing laws and social systems are evaluated in terms of the degree to which they uphold and protect these values. The right thing to do is to uphold the rules if they serve to protect human rights and social welfare values. The social system is seen as a contract freely entered into by individuals. In addition to deontological features, this stage is said also to have utilitarian elements since the reason for doing right is the welfare of all and the protection of everybody's rights. The socio–moral perspective is the perspective of rational individuals who are aware of values and rights underpinning contracts and social attachments. The morality at *stage six* is characterized by universal ethical principles. The right thing to do is to follow self–chosen ethical principles, and these principles are universal principles of justice. The reason for doing the right thing is the belief in the validity of universal moral principles, and one's commitment to them (Kohlberg 1987:19–31; Walker 1993:158–159). *Stage six* has occupied a controversial place in Kohlberg's theory due to the lack of empirical evidence to support it (Habermas 1990; Kohlberg 1990; Puka 1990).

In order to measure moral development, Kohlberg used his stage theory to evaluate his informants' response to hypothetical moral dilemmas. He ranged them along different stages depending on apprehended moral maturity. Until the early 1970s only males served as informants in Kohlberg's research, but when girls started to take part in the experiment, it turned out that their solutions differed from those of the boys. Girls emphasized responsiveness and connectedness with others, on preventing harm and maintaining relationships. Boys valued independency, justice and abstract reasoning. The girls' responses were given a lower score in Kohlberg's stage theory because their reasoning were embedded in the contexts of particular others rather than in abstract rules of justice. And since Kohlberg's theory was meant to be universally applicable, this result led to the conclusion that girls are less morally mature than boys. Gilligan refused to go along with such a conclusion. She blamed Kohlberg's research, not the girls, for their low scores. She accused Kohlberg's model sex–bias: It was unable to appreciate the moral reasoning of the female informants in a balanced and adequate way.

Gilligan's Critique of Kohlberg

Gilligan's critique of Kohlberg's theory can be sorted along three veins, each with a different source. First, Kohlberg may have inherited prejudices against women and their moral reasoning from his ancestors in psychology Sigmund Freud and Jean Piaget, prejudices that determined the interpretation of his data. Freud portrayed differences between the sexes to women's disadvantage, and his critique of women's sense of justice reappears, according to Gilligan, in the works of both Piaget and Kohlberg (Gilligan 1982:18). For instance, Freud, in "Woman as a Castrated Man" (1933), says that women must be regarded as having little sense of justice, and this, in turn, is related to the predominance of envy in women's mental life. What justice demands is a modification of envy. It therefore demands that envy be put aside, something he finds women incapable of doing (Freud 1977:108). Piaget, when observing the behavior of males and females, characterized the differing behavior of women, as being at variance with the norm. According to Gilligan girls were of interest insofar as they were similar to boys and confirmed the generality of Piaget's findings. The differences noted were considered uninteresting, and, therefore, of no significance for the study of children's moral judgment (Gilligan 1987:21–22). Piaget's findings on girls were comprehended as diverging from the traditional research paradigm, and Kohlberg's observations on girls' moral reasoning subsequently interpreted as if girls were less mature. It is these "anomalies" that formed the background to Gilligan's own research, and, in turn, her ethics of care. Both Piaget's and Kohlberg's approaches to sexual differences accord with an old tradition in western thinking, the source of which is probably Aristotle's

De Generatione Animalium, and *Politics*. Here, observed sexual differences are listed in hierarchical order, in favor of men (Pettersen 1996).

Second, in addition to critiquing the gender–biasedness of Kohlberg's interpretations of the data, the whole construction of Kohlberg's stage theory has been questioned. The longitudinal data that formed the theory's empirical grounding contained only male samples, which clearly undermines the universalizability of the model (Gilligan 1987:22; Walker 1993:161).

A third possible source of the male bias lies in Kohlberg's understanding of morality. His model of moral development is based on a deontological conception morality (Kohlberg 1987:23–24). Kohlberg has admitted that he assumed the core of morality and moral development to be deontological: a matter of rights and duties or prescriptions. This assumption is linked to his view on mature moral judgment as based on principles of justice (Kohlberg 1984:225). This moral approach has been criticized for representing traditionally masculine values and skills: the ability to abstract from the particular, to deduce from rules and principles rather than focusing on context, to put reason over emotions, to rely on a concept of self as independent rather than interdependent etc. (Gilligan 1982; Noddings 1984; Tong 1993; Held 1993; 2006; Pettersen 2004; 2006; Walker 1998). These structural features serve to demarcate the content and scope of moral theories, and help explain why experiences associated with female behavior are excluded from the dominant moral tradition.[4] Sexual bias is suspected innate to Kohlberg's moral and psychological frameworks, and affects his interpretation of gender difference in moral reasoning. Gilligan recognizes the differences between the sexes in their moral reasoning, but argues that women's responses should not be taken as moral deficiencies. The reason girls are considered less morally mature in Kohlberg's model is, she says, because the model was unable to adequately accommodate deviations from the sex–biased norm (Gilligan 1982:25).[5]

An Illustration of the Two Voices: Jake and Amy's Response to Heinz's Dilemma

At this point, an illustration of the alternative types of moral reasoning Gilligan draws attention to might be illuminating. For this exercise we will use "Heinz's dilemma". It is one of the hypothetical dilemmas Kohlberg gave a couple of eleven–year–old children, Jake and Amy, to resolve in order to measure moral development (Gilligan 1982:25). In the dilemma a man named Heinz considers whether to steal a medicine which can save his dying wife from the druggist or not, a medicine he cannot afford to buy.

The children were asked "Should Heinz steal the drug?", and this is Jake's answer:

> For one thing, a human life is worth more than money, and if the druggist only makes $1,000, he is still going to live, but if Heinz doesn't steal the drug, his wife is going to die. (*Why is life worth more than money?*) Because the druggist can get a thousand dollars later from rich people with cancer, but Heinz can't get his wife again. (*Why not?*) Because people are all different and so you couldn't get Heinz wife again. (Gilligan 1982:26)

Amy's response to Heinz's dilemma is different:

> Well, I don't think so. I think there might be other ways besides stealing it, like if he could borrow the money or make a loan or something, but he really shouldn't steal the drug—but his wife shouldn't die either. (*Why not?*) If he stole the drug, he might save his wife then, but if he did, he might have to go to jail, and then his wife might get sicker again, and he couldn't get more of the drug, and it might not be good. So, they should really just talk it out and find some other way to make the money. (Gilligan 1982:28)

In the light of Kohlberg's theory of moral development, Amy's resolution of the conflict is interpreted to be a mixture of levels two and three. Since this is one level lower than Jake's, it indicates that her response is less mature than his—not merely different—because Amy, in Kohlberg's framework, is neither thinking logically nor reflecting independently. Her response could be described as evasive. Jake's reply, on the other hand, shows greater maturity because of his ruminations: He justifies his answer in a logical way; he is able to distinguish between moral and legal right (Gilligan 1982:27).

Gilligan offers a different interpretation of Amy's response. Amy, says Gilligan, perceives the dilemma as a story of human relationships, and considers things in perspective. The dilemma for Amy is not an isolated problem about a choice between sanctifying property and preserving life. The problem is how to maintain the relationship between the persons involved, and to prevent harm. She perceives, namely, the world as comprised of connections, rather than of isolated individuals. And in consequence, she constructs the problem differently. Amy does not ask "*should* Heinz steal the drug?" but rather, "should Heinz *steal* the drug?" Applying Kohlberg's theory to Amy's reasoning, this is not apprehended (Gilligan 1982:28–32).

Gilligan gives substantial weight to Jake and Amy's response to Heinz's dilemma. She sees Jake's way of reasoning as expressing the logic of a perspective of justice; Amy's, on the other hand, she takes as reflecting an insight central to an ethics of care (Gilligan 1982:30). Gilligan sees these two moral approaches as representing different priorities and focuses. Let us examine Gilligan's portrayal of these two perspectives.

The Perspective of Care and Justice

Availing herself of her empirical studies, Gilligan paints a more general picture of the two perspectives and the differences between them.[6] The differences pertain mainly to the ways in which moral problems are conceived, the ideals upheld, the moral reasoning and the moral injunctions that follow from them (Gilligan 1988:73). The differences between the two perspectives reflect different dimensions of human relationships and give rise to two moral concerns:

The care perspective emphasizes empathic association with others, being responsible and caring. Individuals are seen as connected in relation to others. The others are seen and understood in their own situations and contexts. Within this perspective, moral problems are generally constructed as issues of relationships, or of responses. The problem consists in how to respond to others on their particular terms. One resolves moral problems through care. Furthermore, when approaching problems one endeavors to maintain the relationships and the connections between interdependent individuals, or promote the welfare of others, preventing harm coming to them, or relieving their burdens, hurt or suffering. When one decides what to do (or evaluates a decision) from this point of view one is concerned about what will happen (or happened), how things will work out (or have worked out), or whether relationships were/are maintained or restored (Gilligan et al. 1988:35).

Within *the justice perspective* individuals are defined as separate in relation to others. One tends to see others as one would like to be seen by them. Moral problems are generally constructed as issues of conflicting claims between self and others (including society). These problems are resolved by invoking impartial rules, principles, or standards. When resolving moral problems, in focus are one's role–related obligations, duties or commitments or standards, rules or principles for self, others, or society. This approach to conflict–solving includes reciprocity, and that is *fairness*. "Fairness", for Gilligan, means that when we consider how to treat another, we are considering how we would like to be treated if we were in that person's place.[7] From the justice viewpoint, when we are deciding what to do (or evaluating decisions) we consider how decisions are thought about and justified, or whether values, principles or standards (especially fairness) were/are maintained, Gilligan continues. Also, we tend to see others from an impartial point of view, and use a morality of justice as fairness that rests on an understanding of relationships as reciprocity between separate individuals. This understanding of relationships, as reciprocal, is grounded in the duties and obligations of the agent's role in the relationships (Gilligan et al. 1988:35).[8]

To sum up, the perspective of justice draws attention to the problems of inequality and oppression and holds up an ideal of reciprocity and equal respect. The perspective of care focuses on problems of detachment or abandonment and holds up an ideal of attention and response to need. From these ideals, two moral injunctions emerge: "[. . .] not to treat others unfairly and not to turn away from someone in need" (Gilligan et al. 1988:73). Indeed, several aspects concerning the portrayal of the two moral perspectives could be further discussed and analyzed. This will be done in subsequent chapters. We now need to consider Gilligan's claims concerning these moral orientations, and show how she explains their origin.

Gilligan's Two Major Hypotheses

In *In a Different Voice* Gilligan sets out two major hypotheses. The first asserts the existence of two different types of moral reasoning, the care and justice perspective. The other hypothesis claims, additionally, that women typically hold the care perspective, while the justice perspective typically is the moral voice of men.[9] The first claim can be termed "the different voice hypothesis", the second "the gender difference hypothesis" (Friedman 1993:260). These hypotheses are both separately problematic, as is the relationship between them, and this has given rise to much debate. As to the "gender hypothesis", Gilligan emphasizes in the introduction to *In a Different Voice* that this association with care and women is not absolute, and is not to be taken as a generalization of either sex. Gilligan describes the contrasts between male and female voices to highlight, she says, a distinction between two modes of thought and to bring a problem of interpretation into focus (Gilligan 1982:2). She also stresses this point later, saying that the title of her book was deliberate; "it reads, 'in a *different* voice', not 'in a *woman's* voice'", she points out. The care perspective is, Gilligan underlines, "neither biologically determined nor unique to women" (Gilligan 1993:209). One question worth raining in respect of the different voice hypothesis is whether Gilligan holds the view that only two moral perspectives exist. In *Mapping the Moral Domain* she says that "there are *at least* two different moral orientations", while identifying a few pages later justice and care as "*the* moral coordinates of human connections" (Gilligan et al. 1988:136,144, italics added).[10] Gilligan's remarks on this topic allow for different interpretations both concerning her view on morality as well as the relationship between justice and care. Nevertheless, many of her readers are inclined to believe that she operates with a dichotomous view of morality (Nunner–Winkler 1993:143; Flanagan and Jackson 1993:75; Blum 1994:240–241; Vetlesen 2002:218). I offer, however, several instances of Gilligan transcending dichotomous thinking.

As to the relationship between the two hypotheses, Gilligan does not discuss their possible (inter–) independence. It is nevertheless possible to consider the "different voice hypothesis" as independent of the "gender hypothesis" since we can assert the different moral voices without gendering them. It is not so the other way around; there must necessarily be two different moral voices if one believes there are two separate moral voices typical of males and females respectively. Hence, the "gender hypothesis" is dependent on the "two different voice hypothesis". It is nevertheless difficult to treat "the different voice hypothesis" as completely independent of gender, not least because Gilligan explains the origin of the different voices with reference to a gender–related psychological hypothesis. Therefore, we need to take a closer look at her psychological hypothesis, her concept of gender, and how she deals with the statistic correlation between gender and moral orientation.

The Connected and the Separated Self

In addition to characterizing two different moral voices, Gilligan explains their origin by means of psychological theory, where early childhood experiences are particularly relevant:[11]

> Predispositions towards justice and towards care can be traced to the experience of inequality and of attachment that are embedded in the relationship between child and parent. And since everyone, thus, is vulnerable to oppression and to abandonment, two stories about morality recur in human experience. (Gilligan et al. 1988)

Since no child can survive without being in a relationship, interdependence is a common human experience, says Gilligan. As children grow up, they continue to exist in a web of relationships, and throughout life, the connections between self and others are important (Gilligan 1982:98). These fundamental assumptions about human nature are constitutive features in Gilligan's way of perceiving the world, and I characterize them as her ontological starting point. Gilligan conceives relationships as a basic feature of human lives, and considers them to be of fundamental importance. Despite the common experience of being related in early childhood, she posits two main ways of perceiving oneself: as interdependent and connected with others, and as independent of others. They constitute two quite different concepts of self the "connected", "interdependent" self on the one hand, and the "separate", "autonomous" self on the other.

The different conceptions of the self affect the perception of relationships. A separate self tends to regard relationships as an interaction between separate and equal autonomous individuals. The connected self tends to perceive relationships as an interaction between connected and interdependent persons (Gilligan 1982:8; Gilligan et al. 1988:33). Gilligan often emphasizes the contrasts between the separate self and the connected self, but, as we shall see later, the self Gilligan describes is not inflexible or submissive; on the contrary, also independency is required to develop and change in order to attain maturity. Other modes of self–definitions are also possible (Gilligan et al. 1988:41,42).

The reason why people hold different conceptions of self and relationships is, very roughly, due to differences in the process of separation in early childhood. Gilligan's emphasis on psychology does not mean that she is unaware of other factors that influence gendering. She mentions race, ethnicity and class (Gilligan 1982:169), but clearly her major thrust lies in her psychological theory of ego and identity development. Here Gilligan draws on the psychological theories of Nancy Chodorow, Erik Erikson Sigmund Freud, Lawrence Kohlberg and Jean Piaget, as well as her own empirical research (Gilligan 1982:10–28). However, the object–relation theory of Nancy Chodorow is particularly important in explaining the care perspective (Gilligan 1987:28,29). In *The Reproduction of Motherhood* (1978) Chodorow tells how a basic common experience in early childhood may result in a gender–divided concept of self, as well as perception of others, relationships and moral orientation. As Chodorow sees it, the early relation to a primary caretaker provides children of both genders with the basic capacity to participate in relationships sharing features of the early parent–child relationship and the desire to create this intimacy. However, as women mother, the early experiences in the pre–oedipal phase of the relationship differ for boys and girls.[12] Girls, Chodorow believes, maintain more concern with early childhood issues in relation to their mother, and a sense of self involved with these issues and their attachments therefore retains more pre–oedipal aspects. As a result of the greater length and different nature of the girls' pre–oedipal experiences, as well as their continuing preoccupation with issues common to this period, women retain capacities for primary identification and their sense of self is continuous with others. This enables them to feel, among other things, the empathy needed by a cared–for infant. In men, however, these qualities are curtailed, as their mothers start to treat them at an early stage as an opposite, and also because their attachment to her must be repressed in time, says Chodorow. The relational basis for mothering is therefore extended in women, and repressed in men, as men experience themselves as more separate and distinct from others (Chodorow 1978:206–207).

Chodorow and Gilligan share structural similarities as they both explore how early childhood experience affects our subsequent attitudes and actions. Their views of the content as well as the significance of object–relational experience bears resemblances as they both emphasize the experience of detachment and attachment. Nevertheless, they differ in their focus. Chodorow focuses on how the pre–oedipal experience influences mothering and the reproduction of mothering in particular, while Gilligan explores its moral implications. Those who conceive the self as autonomous regard relationships in a reciprocal way and tend to use a morality of justice. Those who perceive the self as connected tend to regard relationships in the responsive and connected way and tend to use a morality of care. The connected self typically holds care as an ideal, while justice tends to be the ideal of the separated self (Gilligan et al. 1988:36–41). The origin of these two moral voices, Gilligan says, lie in differences in early childhood separation, something that leads to a different conception of self, others and the relationships between them. Since early separation is taken to differ for girls and boys, this explains the statistical correlation between gender and different concepts of self and others. Furthermore, the comprehension of human interaction influences moral perception and, since this comprehension is gendered, it also explains why females tend to have a different moral orientation than males. This brings us to Gilligan's own theory on moral development, i.e. the process through which the agent may develop towards becoming a carer.

Gilligan's Theory on Moral Development

Beyond the two different moral voices we find two distinct psychological development patterns, related to one's conception of oneself as connected in relationship with others, or as separated in relation to others. Each leads towards a particular moral orientation. One of these lines of development, says Gilligan, is taken account of in psychology and acknowledged in moral theories. It is the development of the autonomous self, associated with the perspective of justice. Not so with the other path, the development of the related self, with its associated perspective of care (Gilligan et al. 1988:14).

The moral development Gilligan outlines appears in her *Abortion Study* (Gilligan and Field Belenky 1980; Gilligan 1982).[13] She finds that her female informants often start by focusing on their own interests only. The overriding concern is survival and satisfaction of need; the interests of others are neglected. Then there is a shift to the consideration of the needs of others, on the costs of their own interests. When a decision finally is made, it is often through the recognition of both the interests of self and others. Through shifting perspective once more, a solution is found, ensuring that both other's and own interests are taken account of (Gilligan and Field Belenky 1980: 83–85).

More precisely, Gilligan identifies *three levels* in the developmental process towards the moral perspective of care.

> The sequences of women's moral judgment proceeds from an initial concern with survival to focus on goodness and finally to a reflective understanding of care as the most adequate guide to the resolution of conflicts in human relationship. (Gilligan 1982:105)

On the *first level* in her developmental theory, the most important thing is to survive. Taking care of oneself is declared to be the overriding concern (Gilligan 1982:75). Care on level one is self–care. Self–care and self–love at this developmental stage is primarily understood as self–protection against hurt. A transition follows, due to awareness of one's "attachment or connection to others" (Gilligan 1982:76). On *level two*, self–interest is no longer the basis for judgments, but social norms and other people's expectations. Other people's interests are now the overruling concern; hence this stage can be termed altruistic. Along with altruism comes the problem of self–sacrifice, which might incite a new change. Moving to *level three*, a reconsideration of the relationship between self and other becomes important. The agent begins to ask, "whether it is selfish or responsible, moral or immoral to include one's own needs within the compass of her care and concern". The type of care that appears on level three is characterized by ego taking into account both the interest of others and of the self (Gilligan 1982:82).[14]

Now, there are several ways of understanding and defining both "altruism" and "self–care/self–concern". Here we must confine with a suggestion on how Gilligan may understand them. She seems to use "altruism" as interchangeable with "selflessness" and "self–sacrifice", something that indicates that she by "altruism" means what Nagel (1978:80) terms "pure altruism", i.e., "the direct influence of one person's interests on the actions of another, simply because in itself the interests of the former provides the latter with reason to act". "Self–care" may correspond with Nagel's definition of "egoism" (1978:84); "that each individual's reasons for acting and possible motives for acting, must arise from his own interests and desires, however those interests may be defined". Gilligan believes that humans have the capacity for both egoism (self–concern) and altruism (other–concern), and furthermore that egoism and altruism represent stages in the moral development—stage one and two, that is. At level three, egoism and altruism are balanced, or, we could say modified; instead of a pure altruism, which means that the carer's own interests are neglected, the carer's other–concern endures, but it is not unlimited. Self–concern, within limits, is at stage three considered legitimate. Questions concerning the relative weight of the interests of self and other are of course important, and will be discussed several times in the proceeding chapters.

For Gilligan then, there are three types of "care". The types of care found on level one and two, i.e. selfish care and selflessness care, are immature care. Mature care appears on level three, and this "right kind of care" pays attention to as well as weights the interests of self and others. Furthermore, this is why awareness of connection and a contextual sensitivity is, as we shall see, important; a moral person is defined as one who, when acting seriously, considers the consequences to everybody involved (Gilligan 1982:54). Probably as a result of the unawareness of the different types of care, the concept of care and the ethic of care, are sometimes mistakenly understood as a morality of self–sacrifice.[15] The ethics of care advanced is built on the type of care found on level three, not on the selfless care of level two. On this she is crystal clear: "I describe a critical ethical perspective that calls into question the traditional equation of care with self–sacrifice" (Gilligan 1993:209, Gilligan 1987:29).

An understanding of "care" as "mature care" will be central in the later discussion of the ethics of care, but it might be illuminating to examine already the significance of this particular understanding because it differs from what I take to be a common understanding of "care". Intuitively we tend to understand "care" as care for others, and that the more other–directed care is, the better. The notion of mature care, however, involves as much concern for oneself as it does for others. Mature care implies a balancing between the interests of self and others.[16] More generally, the tendency to harmonize opposites found in the concept of mature care is also discernable in other ideas put forward by Gilligan. My presumption that Gilligan attempts to raise above dichotomies marks my reading and interpretation of her ethics of care.[17] The fact that Gilligan's theory should promote a balanced notion of care, gives her version of care ethics, on my view, important advantages compared, for instance, to Milton Mayeroff's (1972), Nel Noddings's (1984), and Kari Martinsen's (1989, 2000). None of which, in my view, take sufficient care of the carer.

Gilligan's theory on moral development and the concept of mature care will become central when we in the proceeding chapters elaborate on the philosophical problems and possibilities in the ethics of care. First, however, we shall survey some criticism leveled at Gilligan, and address some issues concerning gender.

Notes

1. Summers article was first published in *The Atlantic Monthly* in May 2000, and then in June 2000 in *The War Against Boys: How Misguided Feminism Is Harming Our Young Men*, New York: Simon and Schuster.

2. http://www.waynebesen.com/2006/12/dobson–slammed–for–distorting –research.html [tp/09.04.07]

3. This stage can also be found in "some adolescents, and many adolescent and adult criminal offenders" (Colby and Kohlberg 1987:16).

4. However, the idea that ethics is gendered has been central to many philosophers. For instance, Plato has Socrates and Meno discussing the connection between virtues and gender (in *Meno*). Discussions were florid in the eighteenth and nineteenth centuries, some key works being Mary Astell: *Some Reflections upon Marriage* (1700), Mary Wollstonecraft: *Vindication of the Rights of Women* (1992), Harriet Taylor: *Enfranchisement of Women* (1851), Jean–Jacques Rousseau: *Emilie* (1762), and David Hume: "Of Chastity and Modesty" (1739/40). Immanuel Kant advanced in his early work *Observations on the Feelings of the Beautiful and the Sublime* (1764), a gender–divided norm system where women are regarded as less capable of the type of moral reasoning requiring universal principles (Kant 1977:129–144; Grimshaw 1991; Wiestad 1995).

5. Kohlberg has responded to Gilligan's critique, as to the critique of others (Kohlberg et al. 1983). Since the central topic of this book is Gilligan's ethics of care, I will not pursue the Kohlberg–Gilligan debate further. For the record, however, Kohlberg's strategy towards Gilligan can, according to Seyla Benhabib (1987:155–156) be summed up as follows: Kohlberg argues 1) that her data do not support the conclusions she draws; 2) that some of the new conclusions can be accommodated by his theory; and 3) that Gilligan and he have different objects and domains and are therefore not explaining the same phenomena. Benhabib interprets Kohlberg's defense against Gilligan as an example of Thomas Kuhn's portrayal of the defenders of an old scientific paradigm, defending the old paradigm against a revisionist.

6. In referring to the two voices, Gilligan uses a variety of terms, as do others in the post–Gilligan debate. Most common are probably "the care perspective and the justice perspective". "Perspectives" are sometimes replaced by "orientations" or "focus", and sometimes one speaks about "the morality of care" and "the morality of justice" or "the ethics of care" and "the ethics of justice". "Different voices" and

"different ways of moral reasoning" as well as "lines of thought", "moral positions" and "moral approaches" are also used. These terms are used interchangeably. No differentiation is made, to my knowledge, in respect of the empirical findings, interpretations of these findings, or general reflections concerning the structure and implications of the two ways of moral reasoning. In the following I will use "the ethics of care" and "the ethics of justice" only when referring to these voices comprehended as being, or, at least aiming to be, normative ethical theories. The other terms are used more broadly, i.e., when characterizing general aspects of moral reasoning.

7. We could notice the resemblances with Kant's categorical imperative as well as Rawls' veil of ignorance here.

8. These features capture some fundamental structures in classical deontological ethics as well as in Rawls' theory, and probably in utilitarianism too which will be discussed later.

9. "Typically" implies that women are thought to hold the perspective of care more often than men, and that men more frequently than women hold that of justice, but also that some men apply the perspective of care while some women apply that of justice.

10. See also Gilligan 1987:19–33.

11. Lawrence Walker's (1993:160) claim that Gilligan has not provided an explanation as to why men and women may develop different moral perspectives appears thus to be incorrect.

12. Chodorow relates here to the Freudian stages of psychosexual development, where the pre–oedipal phase is taken to be between the ages of 0–3 years.

13. See in particular Chapter 4 "Crisis and Transition" in Gilligan's In a Different Voice (1982).

14. See also Bill Puka 1993 for a discussion of these levels.

15. Michael Slote for instance says: "An ethics of care or concern exclusively or even primarily for favored others seems, then to be morally retrograde [. . .]. Perhaps, morality as caring should say, then, that it is best and most admirable to be motivated by concern for others in balance with self–concern and that all and only actions and activities that are consonant with and display such balance are morally acceptable" (Slote in Baron, Pettit and Slote 1997:227–228). Michael Slote fails to see that this is exactly what Gilligan aims at. What is more, it is the "altruistic care" of the second level that confirms the traditional gender roles, not the mature care on level three.

16. See Chapter 5 for a discussion of this balance.

17. Thus, my reading differs from, among others, Arne Johan Vetlesen's (2002:218), who says that Gilligan does not transcend the traditional dichotomies.

CHAPTER TWO

~

Gender Issues and Criticism

Even if Gilligan and her research have been celebrated and praised, she has also attracted sharp and widespread criticism. In the following, I present some of the objections put forward in the debate as they form part of the background to my own discussion of Gilligan's ethical position and the ethics of care. As we shall see, much of the criticism she directed at Kohlberg rebounds back on herself.[1]

Gilligan's Theoretical Gender Bias

Now, if Kohlberg's theory is suspected to be male biased due to possible misogynistic prejudices inherited from his theoretical predecessors, it must also be possible that Gilligan's theory contains a bias against men. As mentioned, Gilligan relies on the works of the feminist psychoanalyst Nancy Chodorow, who according to Gilligan "writes against the masculine bias of psychoanalytic theory" (Gilligan 1982:8). Chodorow is further said to be the source of Gilligan's belief that caring originates in the mother–daughter dyad (Larrabee 1993:13). The central claims of the object–relational psychological approach, that women are more capable of care and affective relationships (Chodorow 1978:176,126,209),[2] resembles Kant's claim in *Observations on the Feelings of the Beautiful and Sublime* that women have many sympathetic sensations, such as good–heartedness and compassion. The difference lies primarily in the evaluation of these alleged female qualities; for Kant they are partly morally inferior, in Gilligan they can be interpreted as being, in some situations, morally superior. Just as gender differences in Kant and Freud are described in terms that portray women as deficient in relation to men, the feminist psychological theories that form the background to Gilligan's theorizing also portray gender differences in evaluative terms.

The reading of Gilligan's theory as gender biased is not the only possible interpretation of her view on gender issues, but it is a major objection to her theory (Moody–Adams 1991:199). One protagonist of this interpretation is Christina Sommers. She claims that Gilligan's theory of boys' development contains three assumptions: Boys are being deformed and made sick by a traumatic and forced separation from their mothers, that apparently healthy boys are cut off from their own feelings and damaged in their capacity to develop healthy relationships, and that the well–being of society may depend upon freeing the boys from what Gilligan, says Sommers, describes as a culture that values or valorizes heroism, honor, war and competition—the culture of warriors, the economy of capitalism (Sommers 2000). According to Sommers, Gilligan and her followers wish to civilize boys by diminishing their masculinity, by raising them as girls: "This approach is deeply disrespectful of boys. It is meddlesome, abusive, and quite beyond what educators in a free society are mandated to do" (Sommers 2000).

In addition to pointing at the harmful individual as well as political consequences of the maternalistic tendencies in Gilligan's work, Sommers also objects to the scientific validity of Gilligan's basic psychological assumptions. Gilligan's psychological views are attractive to many who believe that boys could profit from being more sensitive and empathetic, she says. However, anyone thinking to join in what she terms "Gilligan's project of getting boys in touch with their inner nurturer" should note that her central thesis is not a scientific hypothesis. As Sommers puts it, Gilligan's central thesis is "that boys are being imprisoned by conventional ideas of masculinity". It fails to be scientific since Gilligan, in Sommers' view, presents no data to support it, and she continues: "It is, in fact, an extravagant piece of speculation of the kind that would not be taken seriously in most professional departments of psychology" (Sommers 2000).

Although I share Sommers's concern for boys and approve her attempt to draw attention to their situation, I find her critique of Gilligan to be far off the mark. True, in In a Different Voice, as well as other works, Gilligan has been preoccupied with females, not males. Such specialization has weaknesses as well as advantages, but a sharp focus has never, as such, been scientifically illegitimate. Furthermore, a researcher's focal point may also be contextually comprehended: As many other female researchers during the 1970s and 1980s, Gilligan took an interest in the study of girls and women because it appeared to be unexplored territory. In these decades she was concerned with psychological development and ethics; others were preoccupied with discovering the history of women, exploring the relation between gender and science, gender and language, art and politics. It may be worth noting that Gilligan, in her book *The Birth of Pleasure* (2002) pays substantial attention to men, masculinity, and the difficulties connected to establishing a masculine identity. Now, her opponents may say this is in response to critique, which may be correct. It could also be understood as Gilligan's desire to keep up with the times: in the 1970s and 1980s gender studies meant the study of females, while from the 1990s males have tended to be the new focus. There is exactly 20 years between the publication of *In a Different Voice* and *The Birth of Pleasure*. Both books offer a picture of their time; each reflects the leading traditions in gender studies, and together bridge developments within the discipline over the years. Summers also criticizes Gilligan for not providing data in support of her hypothesis. Gilligan and her co-workers refute this (Gilligan 2000), though, as we shall see below, the data she has published can be criticized on several accounts. Finally, we are not told what Sommers requires of a hypothesis for it to be scientific. It appears as if she fails to see that psychological hypothesis cannot be confirmed in the same way as hypothesis in the natural sciences.

Gilligan's Gender–Biased Data

Gilligan's two moral perspectives, as well as the link to gender set forth in *In a Different Voice*, are based on three studies: *The Abortion Decision Study*; *The College Student Study*; and *The Rights and Responsibility Study* (Gilligan 1982:2–3). In "The Abortion Decision Study" twenty–nine women were interviewed once, and twenty–one were interviewed twice about decision–making in relation to abortion (Gilligan 1980:76; Gilligan 1982:3). "The College Student Study" is a longitudinal study, for which she interviewed twenty–five students twice. For "The Rights and Responsibility study" Gilligan interviewed males and females aged from six to sixty (Brabeck 1993:38). Gilligan has claimed that these studies provide empirical evidence to back her hypothesis on moral reasoning (Gilligan et al. 1988:118).[3] The fact that her original study (i.e. *The Abortion Decision Study*) consisted only of female informants, and that the dilemma they were to consider was a "typical" female dilemma (whether to have an abortion or not), raises the question of how representative her data is. The discussion concerns whether these studies provide an adequate basis for generalizing about the existence of two moral ways of reasoning, and to link the two "voices" to gender, or whether they should be understood as qualitative interviews merely illustrating her hypothesis about two different moral perspectives. Gilligan's reservation as to the possibility of generalizing her findings is, in my opinion, lost sight of in clamor of the post–Gilligan debate. Gilligan has been quite explicit in her emphasis that we "suspend any claims as to the generality of these findings". It is clearly necessary, she continues, to examine the vicissitudes of the perspective of care and the perspective of justice as well as a wider range of moral problems, in relation to the different socio-economic, educational and cultural contexts men and women are embedded in (Gilligan et al. 1988:119).

A further criticism has been directed at Gilligan's interpretations of her informants (Romain 1992; Dancy 1992). Jonathan Dancy, for instance, claims that Gilligan forces Jake and Amy's response into the care and justice perspectives, and argues that they can be interpreted in a different way (Dancy 1992:459–463). This implies the presence of the "Rosenthal Effect" in Gilligan's studies, i.e., that the researcher's bias tends to sway the results in the direction of what the researcher wants to find. Another risk to be considered when discussing the empirical existence of the two moral perspectives is the "Hawthorne Effect": here, informants may try harder to be "moral" simply because they are being interviewed about their moral judgments. These are, in my opinion, relevant concerns in respect of Gilligan's data—indeed in respect of any research based on interviews.

There is a final, but fundamental critique of Gilligan's work linked to the publication of her data. According to several critics, no quantitative data have been reported from these additional studies, and standardized interviews have not been published (Brabeck 1993:38; Walker 1993:160; Sommers 2000). In 1993, Mary Brabeck (1993:38) claimed that "evidence for Gilligan's theory currently rests on quoted excerpts from interviews and her interpretations of these selected excerpts". Still, Gilligan's original data and interpretation is an issue (Gilligan 2000; Sommers 2000; Friedman 2000). The doubt that has been created about Gilligan's data has led some of her critics to characterize her works as "politics dressed up as science" (Sommers 2000).

The Sex/Gender Distinction in Gilligan's Work

How should the statistic correlation between gender and care observed by Gilligan be perceived? Is the correlation accidental, or is it essential? In Gilligan's own work there is a tension in the matter: Some of her passages on the relation between care and gender might be read as expressing essentialism[4]

(Gilligan 1982:171, 173)[5]—others not (Gilligan 1982:2; 1993:209)[6]. I have two suggestions on why Gilligan is not lucid on this, and we shall explore both views: First, I will argue that she does not deal with the phenomenon of sexual difference in a philosophical satisfying manner. Second, I assert that even if Gilligan noticed a correlation between gender and moral orientation, she has failed to articulate if, when, and how, the correlation is significant for ethics.

In *What Is a Woman?* Toril Moi (1998:87) maintains that Gilligan's distinction between "sex" and "gender" follows what Moi terms "the 1960s' manner". Moi means here that "sex" is understood as referring to the body (a biological category), while "gender" is conceived of as mind or as identity (a cultural or social category). I am inclined to go along with Moi's assumption here, for several reasons. First, Moi's illuminating reconstruction of the "history of the notions of sex and gender" makes it, in my opinion, plausible to presume that Gilligan uses gender in "the 1960s' manner". Second, because Gilligan uses psychological theory to explain the male–female differences emerging in her empirical findings, she is obviously linking the perspectives of care and justice to gender, not sex. These processes give rise to a gendered identity that affects moral orientations. Finally, Gilligan rejects out of hand biological determinism, and, in consequence, a link between sex and gender (Gilligan 1993:209). So despite some ambiguities, there are reasons to believe that Gilligan does not take the connection between women and the care perspective to be essentialistic and related to sex, but rather to gender.

Now although many feminists approve of the distinction between sex and gender as it is taken to be a defense against biological determinism, this dichotomization creates difficulties. The body is separated from the mind, reduced to a passive object ruled by the mind. Bodily sensations and experiences can be more or less ignored in the formation of the self if we persist in separating sex and gender as Gilligan apparently does. And what exactly does "sex" in this context mean? Does it refer to hormones, chromosomes or reproductive organs? What about transsexuals? How do bodily experiences affect our gender identity (Moi 1998:138)? We would do well to recall how troubled Descartes became by his own distinction between body and mind, and it has attracted much debate also within feminist theory. Suffice it here to mention Judith Butler's *Gender Trouble* (1990) and *Bodies that Matter* (1993). There is a tradition of opposition in philosophy as well, prominent names being Edmund Husserl, Maurice Merleau–Ponty and Simone de Beauvoir (Heinämaa 2003). The ethics of care, with its critique of rationalistic prevalence and the restricting dualistic categories common to mainstream moral philosophy and ethics, risks accusations of inconsistency if it continues to rely on the sex/gender distinction in dealing with variation in the moral outlooks of men and women.

Furthermore, even if we accept privileging gender over sex for the sake of keeping biological determinism at arm's length, also the concept of gender as used by Gilligan can lead to essentialism; from the cultural and psychological processes that form gender identity flow a particular female and masculine psyche. This gendered psyche might turn out to be so constitutive of identity formation that we in fact can speak of a *psychological* determinism, no less problematic than is biological determinism. There are other ways of avoiding biological determinism than applying the sex/gender distinction: according to Moi all we have to do is to deny that biological fact can justify social arrangement (Moi 1998:69). Another problem associated with the gender–sex distinction is its inadequacy in explaining differences between people. However we understand the two categories, and the relation between them, identity and differences can hardly be reduced to sex/gender only. A person is more than sex and gender; she belongs to a social class or caste, a race, often has a nationality and sometimes a religion on top of a collection of a unique personal experience (Moi 1998:47–60). Gilligan has been roundly criticized on this point. By singling out the domestic life "typical of white, middle–class, heterosexual women" and "fail[ing] to capture the experience of the lesbians, black women and working–class women". Pierce and Nicholson both see her theory as deeply culturally situated (Pierce 1991:62; Nicholson 1993:98). Claudia Card argues similarly, accusing Gilligan's ethics of care of "conservatism" because it reinforces traditional middle–class conceptions of femininity (Card 1991:17). Annette Baier on the other hand, finds in Gilligan's ethics of care a counterweight to Western individualism through its emphasis on connections and the importance of the family (Baier 1995: 57).

Toril Moi (1998), it should be noted, does not address Gilligan as such; indeed, Gilligan is mentioned only twice and then very briefly. Moi deals with tradition—thirty years of feminist theory which, she maintains, is based on the sex/gender distinction, and which, she believes, Gilligan is part of. But that "1960s manner" of applying the categories in question is too narrow to adequately explain why males and females tend to hold different moral orientations, Moi contends, suggesting that we learn from Simone de Beauvoir. In *The Second Sex*, (1949) instead of the distinction between sex and gender, Beauvoir uses a notion of "lived experience" (*l'expérience vécue*). It lets her tread a path between those who, on the one hand, contend that sexual difference has little relevance (such as Judith Butler in *Gender Trouble* [1990]) and those (such as Luce Irigaray in *An Ethics of Sexual Difference* (1984)) who argue that sexual differences are almost all-pervading. Beauvoir's lived experience refers to the accumulated subjective experience of individuals. According to Beauvoir, you are your lived experiences, and your experiences are related to having a certain body in a certain culture. Some experiences are indeed connected to sex as well as to gender, but others are not. A group of people may share certain things, but not others. The relevance of sex to lived experiences, and the manner of its impact, depend on the situation. Some cultures may accentuate sexual difference in some situations, while ignoring it in others (Beauvoir 2000:3)

Beauvoir's concept of lived experience is more open than the sex/gender distinction, allowing us to take into account varieties of experience while remaining contextual sensitive. I suggest that we read *In a Different Voice* a phenomenological inquiry into the lived moral experiences of women in a certain socio–cultural situation, not as a testimony of what it means for women to be moral agents. Then it should be possible to transcend both the discussions on whether Gilligan is essentialist or not, and the constraints the sex/gender distinction puts on any attempts to explain women's tendency to associate with the care perspective, and men's to correlate with the justice perspective. In what follows I will nevertheless consider some feminist views on Gilligan's ethics, and thereafter discuss how her version of the ethics of care compares with feminist ethics.

Feminist Views on Gilligan's Ethics of Care

The feminist response and debate on Gilligan's work and theory has been extensive and my approach of Gilligan's ethics in light of different feminist views is not exhaustive. Instead of spending time surveying every single feminist approach to Gilligan's ethics of care, I would focus on a feature shared by all feminist views. That is a commitment to gender equality and a desire to achieve such equality (Kourany et al. 1993:1). Feminism in ethics, as in other disciplines, aims at "ending oppression, subordination, abuse and exploitation of women and girls, wherever these may arise" (Friedman 2000: 205). And while opinions on the sources of oppression, and on the strategies most likely to bring sexism to an end vary, I want to apply the minimalist definition of feminism to Gilligan's ethics of care and ask: Does Gilligan's ethics of care oppose or sustain feminism i.e. does it promote or discourage inequality and sexism? What we need to know here is that Gilligan does not only claim for her research an empirical correlation between women and care. She takes it to a normative level, where she embraces the value of care, and gives it ethical relevance. In fact, the value Gilligan finds empirically correlated with women she takes as the core of her normative ethics of care. This praise of care is one of the causes of the intense debate among feminists, where some maintain that her ethics of care contributes to end gender oppression, and others that it sustains and even reinforces traditional constraints.

Historically, culturally, politically and economically, care is linked to women. Care is a value and a virtue associated with women's work, with their nature and their purpose in life. Aristotle, Augustine, Thomas Aquinas, Rousseau, Kant and Hume have all contributed to such a view. The genderization of care explains why Gilligan's theory of care is called a *feminine* ethics. A feminine ethic is one that focuses, expresses and defends virtues and moral ideals that are *culturally identified* with women. A *feminist* ethic is an ethic that focuses on suppression and dominance, and often pursues political aims (Tong 1993:4–12). Gilligan's ethic of care in this sense *is* therefore rightly termed a feminine ethics. The crucial question, however, is whether Gilligan's feminine ethics of care is also a feminist ethics since it is based on a value that culturally is identified with women? Some feminists would say yes, it is, others that women should be very careful with this theory.

For example Joan Tronto argues in "Women's Morality: Beyond Gender Differences to a Theory of Care" (1987) and in "Women and Caring" (1995) that the care voice discovered by Gilligan may be a reflection of a survival mechanism for women and others who are dealing with oppressive conditions. Tronto also argues that Gilligan's ethics of care probably is most appropriate for those in a subordinate social position, as it can be understood as expressing the necessity to anticipate the wishes of one's superior (Tronto 1995: 112).[7] Virginia Held warns us against equating the tendencies Gilligan's women in fact display, with feminist views. The reason, says Held, is that their tendencies, for instance to care, may well be the result of the sexist, oppressive condition in which women's lives have been lived (Held 1995: 2; Held 1998: 336–337). Both Tronto and Held are prominent care ethicists; their contribution to the ethics of care is highly significant, as we shall see later. What they are critically towards is Gilligan's version of the ethics of care.

Let me also mention Catharine MacKinnon as an example of those who responded particularly skeptically towards Gilligan's ethics of care. In an exchange with Gilligan, MacKinnon says she found *In a Different Voice* politically infuriating because Gilligan, according to MacKinnon, does not sufficiently explain how the care perspective came into being in the first place. MacKinnon thinks she knows why.

> *Why* do women become these people, more than men, who represent *these* values? For me, the answer is clear: the answer is the subordination of women. . . . [Gilligan] has also found the voice of the victim—yes, women are a victimized group. . . . What bothers me is identifying women with it. (MacKinnon quoted in Benhabib 1994).

According to Benhabib (1994) the exchange between Gilligan and Mac-Kinnon exemplifies a type of "paradigm clash" within feminist theory on whether women carry a set of different and unique values that should be promoted, or whether they should focus on gaining power and equality in the existing society. What MacKinnon is afraid of is that woman's voice is an expression of woman's *false consciousness*, as are Joan Tronto and Virginia Held. In these warnings I hear the echo of another philosopher: Simone de Beauvoir. Introducing *The Second Sex*, Beauvoir discusses the difficulties involved in knowing what it means to be a "woman"—as defined by a gendered culture (Beauvoir 2000:33–48). Indeed, adopting Beauvoir's existentialist feminist terminology one could say that the issue is whether the concerns of Gilligan's female informants relating to care and private relationships should not more accurately be understood as testimonies of women consigned to immanence by an oppressive male culture, as the second sex's touching attempts to gild their prison. Beauvoir, writing almost 60 years ago, drew attention to women's tendency to care and repair. Since woman's situation is confined and suppressed, it is easier, Beauvoir explains, for them to create a fragile happiness within the home, rather than outside (Beauvoir 2000:703–704). Beauvoir's point is not to dismiss care or neglect its importance, but to show how gendered structures confine women's freedom (Pettersen 2006).[8]

Some of the feminists who emphasize that Gilligan's ethics of care reflects a traditional gendered norm system, reject her ethics as a feminist ethics, or are at least skeptical to it, because they believe that it sustains and reinforces traditional gender structures—structures that disfavor women. These critical reflections deserve attention. But paying attention to something is not identical with passivity. We should make use of this insight and turn the question of false consciousness around and ask instead: Where is the Archimedean point from which it can be claimed that women's lifestyles are inauthentic, from which we could determine whether some women's values are wholly or partly the result of false beliefs, false consciousness, oppression, subordination or victimization, while others are not?

The fact is that not all feminists view the feminine as an expression of victimization and subordination. Some feminists want to turn their back on what to them is a masculine culture, and search instead for a genuine female nature or essence. From this feminist perspective, the different voice of women becomes a viable alternative to what they consider the masculine voice of justice. Instead of criticizing or questioning the feminine aspect of Gilligan's ethics of care, these feminists applaud the feminine. They assert that care, which has defined the life of most women for centuries, has been neglected and devalued too long, and that it is time to upgrade and celebrate care. These feminists see no difference in value between the ethics of care and other moral theories; some even believe it is *better*. Nel Noddings holds in her book *Caring: A Feminine Approach to Ethics and Moral Education* (1984) the view that an ethics of female care is superior to what she portrays as a masculine ethics of principles. The ethics of care, she says, is a feminine ethics, it expresses the mother's voice, a voice which has been silenced by the voice of the father, and the father's voice is a voice guided by Logos, the masculine spirit (Noddings 1984:1) The difference between being guided by the father's and the mother's voice, Noddings suggests is that "The father might sacrifice his own child in fulfilling a principle; while the mother might sacrifice any principle to preserve her child" (Noddings 1984:37).

For Noddings the feminine voice of care is superior to the masculine voice, and her views on the ethics of care recall a debate within feminist theory on essentialism and anti–essentialism, a debate which culminated during the 1980s. One can draw from this debate, connections to feminist debates on postmodernism, multiculturalism, relativism and globalization. Here is obviously not the place to discuss all these aspects, only to mention that some feminists agree on that Gilligan's ethics of care can work to hasten the fall of modernity and encourage postmodern plurality (Hekman 1995). Others find affinities with communitarianism, and some would like to globalize care.

The Ethics of Care—a Feminist Ethic?

Now, as we have seen, of the different feminist views on Gilligan's ethics of care, some hold that the feminine aspect of this theory fails in terms of generally held feminist goals while others claim that it represents a superior moral voice and that feminists should work towards upgrading the status of the feminine. My own view on the matter is that I take Carol Gilligan's ethics to be a feminist ethics. It is a feminist ethics because it reveals how recommendations, values and categories used in traditional normative ethics are not gender neutral, but constructed in a way that fails to adequately accommodate the feminine aspect of our lives. By drawing attention to gender–blindness and sexism in moral philosophy, Gilligan's ethics aids the effort to eradicate the neglect, disregard and devaluation perpetrated by traditional theories. Her works also pave the way, as we shall see, for the development of alternative concepts and analytical categories in moral philosophy and ethics. This is indeed in accordance with the goals of feminism in ethics.

Although we rightly in my opinion find in Gilligan's ethics of care a feminist ethics, I want to end this chapter by reflecting on some of the pros and cons of using the term "feministic" on the ethics of care. A relevant counterargument is that if this ethical theory has any bearing on ethics and moral philosophy in general, it is unnecessary to speak of it as "feministic" (Schott 2004:28), as it would only make the ethics of care seem totally irrelevant to the mainstream discourse. One might also argue that the best antidote to gender–bias in moral philosophy is to aspire to a nonsexist theory, a theory which can avoid discrimination, constraints or stereotypes based on gender. When developing an ethics of care in the field of moral theory, we need to take special care not to gender the theory, and the term "feministic" can be comprehended as a way of continuing the genderization in ethics and moral philosophy. If we believe that care is a value that deserves to be appreciated more and protected, the best way of achieving this would be to insist on a gender–neutral ethics of care. If care is a valuable moral ideal, it is valuable for women as well as for men. Of course, simply by naming the ethics of care feministic one risks cleaving "research" and "philosophy"—considered an expression of pure reason, untouched by sex or society—from "gender research" and "feminist philosophy"—thought of as infused by subjectivism and political goals but little scientific validity. Another danger lies in the likely stigmatization and devaluation of research labeled "feministic" insofar as academic fields that are dominated by women tend to suffer from low prestige. Women often find recognition more readily dispensed when their co–authors are men (Cudd and Jones 2005:110). "Feminist" ethics also risks being seen as politically motivated research; anathema to many philosophers and researchers, further isolating the ethics of care from relevant arenas. And if it gains a reputation of being of interest only to women or dedicated feminists, its substantive concerns will suffer from lack of attention.

On the other hand, advocates of a "feminist" ethics of care may respond by pointing out that "feministic ethics" simply means the use of insights gained within feminist philosophy to analyze ethics and moral philosophy.

And as the ethics of care investigates traditional female values and practices, and explores the gender bias of normative theories, its name should reflect that endeavor. For some, to call something "feminist" is to take a stance: Research is always influenced by politics and motivated by particular interests anyway; exposing and eradicating gendered power–structures in ethics and moral philosophy are therefore perfectly legitimate aims. In this way, the assertive use of "feminist" serves as a counterweight to devaluating tendencies.

Now, whether the different voice Gilligan heard is a victimized voice, the voice of the slave trying to please her master, or an expression of a superior uncorrupted female nature may be an interesting question in some respects, as is the debate on whether the ethics of care in fact is a feminist ethics, and whether it is wise to name it this way. However, for those who advocate care as a normative value, and want to investigate the moral–philosophical implication of the perspective of care, these issues are not the most essential issues. Whether we approve or disapprove of the ethics of care should in my view be based on whether or not we can argue convincingly for the normative plausibility of the theory, not be conflated with debate on the empirical and cultural correlation of women with care. So even if the ethics of care is deeply rooted in what culturally is defined as feminine, both feminist and non–feminist philosophers would be well advised not to let gender issues overshadow other important aspects of care ethics, but direct their efforts at developing this moral theory in the hope that care will be appreciated by men and as well as by women, in practices as well as in moral philosophy. Hence, we shall leave the strong focus on gender behind, and turn our attention to some of the meta–ethical challenges crucial for an ethics of care.

Notes

1. This exposition is not exhaustive; the point is to set out information of a general nature as on a backdrop to her theory, and, at the same time, determine where in the ongoing debate the focal point of this book lies.

2. Chodorow says "[b]ecause women are themselves mothered by women, they grow up with the relational capacities and needs, and psychological definition of self–in–relationship, which commits them to mothering. Men, because they are mothered by women, do not. Women mother daughters who, when they become women, mother" (Chodorow 1978:126).

3. "Evidence that the two moral orientations we have described structure people's thinking about the nature and resolution of moral conflicts come from studies of the way people describes moral conflicts they have faced. Analysis of such descriptions indicates that people tend to raise consideration of justice and of care in recounting experiences of moral conflict and choice" (Gilligan et al. 1988:118).

4. Essentialism is the argument that there is some foundation for the category "women" grounded in female nature; women share common characteristics upon which political action can be based. Anti-essentialism is the view that the category "women" is a historically specific and socially constructed category. Categories such as "female" and "male" are from this point of view not fixed by nature and cannot be located in some unchanging natural essence. Instead, they are socially constructed and vary considerably across cultures and historical moments.

5. The following quote exemplifies a relatively close connection between women and care: "In view of the evidence that women perceive and construe social reality differently from men and that these differences center around experience of attachment and separation, life transitions that invariably engage these experiences can be expected to involve women in a distinctive way. And because women's sense of integrity appears to be entwined with an ethics of care, so that to see themselves as women is to see themselves in a relationship of connection, the major transitions in women's lives would seem to involve changes in the understanding and activities of care [. . .] in the different voice of women lies the truth of an ethic of care, the tie between relationship and responsibility, and the origins of aggression in the failure of connection" (Gilligan 1982:171,173).

6. The following quotes exemplify passages where the link between gender and care is presented as downplayed: "The different voice I describe is characterized not by gender but theme. Its association with women is an empirical observation and it is primarily through women's voices that I trace its development. But this association is not absolute, and the contrasts between male and female voices are presented here to highlight a distinction between two modes of thought and to focus a problem of interpretation rather than to represent a generalization about either sex" (Gilligan 1982:2).

7. "[I]nsofar as caring is a kind of attentiveness, it may be a reflection of a survival mechanism for women and others who are dealing with oppressive condition" or it is "an ethics most appropriate for those in a subordinate social position, the necessity to anticipate the wishes of one's superior" (Tronto 1995: 112).

8. In her essay *Une mort très douce* (1964) for example, Beauvoir analyzes the application of care in relation to her terminally ill mother.

~

CHAPTER THREE

Normative Foundations
and Formal Features

Why is the perspective of care comprehended as a normative theory and not merely as a description based on test results in the field of developmental psychology? An inquiry into morality can be descriptive as well as normative, and the perspective of care can be read as non–normative, i.e. as a factual description supported by an explanatory psychological hypothesis concerning difference in moral beliefs, reasoning and judgments. Gilligan nevertheless claims that the care perspective entails a normative ethical theory, but it is not clear on what grounds she rests her claim. In this chapter I will explore the normative basis for the ethics of care, as well as some formal, theoretical features characteristic for this ethical theory.[1]

"Bottom Up" and "Top Down"

The ethics of care, and Gilligan's theory in particular, can be characterized as a "bottom up", or "inductivistic" model, in the sense that its points of departure are concrete cases, particular situations and certain experiences. Certain features of behaviors and actions are extracted, systematized and explicated: Gilligan sees a pattern in women's way of approaching concrete moral challenges, expressive of norms and values related to care that are ignored in mainstream moral philosophy. But after pointing to resemblances between the individual woman's moral experiences and ways of reasoning, Gilligan pretty much leaves the ethics of care at this theoretically undeveloped stage. This is understandable because it is the moral philosopher's task, as opposed to the moral psychologist's, to develop a philosophically sound moral theory of care. Such moral–philosophical scrutiny is compulsory because the norms and values in question are extracted from experience, in this case the historic experience of women, and possibly based on prejudice, ungrounded privilege and parochial preference.

Chauvinism is one weakness of the "bottom up" model, which is frequently contrasted with a "top–down" model or a "deductivistic" approach to ethics. Gilligan depicts traditional moral reasoning as deductivistic; the moral agent takes an ethical principle or theory and asks whether it is morally forbidden or permissible to act in certain ways. She illustrates the process with the reasoning of an eleven–year–old boy, Jake, confronted with Heinz's dilemma (see Chapter 1). The "top–down" structure of reasoning is also termed "the theoretical–juridical model" (Walker 1998:2002). The model is "theoretical" because it evaluates theories according to their logical and theoretical accuracy, not in regard to their applicability. It is "juridical" in the sense that it is used to give judgments on concrete cases. Established norms and principles are given priority in the deductive model, and practice is pretty much ignored. If these norms, principles and categories are inadequate, and/or unrepresentative, the ethical theories and moral philosophy relying on them will disregard and neglect certain ways of approaching moral questions and moral issues. This is exactly Gilligan's point, a point echoed by moral philosopher Annette Baier in her critique of most prevailing ethics. Let's pick up on Baier's critique of the deductive model, as it encapsulates the sense of discontent felt by Gilligan and other care ethicists about the dominant ethical theories.

In her article "Trust and Distrust of Moral Theorists" (1993a), Baier criticizes moral philosophers for adopting a–historical and non–personal points of view. By so doing, she says, they create the impression that statements on right and wrong, good and evil can be given from a (value) neutral position. This is misleading, says Baier, because such a position does not exist. All of us are situated in a particular culture and class, and we all have our personal experience and indeed gender. Individuals' experiences vary in relation to biological sex, wealth, status as suppressor or suppressed. An individual's experiences affect her conceptions of right and wrong, the construction of ethical theories and doing of moral philosophy. If moral philosophers conceal personal information while claiming to speak on behalf of everybody, they should not be trusted, says Baier. She instances her case with Thomas Nagel and his *The View from Nowhere* (1986). This is precisely not a view from "Nowhere", she contends, but probably from around New York University or Brasenose College, Oxford (1993:135). But if the perspective of care represents the values and behavior of heterosexual, middle–class American women—we still need to know why should we prefer the care point of view before the viewpoint from Brasenose College.

The Flourishing Strategy

One of the reasons Gilligan gives for why care is recommended is its assumed beneficial consequences—for individuals as well as for society. Gilligan says that the perspective of care "not only provides a better understanding of re- lations between the sexes" but it "also gives rise to a more comprehensive portrayal of adult work and family relationships". It could "lead to a changed understanding of human development and a more generative view of human life" (Gilligan 1982:174). It could "chart the course of moral development", and also, "as the contemporary reality of global interdependence impels the search for new maps of development, the exploration of attachment may pro- vide the psychological grounding for new visions of progress and growth" (Gilligan et al. 1988:157).

Several philosophical questions can be raised concerning Gilligan's at- tempt to justify the merits of care and formulate an ethics of care by referring to beneficial consequences. Such questions relate to the content of the con- sequences as well as her attempt to found a normative theory on assumed consequences as such. As to the content, one may ask what "good conse- quences" means, i.e. what does "good" signify—the enjoyable, the useful, the skillful, a condition or state of well–being or welfare? Is "good" a property that all good things have in common, or is it relative to a certain standard or situation? How is moral goodness related to the variety of other goods and concepts of goodness? These or other meta–ethical questions shall not be dis- cussed broadly since our concern is how "good consequences" in the ethics of care can be comprehended.

When Gilligan points to the good consequences that follow from care, good relates to well–being (Gilligan 1984:78). But what does "well–being" signify? Since there is no exact answer or definition in Gilligan's work, it needs to be discussed. From what has been said so far in this study, it seems reasonable to suggest that well–being relates to a particular feature of human welfare; inter- personal interaction. Given Gilligan's relational point of departure—the inter- connectedness of people—her concept of "well–being" concerns relationships. I understand Gilligan's "well–being" as meaning "long and short–term well– being–in–relationship". Since being connected is good, and caring sustains, nurtures and promotes relationships, caring is thought to have good conse- quences. "Well–being" is nevertheless not understood in a hedonistic sense; it does not signify pleasure, but to thrive and grow.[2] Therefore, "flourishing" would seem to be an adequate term for Gilligan's "well–being".[3]

Objections to this reasoning are several: (1) Gilligan's understanding of well–being seems very narrow since it primarily focuses on relationships and connectedness; (2) Her argument appears to beg the question; (3) The claim that relationships are necessary to personal well–being and flourishing seems both trivial and disputable. As to (1), the narrowness of her "well–being", I presume that it is not meant to be exhaustive. As I see it, Gilligan has no intention to give a complete theory on human well–being and flourishing. She is interested simply to focus on a particular aspect of well–being; our connectedness. True, relationships are not the only ingredient in personal well–being and flourishing, but connectedness is nevertheless a constitutive element in her theory. In fact, the assumption of human connectedness and dependency are central ontological features of Gilligan's theory and part of what I choose to call the "relational ontology". I take this relational ontology to be a very important dimension of her ethics of care, and it will play a central role in the subsequent discussion. It explains why connectedness has such central place in her understanding of "well–being".[4] Objection (2) will be considered below, but first some remarks on (3), the assumption that relationships and connectedness are necessary for well–being and flourishing.

Anti–Caring Arguments

Even if Gilligan does not consider interpersonal relationships as sufficient for human well–being and flourishing, their value can nevertheless be disputed because we know that abusive, exploitive and destructive relationships exist. Gilligan is aware of this (Gilligan 1982:109–115), but does not respond to the problems they give rise to, as she does not encounter directly the mistreatment that may take place within relationships. However, she might be read as indirectly dealing with these problems. She advocates care in close relationships because it's lack contributes to human misery. Brutal relationships can partly be understood as a result of failing to care.[5]

Another argument against Gilligan's presumption that connectedness is required for human well–being is that certain activities, intellectual and creative activities in particular, which contribute substantially to many persons' sense of well–being and flourishing, may be antagonistic to relationships. People pursue such activities, such as writing and painting, mostly alone. Often they require contemplation, a solitary endeavor that most likely will detract from the time and effort available to spend on relationships. Diane Romain portrays this in a pertinent way:

Intellectual and creative work gives me the most pleasure and satisfaction. [. . .] I love to be alone in my study all day with only the hum of my Mac to keep me company. I love to read my writings again and again, to find thoughts to elaborate, structure to develop. I love to sound my words and sentences, to listen to the pattern of phrases. I could append hours on a single paragraph. But I rarely do. I rarely spend hours on a single essay or story. And why? [. . . Because] I focus more on relationships than on writing. (Romain 1992:30,31)

Moreover, if care and connectedness are coupled with women's activities the objection that caring relationships are not equivalent with human flourishing gains even more force. We could use women's history as an illustration of how the occupation with relationships has constituted an obstacle to women's participation in different spheres of life. Several influential works have drawn attention to the concern: In 1928 Virginia Woolf published *A Room of One's Own*, where she explained the dearth of women in the arts and sciences with the lack of space and time available to them to carry out such work. Alexandria Kollontay portrays in *A Great Love* (1929) the difficulties women experience when trying to combine the involvement in political work with romantic and intimate attachment. In *The Obstacle Race* (1984) Germaine Greer put forward a hypothesis as to why there are so few great female painters in history of art: Women of talent became personally involved with their (male) teachers, a relationship that consumed their time as well as their creative resources. In *The Second Sex* (1949), Simone de Beauvoir claimed that the only way of ending the oppression of women would be for women to free themselves from their roles as mothers and wives and appropriate the rationality and independency of men. And in her lecture "Women and Creativity" (1966), she asserts that women, in order to become writers, must not belong to men and children, but to themselves only (Beauvoir 1987:17). Many other feminist contributions could be mentioned, but my point is that even if a variety of reasons are given for women's subordination,[6] there is consensus among these writers that women must regard themselves as independent, not dependent on others. So the belief that caring is a desirable goal can be counter with political arguments; the ethics of care contributes to sustain traditional gender roles in the family as well as in professional life, it goes against the main achievements of the women's movement. From an ethical standpoint, we could interpret care ethics as confirming a view of women as accommodated by, for instance, Rousseau and Kant, and for founding her theory on a metaphysic which leaves little or no room for individual projects.

Nevertheless, these anti–caring arguments do not affect Gilligan's theory as such. First, because she explicitly warns against relationships that serve as hindrance for women (Brown and Gilligan 1992:29–30), she cannot be claimed to romanticize "female care or the nineteenth–century ideal of pure womanhood" (Gilligan 1982:128–133).[7] She says further:

> Thus in contrast to the paralyzing image of the "angel in the house", I describe a critical ethical perspective that calls into question the traditional equation of care with self–sacrifice. (Gilligan 1993:209)

Her rejection of the "angel of the house" can be deduced from her theory of moral development, in particular her concept of "the right kind of care" which we might remember is the mature care she places on level three of her developmental scale. Characteristic for this type of care is the idea that caring includes concern for oneself as well as others. Care is therefore not completely self–sacrificing, nor totally selfish. In understanding care as mature care, the objections to the idea of care based on the existence of abusive, oppressive and exploitative relationships are weakened because relationships founded on mature care are clearly the opposite of abusive and manipulative relationships. Relationships based on mature care are founded on a balance between the interests of self and others.

With the concept of mature care in mind, we also find in Gilligan's ethics of care the need of a space for people to carry out what they find to be important for their well–being and flourishing. How much they may pursue their interests, however, will be discussed in the next chapters. Among other things, we shall see how Aristotle's discussion on friendship might facilitate our comprehension of mature care. For now I want to claim that Gilligan can be read as submitting an ethic of care where flourishing relationships can be developed—that is without one part, irrespectively of gender, being submissive.[8] For Gilligan, such relationships constitute an important part of human well–being.

Obviously, there are pros and cons concerning the desirability of care, and an ethics based on this value. Gilligan avoids the arguments arrayed against the ethics of care primarily by means of definition: "Care" is understood as the "mature care" on level three in her developmental theory where the interest of both self and others are taken into account. This is a strategy that renders harmful relationships as relationships in which "the right kind of care" is absent.[9] However, even if one accepts this strategy, it does not follow that caring is a *moral* issue. Many activities promote human well–being and thriving: education, art, farming, house–building and so forth. Why then should caring be a moral requirement while farming is not? I believe an answer can be found if we take Gilligan's metaphysics into account: Since individuals are connected in a web of relationships and interdependencies which make them vulnerable, and since caring contributes to sustaining these connections, care should be aimed at. But is this begging the question? Does Gilligan assume what is to be proved? We need to inspect the structure in Gilligan's line of reasoning more closely before she can be acquitted.

Moral Psychology and Moral Philosophy: From Is to Ought

"Being interdependent and connected in relationships is described as common human features which become central to moral understanding", says Gilligan (1982:149). This close connection between Gilligan's view of human nature and her normative recommendations as well as her obscure distinction between fact and value, are reason enough to reflect on the meta–ethical position of Gilligan's ethics of care. Is her theory a variant of ethical naturalism where care is understood to be recommendable because it purports a moral fact, where ethical conclusions are derivable from non–ethical premises? Does Gilligan (and other care ethicists) confuse "is" and "ought"? While this philosophical distinction does not appear in Gilligan's work, from the perspective of moral philosophy, it needs to be clear. We shall ponder this question since her maneuvers might indicate a fallacy in her train of thought.

It appears as if Gilligan draws normative conclusions from her psychological thesis on human nature, thus blurring the distinction between "is" and "ought". The entry point for Gilligan's ethics of care is a combination of empirical studies and psychological theories, both of which are included in the concept of 'nature' (Moore 1993:92).[10] Gilligan's line of argument appears to be that since relationships are a common human feature, necessary for well–being and flourishing, and sustained through care, we ought to care. Now, if Gilligan actually argues from descriptive premises—that people are connected in relationships sustained through care for instance,—to the normative conclusion that care and connections are desirable, her ethics of care may be accused of the naturalistic fallacy. The "naturalistic fallacy" is the allegation G. E. Moore, in his *Principia Ethica* (1903), held against all naturalistic theory: Naturalists are mixing up the two distinct items of fact and value. His thesis is related to a famous passage in Hume's *A Treatise of Human Nature* (ca. 1740), found also in Sophia's *Woman Not Inferior to Man* (1739), i.e. that an "ought" cannot be derived from an "is".[11] It means that no set of descriptive statements can give rise to an evaluative statement without the addition of at least one evaluative premise; without this condition met, the argument is fallacious (Searle 1998:38). Whether it is correct or not has been much discussed, and the stand one takes is relevant to the "autonomy of ethics"; whether ethics is independent or dependent on what obtains in other realms of science such as biology, the social sciences, and, particularly relevant here, psychology. This brings us to the question on naturalism. "Naturalism" is a meta–ethical position, which holds that morality can be reduced to non–moral facts. Non–moral facts are information, or knowledge, of biology, sociology or psychology that are empirically verifiable. In this position, "ought" is reduced to "is", and values are identical with facts. Value judgments can therefore be true or false, just as can factual statements. It is this version of naturalism I now ask if Gilligan's ethics of care can be comprehended as committed to.

Since Gilligan's normative theory stems from her psychological developmental theory, one could expect her not to regard philosophy and psychology as completely separated but rather as working in harness. If this assumption is not too far off the mark, it will influence the way we approach the "is/ought" distinction. In order to explain and support a posited interaction between moral development psychology and moral philosophy and therefore also relate the "is" and the "ought" in Gilligan's theory, I will start by showing why the opposite view is difficult to uphold. By the opposite view I mean the position that psychology is only descriptive, its function being to describe and explain certain facts and not to prescribe or evaluate the worth of these facts, while moral philosophy, by contrast, is primarily concerned with judgment about what ought to be, and aims to clarify and justify its normative and prescriptive claims.

Now, Gilligan's psychological developmental theory cannot be purely a description of some phenomena or other since her moral developmental theory is, as are most developmental theories, based on an assumption that progress and changes take place. Gilligan's three levels are hierarchical, and the transformation from one level to another is a movement upward, towards moral maturity. Each new level is seen as more complete than the last. But there can be no moral development without a perception of right and wrong, good and evil (Thomas 1991). There must be *something* to develop. In Gilligan's psychological theory this something is care. Care is the selected normative criterion that organizes the empirical classification in her research, and provides the "superiority" of level three over level one and two with regard to content. Selfless care is better than selfish care, while mature care is morally most excellent. The "is" in her moral psychological developmental theory is induced by the "ought"; what is described as moral maturity is influenced by the evaluative assertion that care is good and desirable.

Furthermore, in addition to argue against the view that psychological developmental theory is purely descriptive, I also hold that moral philosophy cannot come up with an "ought" without any empirical assumptions about human nature, capabilities and preferences. A glance at the history of ethics illustrates this point: Aristotle, Augustine, Machiavelli, Kant and J.S. Mill each had their particular notions of the nature of men and women, which in turn deeply influenced their ethical theories. This last point can be related to Gilligan's critique against what she takes to be the traditional ethical paradigm: The "ought" relies on a(n inadequate) conception of what human beings are. Human beings in Gilligan's view are both interdependent and autonomous, and this fact is not, according to her, taken sufficiently account of. The apparently inadequate concept of human beings is also part of many feminists' critique of the dominant ethical theories (Walker 1992; Tong 1993:48–80).

As shown, the distinction between ought and is, between facts and values, as well as between moral philosophy and moral psychology, can be disputed, and this brings us back to my questions: is Gilligan guilty of the naturalistic fallacy, and is there a meta–ethical naturalism lurking behind Gilligan's defense of the normativity of care? As I see it, the lack of distinction between is and ought in Gilligan's theory does not have to be understood as amounting to complete identification of is with ought, of values and facts.

Such a reduction would entail the position of ethical naturalism—a position beset with problems (Thomas 1991:429). However, what has been said so far only demonstrates that is and ought, fact and value, psychology and ethics are related, it does not compellingly show how one can get from is to ought without arguing either fallaciously, or accepting ethical naturalism with all its problems. Kohlberg, who struggled with the same problem, said that, "As opposed to naturalism, we hold with Hare [. . .] that moral language and judgments are fundamentally *prescriptive*, not descriptive". Perhaps Gilligan would be well–advised to side with Kohlberg in this particular matter, since prescriptivism is a meta–ethical position that allows moral judgments and language to refer to facts, although it does not exhaust the meaning of moral judgments or statements, insofar as moral judgments have an additional prescriptive element. "Ought judgments" are prescriptive or action–guiding in the way imperatives are as they attempt to guide choices and actions by recommending or condemning, not by making truth claims (Beauchamp 1991:108). Imperatives can be derived from principles or norms a particular agent finds binding. They also seem therefore to allow for a positing of care as a norm. Hare's prescriptivism requires that moral judgments are "universalizable prescriptions" (Hare 1991). Hare's universal prescriptivism relies on a notion of universalizability which is broader than Kant's, as Kant seems to tie universalizability to considerations of justice (Nortvedt 1996:28 n9). According to Hare, justification of moral decisions requires a complete account of the principle employed as well as its effects, and the principle itself is open to modification.[12] However, even if such a complete account could be given one might ask why accept the principle and the effects in the first place. This question is similar to the question *Why be moral?* to which, presumably, no further answer could be given. Or, as Beauchamp portrays it:

> We can only ask the person to make up his or her mind about which way one ought to live. In the end, everything pertaining to the choice of retaining one's old principles or finding new ones rests upon a decision of principle; individuals must decide for themselves whether to accept a course of conduct such as the moral life. (Beauchamp 1991:109)

Related to the formal features and structure of Gilligan's ethics, this might be helpful: The normativity of care cannot be settled merely by pointing to factual descriptions as value–laden, or by referring to the fact that "ought" in traditional ethics relies on an inadequate assumption of "is". The very point at issue, in Gilligan's ethical theory, is that the description given of human beings must be defended further—since what is to be proven is precisely *which* descriptions may be recognized as having normative values. Within the ethics of care there must be arguments for why care and connectedness should be the focus of moral development, and the theory's moral ideal and not a quite different value, such as independency. The question concerning the source of normativity might have an ultimate limit, but for the perspective of care to constitute a *normative* theory, not merely a value–laden, question–begging and fallacious psychological construction, an evaluative premise must be added. The ethics of care needs to be anchored in an ethical ideal or value, if the normativity of the theory is to be justified. I will now suggest how this can be done.

Gilligan's Implicit Normative Assumptions

Even though Gilligan's way of arguing at first sight appears invalid since her normative conclusion seems to be drawn from descriptive premises, one cannot from the lack of explicit normative first premises draw the conclusion that they do not exist. Implicit normative assumptions may very well exist in Gilligan's work. If they do not, one could discuss which normative premises *could* be used to support the conclusion that we ought to care. A certain interpretation of the principle of non–maleficence may answer how one, given Gilligan's theory, can conclude that we ought to care. The principle can be a point of departure for explicating the normative premise in what can be understood as Gilligan's enthymeme. It can serve as the normative first premise that bridges the gap between the descriptive and the normative in her theory. Now, why exactly this premise? Because Gilligan says "the absolute of care, [can be] defined initially as not hurting others", and that "an ethic of care rests on the premise of non–violence—that no one should be hurt" (Gilligan 1982:166,174). I interpret this as an expression of the concern at the normative heart of her ethics of care. The idea of not hurting can be read as having a primacy in the ethics of care, and, if established as the first premise, also occupies a central position in the formal scheme I suggest for this theory. In addition, and equally important, such a theoretical structure explains the origin of the normativity of care. The principle carries the perspective of care into the normative domain, enabling normative conclusions to be drawn from a value premise. The proposed normative first premise in Gilligan's theory of care requires a further elaboration, especially since it is a negative formulation of her ideas.

The Expanded Principle of Not Hurting

If the principle of non–maleficence is understood to mean refraining from inflicting harm or evil on others, I do not take Gilligan's core idea of not hurting to be precisely the same. *Refraining* from harmful behavior implies that we can derive no more than negative duties from the principle of non–maleficence. Caring, however, is not only refraining from harming, it also involves active beneficence. One might therefore assume that it would be more appropriate to establish a connection between care and the principle of beneficence.[13] Related to the principle of beneficence, however, is the problem of determining the extent of our obligation to produce good. Without any restrictions, this principle implies self–sacrifice. This contradicts an important aspect of Gilligan's theory on moral development: mature care pertains to oneself as well as to others. She puts emphasis on this, and this concern is probably not appropriately accommodated if care is connected with the principle of beneficence only. Also, the principle of beneficence can be understood as an injunction to produce a maximum of good, and therefore opens up for inflicting harm on somebody for the sake of producing good for the majority. These implications are incompatible with my comprehension of Gilligan's theory of care and her concept of mature care in particular. As I see it, they can be avoided by linking care to the principle of non–maleficence. However, the principle of non–maleficence, understood as only requiring negative duties, seems inadequate to capture another of what I take to be a main concern of Gilligan—the active participation which care often calls for. Therefore, only a combination of these two principles seems to attend adequately to Gilligan's concerns. When coupled, they protect against what in Gilligan's theory are apprehended as non–desirable implications, implications that seem to follow if each principle alone is thought of as constituting the evaluative premise in her theory. The principle of non–maleficence, expanded to allow for intervening in situations where intervention is required for preventing harm, is what I in the following will term "the expanded principle of not hurting", and which I interpret as a possible first premise in her normative scheme.

The expanded principle of not hurting also has a slightly different focus than both the principle of non–maleficence and the principle of beneficence. What Gilligan draws attention to in her theory is the damage caused in interpersonal interaction due to a lack of mature care. To this one may reply that interpersonal relations are often harmed as a result of the workings of larger structural systems, such as socio–economic and cultural ones. Far from denying these facts, the expanded principle of not hurting serves to highlight the focus of Gilligan's theory; harm caused in relationships. Given her psychological point of departure she focuses on mental and emotional hurt, not so much on physical harm. This should not lead us to conclude that she fails to acknowledge the importance of structural as well as physical injury, but to recognize where her emphasis lies. I shall draw upon these ideas in Chapter 9 when discussing how this focus can be given a normative justification.

One may nevertheless already doubt the significance of emphasizing non–maleficence in relationships by referring to what may seem to be rather trivial: the importance of acting in a caring way towards, say, one's friends and relatives. Certainly, for some people, this may be common knowledge, for others it is not, just as some find it obvious to treat others in a fair and equal way, others do not. These empirical matters are not important here. What is important is Gilligan's claim that only one type of behavior is deliberated and taken into account in ethical theories and given ethical relevance. When the principle of non–maleficence is interpreted as "the extended principle of not hurting", the sphere of features considered morally relevant seems to widen: Caring in relationships is given ethical relevance. If this is not too far off the mark, then Gilligan is right in one of her claims: that the ethics of care induces a change in the way one understands the moral domain.

In introducing the expanded principle of not hurting as a first premise in the ethics of care I take a stand in the discussion on principles in ethical theories. The ethics of care advanced here is not a theory that rejects universal principles.[14] Although my discussion goes beyond Gilligan's account, my conclusion here does not deviate from what there is textual evidence for: In *In a Different Voice* both the ethics of care, and care, are linked clearly to the universal principle of not hurting: "Care becomes the self–chosen principle of a judgment that remains psychological in its concern with relationships and response but becomes universal in its condemnation of exploitation and hurt", she says (Gilligan 1982:74).

Two Normative Strategies

Let me sum up what is said so far in regard to the normative foundation of the ethics of care in order to make them distinct. In Gilligan's works, different ideas can be made out; ideas that sometimes appear to be separate but nevertheless hang together. There is (1) the perspective of care that can be understood as an evidence–based account of a certain way of making moral decisions. As a subdivision of the discussion of this perspective we have (1a) the question of how and if moral judgments are gendered, and (1b) whether moral reasoning can be separated into two major orientations: one of care and one of justice. Furthermore, the perspective of care is explained through the lens of a particular (2) psychological theory on moral development that results in a concept of morally mature care. This psychological theory has its origin in the assumption that the self is related. This assumption is contrasted to the view that the self is separated and independent of others, which is what Gilligan takes to be expounded in the traditional ethical theories. As to the assumption concerning the related self, it is an entry point to Gilligan's ideas, and I have therefore termed it her (3) "relational ontology". Additionally, based on these assumptions, she also claims the existence of (4) an ethics of care, a normative theory that urges us to care. Gilligan neglects to work out philosophical arguments for this injunction, and in this chapter I have tried to suggest one way of doing so. I have confined the attempt to an examination of the possible reasons that could be given for understanding Gilligan's theory as a normative theory—not merely as an account based on empirical findings in developmental psychology. The normativity of care in Gilligan's ethics seem to be justified by two strategies: First, there is the explicit strategy of referring to the anticipated beneficial consequences, and second an indirect strategy that relates caring to a particular interpretation of the principle of non–maleficence. The first strategy entails, and discusses, several problems, such as determining what is meant by "good consequences". For Gilligan, consequences refer to "human well-being" understood as human growth through relationships. Human connectedness is, as I read Gilligan, a necessary but not sufficient condition for human well-being and growth. The main problem with this strategy is nevertheless the conflation of well-being and growth, connectedness and human nature. First, it seems contradicted by the evidence: Being in relationships is not always equivalent with well-being and growth. Gilligan gets round this difficulty by claiming that "the right kind of care" is what is required to make relationships into a desirable end, and what also to some extent gives room for individual projects. Second, and more difficult, is the fact that she seems to be drawing a normative conclusion from factual premises, thereby committing a naturalistic fallacy—something that steers her theory in a naturalistic direction. However, even if the sharp distinction between facts and value, is and ought, moral psychology and moral philosophy is disputed, in fact, they are showed to be related—an ethics of care must be supported by a moral principle that is compatible with the evaluative premises in her theory. I have suggested that such a principle can be found in her theory. It is a variant of the principle of non-maleficence that I have termed "the expanded principle of not hurting". Using this as a strategy for founding the normativity of care, her theory avoids naturalism. By introducing this value premise, Gilligan avoids what may be regarded as fallacious argumentation, i.e. concluding from a descriptive fact that we ought to care and nurture relationships. This strategy saves her theory from relying entirely on an empirical justification.

The Expanded Principle of Not Hurting and the Private/Public Distinction

Different ethical theories emphasize different values, but a common feature of most is that they set out a definition of the scope of the particular values they defend: A just society; human rights for all; professional codes of conduct and so forth. I want to explore here whether the moral values Gilligan advocates are intended for the private or public domain for individuals, institutions, professions or for communities. At first sight, Gilligan appears to take an interest in the personal point of view. By listening to "the different voice", a feature that gives her theory its "bottom up" structure, Gilligan's ethics of care takes its cue from women's experiences in the private domain. Normative theories have, since Aristotle, been founded on the separation of the private and public domain, with the private understood as the household, the public as the sphere of careers, business, politics and art. In liberal theories, like in Rawls's, the private is considered outside the ethical and political domain, and, for that reason, more or less neglected (Okin 1989). Classical ethical theories, like those of Hume and Kant treat the private as inferior to the public domain. Women have been encouraged to adhere to values such as obedience, chastity, compassion and self–sacrifice—virtues that confine women's freedom and access to politicking (Okin 1979; Grimshaw 1991; Held 1993; Beauvoir 2000: 240,780). To traditional moral philosophy the personal point of view is partial and local, exactly the opposite of what morality requires, namely impartiality and universalizability (Friedman 2000: 208).

Focusing on women's experiences, as Gilligan does, is to challenge the blinkered field of ethical theories and moral philosophy, and of "points of view from nowhere" also. In granting the personal an ethical dimension, Gilligan is in sync with the famous feminist slogan of the 1970s, "the personal is political", and most contemporary feminist philosophy. Because women's historical preoccupation with care unfolds in the private domain, the public/private distinction has obscured women's work and concerns. Moral theory envisages the moral agent largely as independent, equal in power and fully rational. These theories are therefore unable to deal with the twin challenges of dependency and vulnerability.

The ethics of care, however, not only challenge the private/public distinction, it cuts across this traditional dichotomy. This ethical perspective is directed towards the relational process—at any level. Care is relevant wherever and whenever people interact, be it within families, friendships or among colleagues. Gilligan takes an interest in all levels; she is concerned with the costs of silencing care, "[. . .] not only in private life but also in professional training", and she worries about the institutions of education as well as the culture of North American society (Gilligan et al. 1988:290–291).[15] Because the normative values of the ethics of care refuse to pair off the public with the ethical and private with the pre–ethical, they subvert the public/private dimension altogether. The moral agent envisaged by the theory is able to transcend the public/private dichotomy. Both the relational ontology and values emphasized extend the theory's scope to human interaction. The concern of the ethics of care is the domain of the interpersonal; the relationship between people on the macro as well as micro level.[16]

The model of the moral agent as relational and the expanded principle of not hurting give the ethics of care an alternative moral ontology, allowing for a wider view of human interaction. The relational moral ontology provides the ethics of care with the resources to throw new light on well–known ethical challenges, bring neglected ethical problems into focus, and assess whether they are ethically relevant with regard to the expanded principle of not hurting. We shall return to this later. Let me now only point out that the ethical perspective is no longer considered a typically female concern, as it was 25 years ago. It is recognized today as having come of age, strong enough to take issue with wider moral theory and ethics. Even if Gilligan herself does not develop an ethics for institutions or the global arena, features of her theory could be expanded in that direction. Several care ethicists have taken the ethics of care outside the private domain. Virginia Held (1993) and Fiona Robinson (2006) are two examples to whom we shall return in Chapter 10.

Since we are concerned with formal features of the ethics of care in this chapter, we should ask whether the care perspective, with its focus on relational processes, is intended to guide interpersonal conduct, or whether it aims at the development of certain character traits. Dominant modern ethical theories, such as utilitarianism, deontology and liberal theories, are primarily preoccupied with how to act, not with the process of developing virtues (Schneewind 1990). We should nevertheless keep in mind that the distinction between character trait and conduct is not sharp; they are certainly not mutually exclusive. Care can be understood as a way of acting and responding towards another (an ethical conduct), as an attitude, a moral virtue and as an ideal of not hurting and promoting flourishing (an ethical ideal). The distinction between character trait, conduct and ideal may nevertheless be useful for scrutinizing the relationship between the perspective of care and other ethical theories. Before we can develop her theory, we need to determine what kind of normative theory it is Gilligan is offering. I shall therefore examine in the next chapter Gilligan's main concept, the concept of care. I hope there to clarify what "responding to need" means, and what role we should assign to emotions, engagement and empathy in the ethics of care.

Notes

1. To examine what gives Gilligan the license to term her findings a normative ethical theory one must overcome several methodological difficulties. First, Gilligan does not clarify the issue of the normativity of the care perspective. Descriptive and normative statements are not clearly distinguished in her works. For example, when writing on a characteristic feature of humans, i.e. being in relationships, no normative elements seem to be present. However, privileging one particular human feature over others is an indirect statement of value, as are her explicit claims that an inclusion of the perspective of care will imply a desirable expansion of the moral domain and shift in the conception of what is relevant to this domain (Gilligan 1982:173–174; Gilligan et al. 1988:119). Due to the shortage of philosophical reflection in Gilligan's work on the desirability of the expansion she envisages, my task

in this chapter will require at least two approaches. First I will have to interpret what she says, and then suggest what she seems to be saying and implying. For this reason, I do not claim that my propositions as to the normative foundation of the ethics of care represent Gilligan's view. They remain my reading of her ethics of care—even if they are meant to be in accordance with what I take to be her main ideas. I use "Gilliganian ethic" to indicate that my interpretation is going beyond what there is textual evidence for. Second, when discussing how and why Gilligan's theory may be considered a *normative* theory, the reader may expect a clarification of what is required of a system of thought to qualify as such. But in this area there is considerable disagreement both in regard to formal structure and content. Contention concerns differences in epistemological and moral positions. A list of criteria that a normative theory must fulfill can be found in the literature on ethics. It is based on the belief that a moral theory has to contain one (or several) ethical principle(s) that 1) overrides non-moral concerns; 2) are action-guiding imperatives; 3) are universalizable; and 4) are other-regarding (Beauchamp 1991:16–22). However, as Gilligan opposes the traditional ethical paradigm, its concept of morality and moral reasoning in particular, an attempt to evaluate her theory on the basis of a "traditional" list seems to be a methodological blunder. But we need some parameters in order to examine her theory in a systematic way. I will therefore adopt a "minimalist" perspective: A normative ethical theory is considered as a philosophical attempt to provide reasons for why one should support certain moral principles, attitudes, conducts and/or virtues. Now, not all reasons given in defense of a normative ethical theory are necessarily "good" reasons. Opinions differ over what it means to give a successful justification of an ethical theory as to, for instance, how premises are produced and how conclusions are drawn (Beauchamp 1991:34–35,83). In this chapter I do not focus on assessing if the merits of the reasons provided are "good", I confine myself to discussing *which* reasons can be given for reading Gilligan's perspective of care as a normative ethic.

2. To some extent Milton Mayeroff has a similar approach to caring, suggesting that care be understood as "helping the other grow" (Mayeroff 1972:1). However, it falls short of Gilligan's notion of care because, inherent in Mayeroff's view of caring, there is what appears to be a one-sided focus on the cared-for. Mayeroff focuses too much on the "flourishing" of the other and thereby neglecting the perspective of the carer. Mayeroff's concept of care has resemblances with Gilligan's care on level two, but the concept of care on which her theory relies on is mature care on level three in her theory on moral development.

3. When I use the expressions "human flourishing", included within it are "to care" and "to be cared for". "Human flourishing" captures Gilligan's two-fold point about caring; that caring activity aims at enabling the other to flourish (or grow in Mayeroff's parlance), and that caring contributes to the carer's own flourishing. Also, Gilligan's concept of care is not only connected to the principle of benevolence, but to the principle of non-maleficence. Mayeroff's concept of care is not fully compatible with Gilligan's.

4. Gilligan herself does not clarify the metaphysical presumption related to her ethical ideas in this way, it should be noted however.

5. True, not all attempts to care are successful, since care requires an adequate reading of the situation, an opinion of what is in the best interests of the person being cared for as well as an adequate response. Gilligan does not address these issues. I deal with them in subsequent chapters.

6. Such as biological, psychological, historical and economical reasons, that is.

7. See also Gilligan 1987:29.

8. As already pointed out above, the statistical correlation between gender and moral orientation Gilligan claimed to have found is problematic, but it does not have to be carried over into her normative suggestions (Gilligan 1982:2, 1993:209). She holds the view that both an ethics of rights and an ethics of care are required for moral maturity.

9. Now, one may understand this strategy as an attempt, not to explain, but to explain away the existence of harmful relationships. It is nevertheless not a philosophically unfamiliar way of dealing with problems, and bears resemblance with Socrates', Plato's as well as Augustine's way of explaining the existence of cruelty; such phenomena exist as a result of the agency of imperfection or defectiveness.

10. This could shed some additional light on my argument set out above, that a certain understanding of the concept of gender, i.e. that the male and female identity is constituted through psychological processes in early childhood and maintained and sustained through cultural processes, might be understood as a parallel to biological determinism.

11. Sophia, probably a pseudonym for Mary Montague questioned the possibility of deriving "ought" from "is" in her book which was published before Hume's *Treaties*. It is possible that Hume was influenced by Sophia's work, as it was rather well known (Wiestad 1994:20-23,100-112).

12. Hare's position has been criticized by, among others, Philippa Foot who asks if it is open for us to choose freely what counts as evidence for moral goodness (Beauchamp 1991:110–111).

13. Kohlberg (1990) makes an effort to establish a connection between care and the principle of beneficence, and in Chapter 5, I examine this attempt closer.

14. Many protagonists of care, such as Noddings (1984), are critical of principles *as such*. In my opinion, this skepticism is exaggerated. It should, nevertheless, be made clear that I understand a "principle" not as an inflexible and rigid rule but as a "guide".

15. As to the last concern she says: "The commitment of a democratic society to an ideal of social justice based on a premise of individual equality makes evidence of differences disturbing. Within an educational system committed to the goals of equal opportunity and individual freedom, ideals of no difference are often sustained by practices of not listening and not seeing. The justification of such practices in the name of justice reasoning, the encouragement of children and adolescents to turn away from the perception of the other's needs and often their own needs as well, points to a central dilemma for American education: how to encourage human responsiveness within the framework of a competitive, individualistic culture" (Gilli-

gan et al. 1988:291). Also in her latest book she touches on the connection between listening, speaking and democracy: "Democracy rests on an ideal of equality in which everyone has a voice" (Gilligan 2002:4).

16. Many central terms in Gilligan's theory are without clear definitions in her works, they are elaborated as I undertake to interpret her theory. The meaning of her term "relationship" is a case in point, it should now be more distinct; what she has in mind is not a causal relation between people. She does not associate "relationship" with a succession of events, where the connection is one-sided. Conversely, the term "relationship" refers to connectedness and interdependency, implying a response back and forth towards each other's needs. Relationships are reciprocal, and they are not mere means to achieve an end. Relationships are also ends in themselves. True, these features are general, but a more precise definition is contingent on its references, of the particular type of relationship in question. If the term refers to the relationship between parents and children for instance, the meaning of the notion will be different than in for teacher–student relation. The point is that a broad use of the term relationship includes various types of relationships of varying depth and vigor, and is probably intended by Gilligan as humans participate in webs of different relationships. A more detailed discussion about caring in symmetric and asymmetric relationships will follow later in relation to a discussion of Robert Goodin's thesis on protecting the vulnerable, of professional caring, and of the Aristotelian notions of friendship.

CHAPTER FOUR

~

Care, Cognition, and Emotions

In order to comprehend and develop an ethics of care, the role of emotions in care needs to be scrutinized. This is what I want to do in this chapter. Emotions are obviously a major aspect of care, but their role is a complex one. Care tends more often to awake connotations of emotions, as opposed to rationality. Gilligan takes issue with what in her view is a misconstrual:

> My critics equate care with feelings, which they oppose to thought, and imagine caring as passive or confined to some separate sphere. I describe care and justice as two moral perspectives that organize both thinking and feelings and empower the self to take different kinds of action in public as well as private life. (Gilligan 1993:209)

In what follows I develop an approach to the interplay between emotion and cognition, to co–feeling, moral autonomy and certain aspects of the care-giver's emotional reaction. Gilligan's view will be discussed in light of theoretical contributions of Lawrence Blum and Nel Noddings. I undertake a couple of detours in the direction of David Hume's and Immanuel Kant's ethics.

The Interplay of Emotion and Cognition

Care, according to Gilligan, has "cognitive as well as affective dimensions" that are not readily separated (Gilligan et al. 1988:151). Care "organizes both thinking and feelings" (Gilligan 1993:209). The unwillingness to dissociate the cognitive and affective dimensions challenges a particular view on cognition within developmental psychology, represented by among others, Jean Piaget. Within this tradition, as Gilligan sees it, cognitive development is comprehended as equivalent to the growth of mathematical and scientific thinking. She says it "conveys a view of people as living in a timeless world of abstract rules" which privileges separation, individuation and autonomy and regards strong feelings as a reaction to detachment, indifference and lack of concern as illegitimate (Gilligan et al. 1988:xi,xii). In her opposition to the approach, Gilligan draws upon, among others, the works of Michael Polyany and Lev Vygotsky, particular Vygotsky's thesis that higher cognitive functions, such as voluntary attention, logical memory and formation of concepts, originate in relations between individuals. The main point is that in the course of development an individual process is transformed into an interpersonal one. Gilligan says further that the tacit, intuitive forms of knowledge, also called "connected knowledge" which originate from interpersonal processes, may lead to differences in morality, such as different ways of perceiving a problem, different reasoning strategies, problem solving, and ways of responding (Gilligan et al. 1988:xxi). The acquisition of knowledge, including morally relevant knowledge, is something that happens within human connections.[1] It is a result of being interdependent rather than independent. Furthermore, cognition is not merely an intellectual ability. The faculty of "care–cognition" results from experiences in relationships, and these experiences are intermingled with feelings. If knowledge of attachment and detachment, of oppression and dependency is based on experiences, there are also emotions related to this knowledge. These feelings, according to Gilligan, define moral experiences and clarify moral violation, but the power of moral feeling coexists with the knowledge that feelings can be understood differently in different contexts (Gilligan et al. 1988:121).

This "connected–knowledge" which relates to social responsiveness and moral concern is often thought of as something that is developed in early childhood. If that is the case, it might change the angle of incidence towards adolescent development, says Gilligan. Rather than asking why such capacities have failed to emerge by adolescence, which would imply immaturity, one should ask why they have been diminished or lost (Gilligan et al. 1988:ix,x). In her later works, Gilligan pays close attention to this question (Gilligan et al. 1990; Gilligan 1991; Gilligan and Brown 1992; Gilligan et al. 1995). Focusing on the development of adolescent girls in particular, she finds that, at a certain age, they experience a split between their thoughts and their feelings. This split helps them to understand and make sense of the world around them, but at the same time leads to internal conflicts, to a sense of alienation and disconnection from felt experience and "bodily knowledge" (Brown and Gilligan 1992:127–128) which often results in silences (Gilligan et al. 1995). The voice that has become silenced is the "different voice", the moral perspective of care.

As to the two different schools in moral developmental theory, a similar pattern is to be found in moral philosophy. Some moral theories are based on emotions, others—the predominating sort—on reason. Actually, much modern philosophy exhibits a distrust of emotions. The distrust of emotions is deeply rooted in Western moral thinking, and can be explained on the basis of several notions: emotions are associated with the body, sexuality, nature and women, which in Western hierarchical thinking are considered inferior to reason, self–control, culture and masculinity. The presence of emotions is associated with being out of control, by having one's judgment clouded and blinded, by being understood as subjective, i.e., they make the moral agent partial. A consequence of justifying morality on grounds of universality and objectivity is that emotions are considered as irrelevant, or an inferior part of morality (Lloyd 1995; Vetlesen 1996:11–16; Held:1998).

Even if though such a view of emotion in moral philosophy has prevailed, it has not been the only one. Several seventeenth–century English moral philosophers, as the likes of Lord Shaftesbury, David Hume, Adam Ferguson and Adam Smith, found the source of morality in feelings such as sympathy rather than in reason. They called attention to the emotive side of human nature and regarded ethical judgment and action as rooted in feelings, not in reason (Thilly 1958:355–356). Contemporary feminist philosophers— Martha Nussbaum, Annette Baier, Sandra Lee Bartky and Joan Tronto to mention a few—have taken an interest in these ethical theories.[2] Philosophies evolving from and inspired by Marx, Kierkegaard, Nietzsche and Merleau–Ponty have demonstrated the impact of context and experience on thinking. Other contemporary philosophers, such as Lawrence Blum (1980, 1994), Martha Nussbaum (1990), Arne Johan Vetlesen (1994) and Diana T. Meyers (1997), have challenged the prevailing view on emotions in moral philosophy.

Now, where in this landscape does a Gilliganian ethics of care fit? Gilligan's unwillingness to distinguish between emotion and understanding places her outside mainstream ethics—where cognition is considered, roughly speaking, an individual achievement and where emotions are regarded with suspicion. In this ethics of care it is not a question of either emotion or reason. It concerns the *interplay* of reason and emotion, between cognition and affection. Arne Johan Vetlesen's thesis that emotions are an indispensable part of a moral agent is therefore of some interest in relation to Gilligan

(Vetlesen 1994:6; 1996:15). However, it should be noted that Vetlesen explicitly says that even if his approach to emotional abilities overlaps in part with Gilligan's interests in care, his analysis of moral performance does not capture the ethics of care better than it captures the ethics of justice (Vetlesen 1994:350). This is because, says Vetlesen, that his thesis assumes that the exercise of judgment presupposes and is made possible by "having" certain emotions, but does not claim that emotions have primacy. On the contrary, moral judgment is a twofold accomplishment that requires a cognitive as well as an emotional aspect. They are equally important (Vetlesen 1994:157). Now, Vetlesen's reservations concerning Gilligan are probably based on her presentation of the perspective of care i.e., her portrayal of her research. True, in Gilligan's research, particularly as set out in In a Different Voice, her informants seem to give emotions priority over reason and therefore making emotions appear more significant for women in moral judgments, a point Vetlesen also takes up, claiming that gender makes no difference on the level of constitution (Vetlesen 1994:15,351). However, what Vetlesen seems to leave out is the fact that there are different levels within Gilligan's theory, as well as different notions of care. The perspective of care, consisting of the research to which Vetlesen is presumably referring, is only one element in Gilligan's theory. It is only a part—the descriptive beginning—of the story, and must be distinguished from her ethics of care, which are Gilligan's normative suggestions. On the normative level Gilligan is not committed to gender,[3] nor does she hold that emotions are prior to cognition. The perspective of justice and the perspective of care describe, and partly explain, gender differences in the agents' moral reasoning and moral feelings, as well as why and how emotions, contextual sensitivity and concern for the related other are considered secondary to the dominating school within moral psychology as well as moral philosophy. However, to prevent promulgating a simplistic view of "male and female", a new theoretical framework is necessary says Gilligan (Gilligan et al. 1988:iv). It is needed because the traditional dichotomies of Western thinking, such as self/other, mind /body, thoughts/feelings and past/present "undermine knowledge of human relationships by washing out the logic of feelings". In her normative ethics of care, she is concerned with transcending this mode of binary thinking also in relation to emotion and cognition, and replace either/or logic with a both/and logic (Gilligan et al. 1990:19; Gilligan 1992: 127–128). On this reading, the ethics of care is not a normative framework where emotion and reason, cognition and affection, care and justice are construed as opposites as Vetlesen implies (Vetlesen 1994:8,152; 1996:149–153). Conversely, in Gilligan's theory, a move towards reconciliation can be found as a way of conquering both binary as well as hierarchical thinking on the relationship between reason and emotion.[4] In an ethics of care, care should be comprehended not as dominated by emotion, but as expressing both emotion and understanding, not readily separated (Gilligan 1993:209; Blum 1993:51–52).[5]

This interplay between cognition and emotion inherent in the comprehension of care has implications for the ethics of care's moral epistemology. Gilligan points to two ways of achieving the knowledge required for acting morally:

> One can take the role of the other or assume Rawls' original position or play Kohlberg's game of moral musical chairs—all without specifically knowing anything about the other but simply by following the laws of perspective and putting oneself in his or her position. The other conception is of knowledge as gained through human connection. (Gilligan et al. 1988:125)

In the Rawlsian vision, one puts *oneself* in the other's position, and asks how *I* would feel and choose if *I* where in that position. From the perspective of care one asks how do *you* feel when *you* are in that situation, and at the aim is to perceive the needs of others in their own terms. The two approaches might result in divergent judgments and consequently different responses. For instance, I might be rather comfortable with situation X, while you might feel miserable. It allows for errors in both approaches:

> The potential error in justice reasoning lies in its latent egocentrism, the tendency to confuse one's perspectives with an objective standpoint of truth, the temptation to define others in one's own terms by putting oneself in their place. The potential error in the care reasoning lies in the tendency to forget that one has terms, creating a tendency to enter into another's perspective and to see oneself as "selfless" by defining oneself in other's term. (Gilligan 1987:31)

The question then is how one is to avoid the potentials for erring. The answer must be to apply an approach that, one the one hand, allows recognition of the other's "otherness", of seeing the other as different from oneself but which, on the other, does not allow that "otherness" to cloud judgment or be confused with the carer's perspective. To avoid the two potential errors, the perspective of the cared–for and the perspective of the carer have to be integrated. Doing so requires co–feeling as well as autonomy—two concepts in need of a closer inspection.

Co–feeling

"Co–feeling" is an important component in the attempt to avoid the potential errors inherent in the perspectives of justice and care, i.e., the tendency to confuse one's own perspective with that of the other or defining oneself in the other's terms. According to Gilligan, co–feeling is what gives access to the feelings of others. Co–feeling is based on our level of affective imagination, i.e., our ability to enter into and understand the feelings of others (Gilligan et al. 1988:120). Gilligan understands co–feeling as a human capacity that can be developed. In its most inchoate form it is demonstrated in the empathic response of infants to the feelings of others. As the child develops, different experiences of human connections expand and refine this capacity (Gilligan et al. 1988:124). The knowledge required for being able to care originates from experience, and experience is twofold: First, there is the universal human experience of being connected with others, as set out above. Such experience enables us to recognize the needs and vulnerability of others, and it enables us in turn to acknowledge the important injunction within the ethics of care; not to hurt. Second, certain relationships give us an opportunity to get to know the particular other, as well as our self. Friendship is one such relationship where we can achieve knowledge of the other person's perspective and emotions, while learning more about our self. This is a type of knowledge that enhances our capacity to give care, thin as well as thick care (Pettersen 2006a). Another possible way of cultivating one's affective imagination is through literary and artistic experience. As readers of stories and watchers of plays, we may be emotionally moved and engaged by the lives and faiths of others through a process of imagination (Nussbaum 1997). This experience may work to develop our faculty for co–feeling, our ability to recognize and identify emotional and psychological reactions, hurt and vulnerability in others in real life.

Co–feeling is one ability required to perform mature care as it informs the understanding of how one should act or what actions constitute care (Gilligan et al. 1988:123). Co–feeling is the ability to participate in another's feelings on their terms, and signifies an attitude of engagement rather than an attitude of judgment or observation. According to Gilligan, co–feeling differs from empathy, because empathy means an identity of feelings, while co–feeling implies that one can experience feelings different from one's own (Gilligan et al. 1988:122). It has been pointed out that Gilligan's distinction between co–feeling and empathy seems rather odd. It is odd because Gilligan's idea of empathy seems inadequate, restricted as it is to the process of identification (Nortvedt 1996:46). Empathy is not confined to identification, it can be understood as a prerequisite for the development of an awareness and understanding of the emotions and feelings of another person (Vetlesen 1994:204–205). Co–feeling is therefore preferably to be understood as an aspect of empathic competence, something that also accords with the research on empathy and moral emotions (Nortvedt 1996:46).

Even if the critique is appropriate, I believe it is nevertheless worth trying to grasp Gilligan's purpose in introducing the notion of co–feeling. She draws attention to what it takes to be a mature carer; an understanding of the other's perspective which does not imply selflessness, or letting oneself be defined in the terms of other. Co–feeling concerns, as does autonomy, the border between self and others. The idea of co–feeling, says Gilligan, goes against prevailing assumptions about the nature of the self and its relation to others: "Co–feeling implies neither clear self–boundaries nor a merging fusion between self and other. Considered on a theoretical level, co–feeling seems to be psychologically impossible". Nevertheless, it is often registered in research, she says. Co–feeling makes the opposition between egoism and altruism disappear (Gilligan et al. 1988:122). Co–feeling does not signify an absence of difference, or a complete identity of feelings which could result in a failure to distinguish between self and others (Gilligan et al. 1988:122–125), or to become selfless (Gilligan 1987:31).

Again we note Gilligan's attempt to find a "third way", a compromise between opposite poles: Co–feeling is the ability to participate in the feelings of others, through the act of "affective imagination", without (con)fusing self with others on the one hand, or, on the other, merely observing the other's feelings from a distance. The capability to uphold integrity, and, at the same time not revert to egocentrism, is a feature of moral maturity in Gilligan's developmental theory.[6] Co–feeling and autonomy are therefore important ingredients of mature care, and significant for solving moral conflicts (to which I return in the chapter which deals with care and justice).[7]

Care and Moral Autonomy

Autonomy is required to maintain distance between self and other. While Gilligan herself does not address moral autonomy specifically, in light of her view of the self as relational, rather than independent and sovereign, there are nevertheless certain implications we can usefully draw from her work.

Etymologically, autonomy is connected to self–government or self–determination. Moral autonomy has to do with "self–determination in moral understanding and decision–making". It concerns "choosing and living according to rules that one considers to be morally binding" (Friedmann 2000:212; 2005:340–341). Many philosophers have taken moral autonomy to require the possession of personal independence. Another feature typically associated with autonomy is a capacity for reason uninfected by the one's desires, emotions and social situation. Autonomy is also taken to correspond with an authentic, unified and inner self (Zimmerman 1991:233; Grimshaw 2005:334–337).

Now, this traditional understanding of moral autonomy seems at first blush to be at odds with key elements of Gilligan's theory including concept of self, emphasis on interdependence (rather than independence), and its insistence on the interplay of reason and emotions. It would also seem to undermine her theory's emphasis on enriching the contextual setting of moral decision making, by including the interests of self and others. Also, it may seem rash to challenge an understanding of moral autonomy which has empowered many women, and men too, allowing them to defend themselves against oppression. By internalizing this version of autonomy, oppressed women and men are equally empowered with a capacity for self–government and self–determination, both of which traits are taken to be a precondition of moral agency and responsibility (Friedman 2000:215,216). It is indeed this kind of autonomy Simone de Beauvoir urges women to acquire in order to become free and independent persons.

What Gilligan challenges, however, is not women's capacity for self–legislation and self–determination, nor does she distrust them when it comes to moral decision–making and responsibility. What she speaks up against is the traditional neglect of the interaction between self–determination and self–legislation on the one hand, and the agent's relationship and interdependency with others on the other. The concept of mature care together with the notion of a morally mature agent can be understood as contribution towards the development of a new notion of moral autonomy. In terms of ethics of care, a morally mature agent is one that balances the interests of self and others. For this, the agent must have integrity, something the selfless carer on level two of Gilligan's theory of moral development seems to lack. The altruistic carer is incapable of self–legislation and self–determination as her actions are dominated by the wishes of others. The mature carer, however, can make decisions and act on them as a free and independent person. This does not mean, of course, that such a mature moral agent has an extreme version of autonomy, i.e., complete freedom of actions and ways of living. The morally mature agent, according to Gilligan's theory, can resist manipulation and exploitation, while recognizing that she does not have complete sovereignty over choices and actions because they impact on related others for whom she has responsibilities. Her acts might hurt others, and as a caring agent she must take their interests into account in addition to her own. Responsibilities are not always chosen; it is not solely up to the agent to determine who is part of her network or how vulnerable they are. Given these limitations, the autonomous agent balances successfully between the interest of self and others, and between first–order and second–order values and considerations, between those that are negotiable and those that are not.

Gilligan's ethics of care, with its implications for moral autonomy, attempts not only to reframe traditional understandings of moral autonomy and moral philosophy and ethics in a wider sense, but to promote a more nuanced and complex concept of moral autonomy, with space for self–determination and consideration, reason and emotion, independency and connectedness. This is theoretically demanding, as it must reconcile apparently irreconcilable opposites. It is on the horizon, however, thanks to feminist philosophers such as Marily Friedman, Jean Grimshaw, Sara Ruddick and Susan Brison. The ethics of care rightfully describes the notion of moral autonomy as feministic, as against moral autonomy in a conventional sense which represents a "preoccupation with self–sufficiency and self–realization at the expense of human connection" (Friedman 2005:339). Also, it echoes thinkers such as Derrida, Foucault, Kristeva and Irigaray who oppose the Cartesian's bodiless, emotionless, isolated and imprisoned self, and work to hasten the fall of modernity and encourage postmodern plurality (Hekman 1995). The ethics of care can also be understood as part of decades of theoretical resistance to traditional western individualism.

Emotion and Moral Motivation

According to Gilligan, a caring agent is motivated to care on the basis of her experience with caring capacity for co–feeling. Other experiences and feelings, however, can have the opposite effect. Why are some motivations, emotions and experiences considered to be moral, while others are not? And how do they interrelate? Let us look more closely at the caring agent, and try to entangle how experiences, emotions and motivation work together, and why some stand out as particularly ethically relevant under the terms of an ethics of care.

The fact that emotion plays a part in caring does not mean that the caring response is a spontaneous and affective reaction. Mature care does not mean acting on impulses; it is based on a reflection of how to act in order to prevent harm or restore health and promote well–being and flourishing in human interaction. Mature care can be comprehended as a cultivatable, relational virtue with social, intellectual and moral aspects. Its performance is guided by the expanded principle of not hurting, it is *not* to act on the basis of sentimentality. The selfish as well as the selfless care are pathological rather than ethical, and are not what an ethic of care should be founded on. Since Gilligan has had little to say on this issue I refer to Lawrence Blum and Nel Noddings to help show how this grasp of the emotional aspect of care can be sustained. As we shall see, the approaches of both Blum and Noddings are helpful in understanding emotional reactions and responses in caring. We need to remember, however, that the balance between self and other required by the concept of mature care is given less prominence in Blum and Noddings.

Blum makes a distinction between altruistic feelings and moods. Moods are understood as the agent's impulse and inclinations, and are unreliable as moral motivations. Altruistic emotions however, are based on an appreciation of the other person's situation regarding her weal and woe. Sometimes this requires the agent to do what she doesn't feel like, or not do what she would like to do (Blum 1980:16–18). Altruistic emotions are a regard for the good of another person for their own sake, or conduct motivated by such regard (Blum 1980:9). Acts following from altruistic emotions are motivated by the concern for the good of others (Blum 1980:122). If we read Blum's theory alongside Gilligan's, his idea of the altruistic response raises questions concerning the extent to which we are supposed to respond. Since care in Gilligan's ethics is emphasized as relational, and not only other–regarding, the interests of both, or all, affected must be taken into consideration. A mature emotional caring reaction is obviously not based on what Blum terms moods, but it is not entirely based on altruistic emotion either. Consideration for the others weal and woe is indeed important, but not decisive. When a balance between the interests of self and others is accomplished, one is able to care both for oneself and for the other. Again, we see how Gilligan's approach endeavors to reconcile opposites: It is not either/or but both/and, an approach which distinguishes of mature care from Blum's altruistic acts.

Nel Noddings follows Blum in explaining the emotional reaction and response. She distinguishes between a spontaneous impulse and a more stable disposition, the one she designates "natural caring", the other "ethical caring". When we act on behalf of the other because we want to do so, we are acting in accord with natural caring, an action characterized by spontaneity. A mother's care of her child can be described as natural caring if based on an altruistic impulse, on "I want". Sometimes, however, there is no "I want", only resentment, selfishness, hostility or indifference. Here the caring agent needs to reflect on how to act in a caring way in the particular situation. Such reflection should help us tackle a situation in which we are not inclined to provide care. Its verbal translation is the imperative "I must". This is ethical caring. If a propensity for natural caring—"I will"—is absent, the duty of ethical caring—"I must"—should take its place. Ethical caring requires an effort that is not needed in natural caring: It requires the agent to respond to the initial impulse with an act of commitment. The agent commits herself either to overt actions on behalf of the cared–for, or refrains from acting if it is thought not to benefit the cared–for (Noddings 1984:79–83).

Obviously there are echoes here of Kantian ethics of *Grundlegung zur Metaphysik der Sitten* (1797). Noddings refers to the Kantian distinction between what is naturally good and what is morally good when explaining natural caring and ethical caring. The conflict between "I–will" and "I–must" resembles the conflict between our empirical inclination and our duty to act according to the categorical imperative. Nevertheless, there is an important difference. Natural and ethical caring do not require the same effort. But ethical caring is not better than natural caring simply for being more demanding. Both are equal in value. Indeed, to Noddings ethical caring depends on natural caring insofar as both have links to emotions (Noddings 1984:80). Noddings is in agreement with David Hume who in *An Enquiry concerning the Principles of Morals* (1748) not only abandons egoism as the sole motivation for acting, but grounds moral judgments in emotions. Hume argues that moral agents can be motivated to act by sympathy for others. Sympathy is a part of a sentiment included in human nature, and therefore as universal as reason. This sentiment—be it approval or rejection—gives rise to our moral responses. Noddings adds that our ability to feel with others is one of the finest qualities of being human, and vital to develop, by ethicists, parents and teachers alike (Noddings 1984:87,103,178; Noddings 2006:4–9,289). According to Noddings, we must establish a philosophical position that attends to these emotion, not disregards them. From our innate sympathy, she concludes, natural caring can flow. But we are not compelled to care even if we feel "I–will". We are indeed able to withhold care. Correspondingly, if the "I–will" is absent, or substituted by "I–will–not", we are not compelled to act on this either. We have a choice. The crucial question is why should I choose to act in a caring way. It is because, says Nodding, previous experience has shown me the significance of caring. By reviving this experience, I understand why I should act in a caring way. It is our deliberate choice to make care the ethical ideal in our life. What we embrace as our ultimate value, however, is not chosen at random. What we select as our first–order value, what constitutes the "I–must" when the "I–will" fails to appear, is related to what we have experienced as valuable and as reprehensible (Noddings 1984:84).

Both Gilligan and Noddings regard experiences as important to an agent's moral development as a mature caring agent, and both presume a capacity to learn how to enter into and understand the feelings of others. None of them base the ethics of care on experience or sentiment alone, but emphasize the importance of establishing care as an ethical ideal that can guide our moral deliberations, in addition to our emotions. Noddings and Gilligan also agree that cognitive abilities and emotions are not developed mainly as an individual process, but in relation with others. Together they show that an agent's moral values are not the result of rational choice alone, but of the interplay of emotions, reflections and experiences. Becoming a mature moral agent is a relational not an individual process.

One objection to both Gilligan and Noddings is that not everybody has experienced care. Some children are not nurtured and cared for by loving parents. Some of them may end up as molesters or killers. Some people seem to feel nothing, or only resentment of others. For these people, Nodding suggests "reeducation or exile" (Noddings 1984:92). She seems, like Bernard Williams (1972) in "The Amoralist". to regard an incapacity for co–feeling as a pathological disorder. For Williams, the problem with most ruthless behavior is not the person's inability to care. Most do care about others, for instance their mother or their lover. The problem is that their sense of care is not extended to the wider community. The remedy, Williams suggests, is to appeal to their (confined) sympathies, to broaden their capacity for "other–concern". For Nodding, broadening our ability to feel with others is the goal of (moral) education. It also informs her pedagogical approach. As a practical illustration, Noddings says that instead of saying to a child, "you should not hurt the cat", one should say, "when you pull the cat's tail, the cat feels pain". Noddings assumes the child, on hearing this, will stop hurting the cat.

Insofar as Noddings relies on Hume, she is vulnerable to accusations of reducing moral judgments to an expression of emotion, making it impossible to judge between right and wrong. Noddings, we should note, insists that she does not hold an emotivistic position. Emotivists (such as Alfred Ayer) identify right as the positive emotions, and wrong as the negative emotions. As I read Noddings, her claim is that emotional approval and rejection are not given, but they are not created *ex nihilo* either. They are learned and encouraged. When I feel resentment towards the suffering of others, I express a commitment to care as a normative ideal. There is reciprocity between my moral sentiment and my moral ideals (Noddings 1989: 90–91). This is one of the reasons education, for care ethicists like Noddings and Gilligan, is a matter of such urgency.

The comprehension of care and caring as a relational activity that involves emotion in several ways, has implication for standard moral theory as well as for our understanding of how a carer meets ethical challenges. In the next chapter we shall focus on some aspects regarding the relation between the ethics of care and traditional moral theory. As we shall see, the ethics of care challenges the moral point of view, i.e. the position or angle from which the moral agent observes and considers the cases in question and determines what is to count morally and what is to be considered an appropriate response. Also, it has deep impact on traditional views moral ontology on moral epistemology.

Notes

1. Additionally, as explained in Chapter 1, differences in the agents' experience with connections and relationships will most likely result in differences in cognition, and partly explains gender differences in moral approach.

2. On Hume, see Annett Baier (1987), for Smith, see Martha Nussbaum (1997), for Scheler, see Sarha Bartky (1997), and for several of the seventeenth–century moral philosophers see Tronto (1993).

3. Or to be more precise, she does not have to be committed to gender. But, as pointed out in Chapter 2, the sex/gender distinction she applies makes it difficult to eclipse gender dichotomizing. It also clouds rather than clarifies the treatment of such matters in her writings.

4. It would therefore be unreasonable to assume that Gilligan's endeavor is at odds with Vetlesen's aims. As he says, "I oppose the philosopher's predilection for hierarchy and suggest that the capacities in question need to collaborate and be in balance for sound moral performance to be attained. In my account, the sequence of moral performance is undermined once one of the two basic faculties in the subject (sex making no difference) is for some reason impaired or impeded, or otherwise overshadows by its counterpart. My notion of interplay is one of equilibrium, if you like; there is no either/or". (Vetlesen 1994:352).

5. It should be added that being aware of another's needs does not have to cause an internal reaction. It is possible to be conscious about other people's suffering without being moved by it. Such a person might fit Arne Johan Vetlesen's idea of an indifferent person. An "indifferent person" is someone who is emotionally unaffected, who does not feel any emotional engagement about what is happening to another person (Vetlesen 1994:211). Also, a person can be compassionate yet blind, shortsighted, or unrealistic (Blum 1980:110). Cognition and affection may be necessary for an agent to act morally, but it is nevertheless not sufficient. The attitude of the agents themselves also impacts on the degree to which actions can be said to be caring or not.

6. Gilligan is not unique in stressing the moral importance of gaining access to the feelings of others. "Co–feeling" and "affective imagination" bear resemblance to Adam Smith's cogitations on the imaginative faculty. In *The Theory on Moral Sentiments* (1759) Smith addresses the question of how we have access to the emotional state of others, and emphasizes the role of imagination: "As we have no immediate experience of what other men feel, we can form no idea of the manner in which they are affected, but by conceiving what we ourselves should feel in the like situation. Though our brother is upon the rack, as long as we ourselves are at our ease, our senses will never inform us of what he suffers. They never did, and never can, carry

us beyond our own person, and it is by the imagination only that we can form any conception of what are his sensations. Neither can that faculty help us to this any other way, than by representing to us what would be our own, if we were in his case. It is the impressions of our own senses only, not those of his, which our imaginations copy. By the imagination we place ourselves in his situation, we conceive ourselves enduring all the same torments, we enter as it were into his body, and become in some measure the same person with him, and thence form some idea of his sensations, and even feel something which, though weaker in degree, is not altogether unlike them. His agonies, when they are thus brought home to ourselves, when we have thus adopted and made them our own, begin at last to affect us, and we then tremble and shudder at the thought of what he feels". Smith also points out that it is our experience which enables us to sympathize with others (Smith 1790:257, 269). Another example is Edith Stein on imagination. In *Zum Problem der Einfühlung* (1917) Stein asks how one subject can have access to the feelings of another subject and answers her own question by pointing to *einfülung*, empathy, which she assumes to be a precondition for insight into others. She also says that empathy is not an identity with the feelings of others, and that the ability to understand the feelings of others is based on experience and developed through a process of learning (Svenneby 1999, 1999a: 146–162).

7. Additionally, even if co–feeling is a general human capacity, its development (or lack of development) will depend upon the understanding of self in relation to others. Seeing oneself as connected and dependent may stimulate and expand the capacity for co–feeling, stimulate a richer understanding of the emotional life of others.

8. As an illustration of this way of characterizing moral theories I quote Noddings: "The traditional approach, that of the father, is to ask under what principle the case falls. But the mother may wish to ask more about the culprit and his victims. She may begin by thinking, 'What if this were my child?'[. . .] The father might sacrifice his own child in fulfilling a principle; the mother might sacrifice any principle to preserve her child" (Noddings 1984:36–37). Noddings also says that this is far too simplistic to be considered as a summary or a definitive portrayal, but in her opinion it is indicative and instructive as it illuminates the differences that places a caring approach in opposition to traditional theories (Noddings 1984:37).

CHAPTER FIVE

~

Care and Traditional Moral Theory

The claim that the ethics of care challenges traditional moral theory and implies a shift in the conception of what is relevant to the moral domain (Gilligan et al. 1988:119) is in the subject of this chapter. I shall argue that the ethics of care contributes and challenges traditional moral theory. Before doing so however, the umbrella term "traditional moral theories" as well as Gilligan's conception of justice are in need of clarification.

Gilligan's Conception of Justice

Gilligan's critique of traditional tenets in moral philosophy originates from her dissension with Kohlberg's understanding of morality and moral development. In particular she disagrees with the following traditional axioms: 1) There is one core value, upon which all rational agents could agree regardless of personal differences; 2) The one core value is justice; 3) The main activity of normative moral philosophy is to define and defend justice; 4) Moral reasoning is necessary and sufficient for moral actions; 5) The yardstick of mature moral reasoning is the universalizability test; 6) What count as morally worthy actions are actions related to rationally principled moral reasoning only; 7) The goal of moral development, and the definition of a moral agent, is an autonomous, independent and rational self (Kohlberg et al. 1983:40,46,52). Kohlberg derived his conception of morality from Hare's neo–Kantian definition of morality (Kohlberg et al. 1983:17), but Gilligan's critique embraces more than Kohlberg's conception of justice. She criticizes a moral tradition she believes is based on these suppositions. Although she does not specifically say so, it seems likely that what she has in mind is the conventional practice of deontology. Gilligan does not adequately account for the fact that there are a variety of theories within this tradition that differ among themselves. This type of blanket critiquing of a moral tradition can itself be criticized for short–sightedness. What Gilligan is out to do however, is to highlight certain features of a particular moral approach. The point is not to give a detailed presentation of different theories of justice, but to draw our attention to certain basic and shared structures between them. In order to do so, a generalization is necessary. In fact, Gilligan's generalization and critique is often understood to ranges wider than deontology, as axiomata like those listed above are taken as constitutive components of liberal theories and some versions of utilitarianism as well (Tong 1993:13–24), even to be concurrent with much of the modern Western moral theories (Nicholson 1993:91–98, Held 1998). "Traditional moral theories", "traditional ethics", "traditional approaches to ethics" and so on are all expressions referring to theories where such constitutive assumptions are taken to be present. This particular way of perceiving moral theories is also what gives rise to the portrayal of traditional theories as masculine and a caring approach as feminine (Noddings 1984:36–37). "Traditional moral theories", and Gilligan's "justice tradition" seem to overlap with what Margaret Urban Walker (Walker 2002) calls the "theoretical–juridical model" of morality and moral theory, of which, according to Walker, the ethics of Henry Sidgwik, Bernard Williams and John Rawls are paradigmatic examples.

As to Gilligan's conception of justice, equality and fairness is what she connects with justice (Gilligan 1982:149,164,174; Gilligan et al. 1988:33,35,144). Understanding justice as a "fair and equal consideration" is common to all theories of justice, traditionally attributed to Aristotle, and is taken to mean that equals must be treated equally. However, "justice" for Gilligan seems to correspond with the principle of formal justice only; similar treatment for similar cases, without reference to discussions on what should be considered relevant similarities and differences. She gives the impression that reasoning related to justice cannot accommodate differences in needs and she does not consider that differential treatment is not incompatible with a moral theory based on justice (Gilligan et al. 1988:36).[1] Consequently, she characterizes moral principles and their application as "the formal moral judgments whose operations [follow] the logic of hypothetico–deductive thought" (Gilligan 1988:154). Gilligan fails, it seems, to notice that hypothetico–deductive reasoning based on principles also makes use of judgments and deliberation. Furthermore, Gilligan appears to understand the theories of justice as originating from self–interest. The motivation behind the justice tradition is taken to be the rational appeal to self–interest: It is in one's own best interest to accept the principles of justice (Gilligan et al. 1988:135–134).

Even if Gilligan's concept of justice is narrow, her understanding and objections correspond with elements in the history of certain reception of the concept of justice. The validity and authority of this reception, as well as its emergence, cannot be considered here. However, to show that Gilligan's understanding of justice is not completely out of step we might note Bill Puka's claim that her interpretation of justice bears resemblance with critical theory, "which exposes and excoriates the competitive and possessive egoism lurking behind individual rights" (Puka 1990:194). Another example of this comprehension of justice is Hume's claim in *Treatise of Human Nature* (1739) that justice originates from selfishness and restricted generosity of men: "Here then is a proposition, which, I think, may be regarded as certain, that it is only from the selfishness and confined generosity of men, along with the scanty provision nature has made for his wants, that justice derives its origin" (Hume 1911:495). Gilligan seems to focus on what Hume in *An Enquiry Concerning the Principle of Morals* (1751) characterizes as the cautious, jealous virtue of justice (Hume 1898:183). Gilligan's concept of justice is not baseless, but confined as most moral theories and conceptions concerned with justice do not appeal to rational individuals' narrow self–interests, but to impartial justifiability. Impartial justifiability may be understood to exclude reference to people's self–interests (Rakowski 1993:20). Justice may also be understood as originating from a compassionate concern for the rights of others (Bartlett 1992). Despite these reservations regarding Gilligan's portrayal of the justice tradition, I believe the ethics of care challenges traditional moral theory. In particular it disputes the traditional moral point of view—the view that universalizability, impartiality, and impersonality are the formal criteria for what count as moral.

Care and the Moral Point of View

In what we have termed traditional moral theories—a collection of theories which includes what Gilligan calls the justice tradition—the moral point of view is taken to require impartiality, impersonality and universalizability. Whether these formal requirements are secured through Kant's categorical imperative, Kohlberg's moral musical chairs,[2] through a discourse which requires an abstraction from Habermasian contexts or from behind Rawls's veil of ignorance, they are regarded as necessary for judgment or recommendation to be moral. Universalizability, impartiality and impersonality as the formal criteria for what counts as moral are rooted in the moral philosophy of Kant: The idea of every person's moral equality; that each person matters equally and is entitled to equal consideration (Kant 1996:30). Universalizability is required in order to secure that moral judgments apply equally to all relevantly identical situations. Impartiality is mandatory since the lack of involvement or particular interests in the case in question prevents people from favoring a particular person or group of persons. The demand for impersonality, i.e., avoiding privileging particular individuals, secures neutrality of moral judgments. Within this framework, the caring concern for the related other might appear to violate all these claims.

Before repudiating this view on care, an important and relevant insight drawn from Gilligan's works should be mentioned: The understanding of morality will depend upon the moral framework applied in the actual case (Gilligan 1987:24). There is no straightforward way of justifying such claims or allegations since different epistemic points of departure influence our comprehension of what is relevant for settling the issue. Moral reflection requires a moral vocabulary, but such a vocabulary will contain ideals and standards that influence our way of asking as well as answering questions. In order to question the moral authority of particular moral judgments and criteria we have to rely on other moral judgments which themselves could be questioned. The moral conceptual repertoire determines the way the moral subject organizes, perceives and interprets morality in addition to moral theories (Walker 2002:174). Gilligan herself acknowledges these epistemological challenges. She emphasizes that the comprehension of moral conceptions will differ according to the framework used, i.e., in her case, the framework of justice or the framework of care (Gilligan 1987:24). Previously we saw how the concept of self and others, and the understanding of the relations between individuals' influences moral conceptions. Jake and Amy's response to Heinz's dilemma illustrated the point, and also served as an example of how moral concepts can be prejudiced and systematically employed to mislabel the moral experience and judgments of women.[3] In Kohlberg's moral framework (i.e., the Kantian), certain features were emphasized and given moral priority while others were not. A change in moral conceptions allows other features to be seen. What seems to be *the* moral point of view then, is not a neutral point of view, but determined by the adopted and practiced moral framework—which in turn decides whether the agent sees a certain situation as requiring a response or not, and what the options are regarded to be among which the agent must choose. Another illustration of how our moral conceptual frameworks impact on our moral judgments of importance to the discussion of care and the moral point of view, is the different conceptions of what it means to be partial/impartial, personal/impersonal, particular/universal. Such variations are rooted partly in the view taken of emotions. Let us therefore, in order to avoid misunderstandings, inspect a traditional approach to emotion more closely before suggesting how the ethics of care may contribute to the debate concerning the moral point of view.

Kantian Emotions

The approach to emotions that underlies the perspective of justice is based on a certain interpretation of Kant's ethics, in particular on the ethics he sets out in *The Doctrine of Virtue* (part II of *The Metaphysics of Morals*, 1797) and "Observation on the Feelings of the Beautiful and the Sublime" (1764). Here Kant defines truly moral conduct as what is done out of duty (for the sake of duty), not out of inclinations such as love, pity and sympathy. These feelings are considered passive, not will–governed, subjective and therefore a threat to universalizability; they are held to yield no morally relevant cognition. Furthermore, Kant considers them to be instinctive and blind, and therefore to blur our moral judgments. Feelings originate in subjective pleasure, says Kant; hence acting upon them is the direct opposite of acting in accordance with the moral principle. According to Kant, a choice determined by inclination "would be animal choice", only choices "determined by pure reason are called free choices". Since inclinations are rooted in subjective likes and dislikes, which are changeable and unstable, a moral choice based on emotion is considered unstable and unpredictable. This view on emotions emerges from Kant's distinction between what is natural and what is moral. Kant distinguishes between pathological and moral feeling, where pathological feeling is what precedes the moral law (i.e. which originates from natural inclination), while moral feeling is what follows the moral law (i.e. is the feeling of duty, originating from reason). Even if care, compassion, kindness and so forth may be praiseworthy, they are regarded as naturally good. Only what is done from duty is considered moral good (Kant 1996:12–14, 141–161).

This reading of Kant has given rise to two generally formulated objections against Kantian ethics. The first concerns the tenability and cost of the reason/nature dichotomy, the other a skepticism with regard to deriving particular duties from an abstract law of practical reason—duties supposed to be adequate to the complexities of human life (Sedgwick 1990:61). These objections underlie Gilligan's critique of Kohlberg as well as her objections to the justice tradition. However, according to Onora O'Neill, this comprehension of Kant's ethics is part of a criticism that recurs so often that it has acquired an independent life as an element of Kant's ethics, but it is nevertheless "a grim interpretation" (O'Neill 1991:182).[4] As opposed to this "grim interpretation", Onora O'Neill, Barbara Herman and Christine Korsgaard among several contemporary philosophers have formulated other versions of Kant's ethics (Sedgwick 1990:61). A closer inspection of Kant's ethics reveals that the acting out of the motive of duty only means that reverence for the laws is a *response* to and not the *source* of moral worth. It is not so that actions we enjoy cannot be moral (O'Neill 1991:183). Moreover, even if emotion cannot be the foundation of morality, Kant's position is not that action in opposition to or in the absence of emotion is morally desirable. As to the concern that Kant's moral law is too abstract and rigorous to adequately accommodate for the complexity and variety of our moral life, Sally Sedgwick argues that his treatment of the four duties in the *Groundwork* (1785) is Kantian moral theory in its most abstract form, not an exercise in applied ethics. It is a mistake to charge him with rigorism because he does not enter into a discussion about the level of application since his analysis is on an abstract level. When working on the level of applied ethics factors such as a person's history, relationships etc. must be taken into account—but even on this level certain contextual information should be left out. According to Sedgwick, exactly where the specific line should be drawn with regard to relevancy is not clear in Kant, but *some* individual features certainly are morally relevant (Sedgwick 1990:64–66). Also, many who use the label "Kantian" in ethics fail to give an account of the role of virtue in Kant's ethics (O'Neill 1991:184). For Kant, it should be noticed, not all emotions are passive, and there is an obligation to cultivate and strengthen the moral feeling of benevolence (Kant 1996:161–162). In Kant's ethics then, not all feelings are without moral value, passive or out of control, nor without implication for moral perceptions. Nor does Kant's ethics deny all of the uniqueness of the object of our moral judgment.

Impartiality

Impartiality, having no direct involvement or interest in the particular case, is required by the traditional moral point of view partly because our judgment is believed to be blurred by the emotions which may occur in a particular context. From what is said so far, we should be in a position to see that it does not follow from the affective component in mature care that caring is to act on spontaneous inclinations. Having emotions does not transform the caring agent into an impulse–driven, non–rational creature. Rather than blurring our judgment, the affective dimension of caring enables us to perceive the needs of others and to apprehend situations in terms of the weal and woe of others (Blum 1980:132). This faculty is evoked by a direct involvement with particular others, and it is this direct involvement that those who advocated strict impartiality worry about; it is associated with a partiality that inclines us to unfair favoring of our related others. We may desire an ungrounded preferential treatment, but we may also act against this inclination if we adopt care as a normative ideal. True, occasionally we are not strong enough to do this; sometimes we are overwhelmed by our emotions, unable or unwilling to carry out what we ought to do. But this is not an objection to the ethics of care as such, since weakness of the will may occur irrespective of whether one is a deontologist, utilitarian, Christian, Aristotelian or a carer. Blum draws attention to the reliability of Kant's duty in particular: As the actual human motive, the sense of duty is no more immune to the distorting, rationalizing self–deceiving and weakening effects of personal feelings than it is to negative modes. Our will is not always strong enough to force ourselves, or, sometimes we simply do not want to act according to our duty (Blum 1980:28–32).

Part of the implausibility of Kant's ideas about duty as the sole worthy moral motive comes, according to Blum, from failing to see that our altruistic emotions can survive our negative mood and state, and can motivate the agent to act counter to the mood of the moment (Blum 1980:22). Consequently, if the decisive moral criterion is the concern for the weal and woe of the other, impartiality is a moral requirement only in certain restricted sorts of situations. In caring for our friends we do not typically violate the duty of impartiality, simply because impartiality is not always required in those situations. Friends have claims that strangers do not have (Lafollette 1991:322; Blum 1980:46,47). We do not necessarily act against others when we do good for our friends, and doing things for/with friends has a particular meaning (for example spending time together), different from doing things for a stranger. Blum holds that relationships such as friendship have a moral aspect— namely the concern for the friend's good and having a beneficent disposition towards him. He claims that our sense of duty is not the only morally worthy feeling on the ground that altruistic feelings are not to be regarded as inclinations. Kantianism is unable to give articulation to all aspects of morality itself, says Blum (1980:57). This critique of Kantianism is echoed in Gilligan's dissatisfaction with the conventional view of justice. Impartiality does not define the moral point of view, nor does it exhaust the moral domain. Conversely, it defines *a* moral viewpoint suitable in certain circumstances, but not in others.

Universalizability

Another feature of the traditional moral point of view is that of universalizability. According to Kant for an action to be moral it must be capable of being universalized, i.e., I can rationally will that the maxim of the act should become a universal law (Kant 1992:421). It must be possible for an act to be universalized if it is to be considered as morally right. However, in order to do a morally good (or worthy) act, the act must, in addition, be done for the sake of duty. This means that for an act to be morally good it is not sufficient to do right, it must also be done for the right reason. We shall leave the motivation out for now

In order to answer the question of whether care fulfills the requirement of universalizability we need to inspect the notion of universalizability more closely: Lawrence Blum calls attention to an ambiguity, which makes two interpretations plausible. First, there is a "strong interpretation" of the notion of universalizability i.e. one must regard one's act as something that everyone ought to perform, or as something that it is wrong not to perform. In other words, either it is obligatory or prohibited. Second, there is a "weak interpretation" i.e. that one's act must be such that one can regard everyone as morally permitted to pursue it, in other words, permissible (Blum 1980:96).

Is care obligatory, prohibited, or only permissible? The responsibility of not hurting as a particular component of care is universalizable in the strong sense; not hurting is a perfect duty. What is more, the benevolent aspect of care is also universalizable in the strong sense because one cannot be willing to universalize a principle of indifference and lack of care and concern if connections and relationships are to be continued.[5] Such maxim may be rejected because it defeats other moral commitments (Pogge 1989:187). It is not inconsistent to universalize it, but the point is that it is something a rational being cannot will. In her concern with the importance and maintenance of connectedness and interdependency for human flourishing Gilligan would probably agree with O'Neill when she says:

> [N]o vulnerable agent can coherently accept that indifference and neglect should be universalized, for if they were nobody could rely on others' help: joint projects would tend to fail; vulnerable characters would be undermined; capacities and capabilities that need assistance and nurturing would not emerge; personal relationships would wither; education and cultural life would decline. (O'Neill 1996:194)

Care, related to the principle of non-maleficence, can be regarded as a universal perfect duty (held by all, owed to all), and the aspect of care related to the principle of benevolence can be considered as a universal imperfect duty held by all, (held by all, owed to none).[6] Hence, as to the first Kantian requirement—that I can will that the maxim of the act should become a universal law—it seems to be met.

Within the Kantian framework, universalizability is a necessary condition for an act to be morally good, but it is not sufficient. "For in the case of what is to be morally good, that it conforms to the moral law is not enough; it must also be done for the sake of the moral law" (Kant 1992:390). For something to be done with good will one must act in a certain way because the moral law commands it. Only when the act is in accordance with the moral law, *and* motivated by respect for this law, is it morally good (worthy).[7] Since care has an emotional aspect, one may question how it relates to the good will. Kant's distinction between pathological and practical love is useful:

> For love as an inclination cannot be commanded; but beneficence from duty, when no inclination impels us and even when a natural and unconquerable aversion opposes such beneficence, is practical, and not pathological, love. Such love resides in the will and not in tender sympathy: and only this practical love can be commanded. (Kant 1992:399)

As pointed out, mature care—which I contend must be the foundation of an ethics of care—is not pathological. Gilligan does not discuss care in relation to the Kantian division between what is natural and what is moral, but I read her theory on the development of care, from selfish care through selfless care to mature care, in terms of this distinction. In the development of care as portrayed by Gilligan, the two first levels share aspects in common both with Kant's pathological love and Noddings's natural caring. Mature care, however, must not be confused with pathological or with natural caring. Nor must it be confused with romantic and erotic love, which are based upon responses to morally irrelevant particularities related to the others, and, by definition, exclusive. Mature care bears resemblances with Kant's practical love and with Noddings's ethical caring.

Another objection against care as a moral concern appeals to the widely recognized claim that "ought implies can". Care cannot be commanded, one may say, since one cannot be blamed for not having certain emotions. Also this objection is rooted in a certain assumption concerning feelings and the role of emotions in care, namely that my feelings cannot be altered or developed. This is a misperception of human emotions. According to Julia Annas, it is up to me to have the right feelings in the same way as it is up to me to have good habits rather than bad ones (Annas 1993:57). Caring is also to do things for others, but caring does not always correspond with our emotions. Caring emotions cannot be *commanded*, but ethical caring can and may in turn develop the carer's emotional capacity. If so, we could perhaps be blamed for not developing our benevolent emotions. According to Kant, it is a duty to develop beneficence:

> If someone practices it often and succeeds in realizing his beneficent intention, he eventually comes actually to love the person he has helped. So the saying "you ought to *love* your neighbor as yourself" does not mean that you ought immediately (first) to love him and (afterwards) by means of this love do good to him. It means, rather, do good to your fellow human beings, and your beneficence will produce love of them in you (as an aptitude) of the inclination to beneficence in general. (Kant 1996:162)

Kant emphasizes here how emotions can be swayed and disciplined by conduct, while Noddings emphasizes how natural caring is the foundation of ethical caring. Again Gilligan stands out; she does not address the issue of succession, but the morally relevant blind spots (Gilligan 1982; Gilligan et al. 1988), the psychological tensions (Gilligan 1991; Gilligan et al. 1995) and the implication that follows when emotions and (expected) actions are at odds. She does not prioritize between emotions and behavior because the ideal is correspondence between them. Gilligan explains how the concept of self and other, our experiences, social reality and moral ideals collectively determine whether our emotions tie in with our ethical conduct. This broad interdisciplinary approach to ethics is an outstanding feature of Gilligan's theory.[8]

Contextualism or Principled Consideration?

The ethics of care can be regarded as a reaction against what are regarded as rigorous applications and a reluctance to reconsider the principles we find in deontological and utilitarian theories (Calhoun 1988; Gilligan 1982, Gilligan et al. 1988). Nel Noddings (1984) asserts that an ethics of care can be an alternative to ethics based on principles, while I have argued that the ethics of care is not to be understood as based on moral sentiments alone, but rather to be anchored in the expanded principle of not hurting. In fact, the ethics of care can be understood as an alternative way of responding to situations where principles collide with our sympathies and intuitive judgments and universal principles seem inadequate. I will now muster other arguments against making the ethics of care a non–principled ethical approach.

In the article "The Conscience of Huckleberry Finn", Jonathan Bennett (1974) discusses cases where general moral principles and particular emotional pulls conflict in different ways. First there is the case of Huckleberry Finn, who is drawn between his sympathies for his slave friend Jim's wish to run away from his owner, and the principle that slave-owning is a just kind of ownership. Huck's sympathy wins over his principles, he helps Jim escape. Most of us would endorse his actions, but Huck himself believes he has acted weakly and wickedly. Bennett's second case concerns Heinrich Himmler. Also Himmler, it is said, experienced a conflict between his principles and his sympathies. Principally, Himmler believed it was right to execute the Jews, but he also entertained moral qualms: "It will be a great burden for me to bear" he is supposed to have said (Bennett 1974:125–134). Nevertheless, Himmler acted against his sympathies, thinking that acting principally was the right thing to do. In this case most of us would not endorse Himmler's choice given the outcome. In both cases, most of us would defend the violation of the principles involved.[9] This connection between rigid and absolute principle on the one hand and fanaticism and individual moral irresponsibility is a central topic also in Hannah Arendt's *Eichmann in Jerusalem* (1963), as well as in Simone de Beauvoir's two essays on existentialist ethics *Pyrrhus and Cineas* (1944) and *The Ethics of Ambiguity* (1947).

Now what determines our reactions and judgments about whether it is right or wrong to follow certain principles is probably whether we endorse the value(s) the principles are assumed to protect. But never being willing to consider, and possibly reconsider, the principles of our moral stance is dogmatism, which may lead to fanaticism. It does not follow from this willingness however, that principles as such should be rejected, or that a viable alternative to principles would be to base moral responses or ethical theories on emotional whims. Not all sympathies are of the caring, compassionate kind. People do hold, say, racist or misogynistic conducts and attitudes. We can easily find cases where most of us would disapprove of violations of principles as, for instance, in a racist motivated attempt to violate the principle of equality. Solving the problem of contextual insensitivity in traditional ethical theories by rejecting principles could lead to other severe problems such as capriciousness, unpredictability and groundless differential treatment. There is, however, an alternative to total contextual sensitivity on the one hand and unconditional principalism on the other—and that is a sincere readiness to recognize that principles as well as judgments and intuitions can be revised. The most persuasive argument for this fallibilist position is empirical: There is no way to be 100 percent certain that our principles, theories and intuitions are correct. Yes, we can be sure that we have calculated or classified rightly, but not that the theory used for calculating and classification is right. When the result of following a principle goes against what we believe, it means that we must examine our theory again. Furthermore, when our intuitions and emotional pulls contradict well–considered principles and theories we must sometimes be willing to let these moral sentiments be over-ruled.

Suggesting a revision of principles and moral sentiments is influenced by Rawls's idea of reflective equilibrium (Rawls 1971:48–51), and Aristotle's attempt to seek agreement between principles and practice. An ethics of care need not be considered as a spontaneous ethics of the emotions, but as granting principles in ethics a flexible role. Noddings' (1984) emphasis on the spontaneous and affective dimensions of caring leads her to reject traditional principles, more precisely a rigid interpretation of the principles found in consequentialism and deontological theories. Nevertheless, even if ethical principles sometimes are understood and applied like algorithms, it does not justify a complete denial of principles if principles can be understood as relatively flexible and combinable with judgments. If care is understood as a virtue, or perhaps as a "considered judgment", there is an alternative to a total rejection of principle–based ethics. Instead of rejecting either principles, moral intuitions and experiences, one can adopt a method that aims at achieving consensus between our practice and our principles. The approaches of Aristotle as well as Rawls seem plausible devices in this respect. By following this route, one also acknowledges Gilligan's resentment of traditional ethical theories for their insensitivity to intuitions and contextual feelings. At the same time, one avoids the difficulties that follow when moral sentiments and inclinations become the decisive element in a theory.

Implication for Moral Theory

First and foremost, the comprehension of care as outlined above disputes the assumption that the Kantian–inspired approach constitutes the one and only benchmark of morality. An ethics of care does not deny that impartiality and universalizability are important features in some moral judgments, but rejects that they are exhaustive for what counts as moral. When the test of universalizability concerns some selected features only, it impinges on the scope of these theories. Gilligan opposes the claim that Kohlberg's theoretical framework is universal and neutral.

> [T]he so–called objective position which Kohlberg and others espoused within the canon of traditional social sciences research was blind to the particularities of voices and the inevitable constructions that constitute point of view. However well–intentioned and provisionally useful it may have been, it was based

on an inerrant neutrality which concealed power and falsified knowledge. (Gilligan 1982:xviii).

Carried over to moral philosophy, one may say that what Gilligan draws attention to is that ethical theories and moral theory reflects particular sorts of social perspectives, roles, and relations, certain types of needs and ego–developmental processes related to gender (Puka 1990:189–190). Other critics have emphasized that justice as portrayed by Kohlberg in his stage six is the favored ideology of particular socioeconomic systems and sociohistorical conditions. Its rights can, according to Bill Puka, be understood as the prolonging of western individualism and the destruction of more communal, joint–responsibility traditions found in other cultures (Puka 1990:210). Such accusations are serious when it comes to the universalism and neutralism claimed in these moral theories.

Gilligan's critique of the justice tradition is directed against the Kantian components in Kohlberg's theory. However, it could also be addressed to other theories where the independency of the moral agent is presupposed.[10] Gilligan's point is that such theories exclude the form of moral reasoning that takes connectedness and interdependency as a point of departure. She shows thereby that the so–called traditional moral theories are founded on one among other possible models of humans, and that this determines the view on how an ethical theory is to be construed, hence what is considered as morally relevant. She argues against the existence of one exhaustive principle, universal and impartial, that can serve as an adequate rule to moral conduct, and to the idea that moral agents are autonomous in the sense that they alone possess sufficient knowledge to decide for themselves what is the morally right thing to do. Second, as far as I can see, no reasonable interpretation of Kant's ethics could change the hierarchy of reason and emotion, and make way for a Gilliganian anti–dichotomous approach. Thirdly, even if Kant does not reject emotion altogether, his ethics fails to account adequately for emotions, and therefore narrows the moral domain in a way that leaves out many of the situations in which we in our daily life experience moral conflicts not to mention situations we consider to be valuable—such as interactions with our related others.

As to traditional ethical theories, the ethics of care challenges some of their most prominent claims. It explicates the inadequacy of the preconditions and narrow assumptions underlying their key conceptions, and draws attention to what is excluded.[11] It represents a challenge to the epistemological and ontological foundations of most traditional ethical theories (Tong 1993:49–80; Walker 1992:1998) and is particularly relevant if these are taken to be morally universal, neutral and exhaustive. Let us inspect the implications for traditional moral ontology more closely.

Care and Implication for Traditional Moral Ontology

A recommendation concerning how one should act or live will be founded on assumptions about what it means to be human. On some readings characterized as traditional moral theories a human being is defined as an independent self disconnected from though equal to others. In some theories, Kant's and Kohlberg's to mention two of relevance here, self–government and autonomy is aspired, even considered the goal of individual development. One implication following from the traditional approach is that being embedded in relationships may be comprehended as dependency, denoting a lack of self–determination and immatureness. By emphasizing the necessity and value of connectedness, the ethics of care (as explained in Chapter 4) shatters the conception of the autonomous self and reveals its inadequacy. It further repudiates the claim that being attached to others is less valuable and mature than being separated from others. By challenging this moral ontological point, the ethics of care also implicates traditional moral theory in, at least, three ways:

1) The autonomous agent, in the sense of a psychological "sovereign" and independent agent, is not taken to be a valid characterization of the moral agent. It is not adequate as an empirical description of a moral agent, nor as a normative expression of what an agent ought to become. Moral theories that take this type of autonomy as the quintessence of moral agency are incomplete. They are also inadequate in that moral reality does not consist of independent individuals only and because acting morally requires more than the quality of autonomy. Co–feeling and empathy are further necessary components in the rendering of a moral mature agent. The self on which Gilligan founds her ethical theory differs distinctively from a Kantian model of a moral agent. Moral maturity signifies, in the ethics of care, more than practical reason; it means to combine practical reason with emotion, to combine integrity with the ability to be connected with others. The traditional understanding of moral maturity, autonomy and agency is too narrow to serve as an ontological basis for moral theory, or to be the sole ideal for moral development.

2) A consequence of understanding the moral agent as independent rather than connected, traditional theories tend to pay more attention to situations in which humans are independent and equal, than to asymmetric relationships. But ethical challenges are not only faced by independent equals

who are free to choose how to act. In fact most of the situations where we are confronted with difficult decisions concerning how to act are to be found in contexts of interdependency and concern our connectedness with others. This is not to say that traditional theories are completely uninformed of situations of inequality (Kant's fourth example in *Fundamental Principles of the Metaphysics of Morals* from 1785 sets out how to act towards people less advantaged than oneself), only that these situations are considered as exceptional—when, in fact, most people experience both dependency and independency in their lives. But claiming that established theory focuses too one-sidedly on independency and self-legislation is not to say that these capacities are to be disapproved of. The point is that independence and interdependency must be combined in order to give us an adequate portrayal of human beings—their relationships, their development and aspirations.

3) Therefore, traditional advice about how to live and how to act is incomplete. An example of how Gilligan's theory on dependency, relational self and care has influenced and widened the debate in moral theory can be seen in Eva Feder Kittay's critique of Rawls's theory of justice. Kittay says that neither the first nor the second principle of Rawls's account of justice secures fairness to the dependent and dependency workers, as he does not take into account their lack of ability to participate in society or their restrictions as to self-realization. In order to attain equality of justice, says Kittay, a third principle of justice is required:

> To each according to his or her need for care, from each according to his or her capacity for care, and such support from social institutions as to make available resources and opportunities to those providing care, so that all will be adequately attended in relations that are sustaining. (Kittay 1997:252)

However, Kittay continues, there is no natural way of converting such a principle into Rawls's principles of justice since the whole theory, like all contractarian theories, is premised on the assumption that individuals are equal in their ability to compete and participate in social life. When the comprehension of our moral (as well as political) responsibilities fails to acknowledge the dependency between self and other and the significance of care for human well-being and flourishing a severe impediment to equality, freedom and fairness remains (Kittay 1997; Okin 1989).

The idea of an autonomous moral agent is a constitutive element in traditional moral theory; it is rooted in Kant's idea on every person's moral equality and upheld in deontological and liberal theories and in the utilitarian principle of equality. Needless to say, an ethics of care would not reject the normative ideal of human equality, but it would shed light on the insufficiency of construing universal principles as if the traditional conception of autonomy, equality and self–governance represented the whole picture of human contingency, or the only goal of human development, or the most important faculty for a moral agent to possess. Such principles, when presented as neutral and universal, are considered by care ethicists and others as wanting idealizations. In addition to the political and social consequences of such a lack, there are also implications for traditional moral epistemology.

Care and Implication for Traditional Moral Epistemology

Inherent in Gilligan's work is both a radical critique of traditional moral epistemology, as well as a latent attempt to transcend it. Both aspects can be framed in the following way:

1) The universal and formal aspect of traditional moral principles apparently leads to a limited comprehension of what is to be considered the *relevant knowledge* for acting morally. Gilligan emphasizes first and foremost that an understanding of abstract principles and ability to deduce and generalize must not be at the expense of contextual sensitivity, the perception of difference and the significance of relational structures (Gilligan et al. 1988:6). Additionally, the traditional strategy of requiring knowledge about the other is based on identifying the other's similarity with one–self. However, the procedure to ask how I would feel if I were in a certain situation may lead one to fall into the trap of confusing one's own perspectives with an objective truth (Gilligan 1987:31). While there is a danger of errors in care–related reasoning as well, a mature care aims at acquiring the necessary knowledge through a process which combines contextual sensitivity and principle–based reasoning.

2) It appears that traditional moral theory tends to accept a narrower conception of the *cognitive ability* required for achieving relevant knowledge for acting morally. The faculty of mature care not only requires the cognitive skill to deduce from abstract principles, nor is the exclusive perception of particularities sufficient either. Mature care requires the ability to interweave these two types of knowledge. Care is hence not only to comprehend a moral virtue, but an intellectual virtue as well; a cognitive disposition, a higher order faculty, which includes many sub–faculties (Dalmiya 2002). It is among these sub–faculties we find several of the abilities Gilligan states are crucial for making moral decisions. They are therefore important components of an agent's moral competence. Listening, for instance, is an aspect of moral perception (Gilligan et al. 1988:x) considered to be key component

in moral problem–solving. Imagination and co–feeling are other cognitive sub–faculties, as is reasoning. Reasoning, including self–reflection is prominent in caring. It contains elements that are taken to differ from traditional moral theory, such as the "connected knowledge" that induces differences in moral reasoning, problem–solving and ways of responding The faculty of care transcends traditional moral epistemology thanks to its anti–dichotomous approach, and opens up for new insights on moral responsibility:

3) Traditional moral theories can be criticized for too narrow an understanding of *moral responsibility*. In the ethics of care, moral responsibility is not merely limited to the justification of actions by appeal to moral principles. It consists first and foremost in acting responsively in relationships, to gain awareness of the needs of the other and respond appropriately to them (Gilligan et al. 1988:7). The responsibility for acting appropriately is placed on the moral agent, not on an abstract moral principle. It says that the application of morality, as well as moral responsibility is relational, not merely a matter for a sovereign agent and her principles. If principles and rules are to be applied without consideration of the special circumstances, the agent will be released from some of the responsibility for his or her own conduct. One of the achievements of "care–reasoning" is then a widened sense of moral responsibility.

4) Consequently, *the focus* of traditional moral theories is challenged by the ethics of care as it aims at achieving a focal point that complies with *in situ* experience of moral challenges: i.e., within interpersonal interaction. According to Gilligan, highlighting the relation between the agent and those who are affected by decisions made by the agent expands the moral domain and adds to what is considered as morally relevant (Gilligan 1982:24–40). We can say that she accentuates the moral significance of care, human interaction and dependency, things that are "under theorized" in most modern moral theories, especially theories concerned with the issues of rights and justice (Nortvedt 1996:95).

5) Traditional moral theories are also comprehended as rigorous and routine based. Since the focus of care is the interactive selves—others as well as our own self—it requires a constant reflection. Such reflection concerns not only how to understand and respond to the other, but also oneself, and is therefore an ongoing process of *self–reflection*. But what is required is not mere introspection, rather an awareness of how one interacts with others, how well one understands and responds towards others (Dalmiya 2002), and how one cares about oneself. The ethics of care implies an epistemological shift takes place which moves the focus from abstract principles to an emphasis on the inclusion of the domains of knowledge and experience, i.e., the

perspective of care, the "different voice", that have traditionally belonged to women and been left out of consideration. This shift in focus challenges traditional theories; it exposes that their neutrality and universality is exaggerated. Notice once again the anti–dichotomous way of proceeding: The object of knowledge, consideration and reflection is neither the self only, nor merely the cared–for but the interaction between the selves. What is more, this theory on care is not based on an idiosyncratic perspective, nor merely on a generalized view, but on our ability to alter our approach. As such it aims at attending to both perspectives. Moral knowing is not merely a tool of pure reason alone, or an element in an agent's hypothetical thought experiment (viz. Kant's categorical imperative, Kohlberg's moral musical chairs, and Rawls's veil of ignorance). Nor is moral knowledge achieved by acceptance of conventionalities and traditions as communitarians and historicists are inclined to believe. Moral knowledge is acquired through a reflective and interactive process, which includes actual dialogue and co–feeling. There is, I believe, in Gilligan's work, a substantial potential for a "third way", for finding a path between epistemological relativism on the one hand, and moral fundamentalism on the other. This potential is in need of further development, and it will be elaborated on in the next chapter.

Notes

1. Within principal–based ethical theories, like deontology, treating people differently is not necessarily morally wrong. Differential treatment can be understood in connection to the principle of equality, first formulated by Aristotle in his theory of justice. This principle is widely accepted among philosophers today. It says that equal cases ought to be treated (or judged) in the same way. In other words, if two cases are treated differently there must be a morally relevant difference between them. Hence, there are two main types of differential treatment, justified and unjustified, and two groups of cases, equal and unequal. Different cases can be treated differently or in the same way, and analogous cases can be treated either alike or in a different way. If two identical cases are unequally treated, it is termed unjustified unequal treatment. If two different cases are handled differently, this treatment can be unjustified or justified. It is the morally relevant features that determine whether the handling of the case is justified or not. If there are no morally relevant differences between two cases they ought to be treated in the same way, i.e. differential treatment is forbidden. If there are morally relevant differences between the two cases, this can justify the differential treatment. Consensus on the principle of equality can be found among philosophers, regardless of the ethical theory they support. The reason for this general agreement is that one otherwise would be allowing for inconsistency: If treatment A is right in case X, then it must, ceteris paribus, be right to give all cases of

type X treatment A. However, since the principle of equality is formal, it does not tell us which features ought to be regarded as morally relevant, nor how to determine whether cases are analogues or not. There is therefore no common understanding on these matters. In moral argumentation, it is nevertheless common to justify what is regarded as morally relevant features by using a certain formal structure. The morally relevant features (and also a particular judgment) are grounded by appealing to a more general rule, a rule derived from what is considered to be a moral principle, which in turn is sustained by an ethical theory. When there is an inconsistency between our judgment and our principles, something has to be adjusted for consistency to be re–established.

2. At stage six in Kohlberg's theory, the person achieves the moral point of view, i.e. the ability to see hypothetical reciprocal role–taking as the universally valid procedure for decision–making in moral conflicts. This procedure is what Kohlberg calls the "moral musical chairs" and it aims at ensuring the universalizability and impartiality of judgment that Kant aimed for (Nunner–Winkler 1990:109–126).

3. For a further discussion of prejudiced and distorted moral perception, as well as the political implications of such, see Diane T. Meyers (1997:197–218). An example on sexual harassment in this article may illuminate my point here, that the moral concept one possesses is determined by the tradition or discourse one is familiar with, and that these moral conceptions are relevant to moral perception: For feminists and many other women sexual harassment is part of their moral conception, while for many men sexual harassment is conflated with office romance, or, woman's definition of this phenomenon is thought of as over inclusive (Meyers 1997:208).

4. According to O'Neill, critics of Kant read his essay "On a Supposed Right to Lie of Benevolent Motives" as a dreadful warning "against the impasse of any ethics of principle" despite the fact that Kantian scholars debate how this essay is to be understood as it represents an extreme view (O'Neill, 1996:156).

5. Care is not identical with the principle of not hurting, nor with the principle of benevolence, but it shares nevertheless some important features with both principles. That is why I have suggested the expanded principle of not hurting. For a discussion on the relationship between care and these two principles, see Chapter 3.

6. Drawing on O'Neill, these four types of duties can be explained like this: "Universal, perfect duties": held by all, owed to all: counterpart liberty rights; embodied above all in legal and economic systems. (In childcare abusing parents will violate these.) "Special, perfect duties": held by some, owed to specific others; counterpart special rights: fixed by structure of specific transactions and relationships; can be distributed universal given appropriate institutions. (In childcare, this will be the care and support parents owe to their own children, but not to all children, which is what neglecting parents violate.) "Universal imperfect duties": held by all, owed to none; no counterpart rights; embodied above all in character and expressed in varied situations. (Virtues like courtesy and concern are examples and in childcare will be what rigid, fanatic or cold parents lack.) "Special, imperfect duties": held by some, owed to none; no counterpart rights; embodied in ethos of specific relationships and practices

and in characters; often, but not exclusively, expressed in action within special relationship. (An example is the certain sorts of love, attention and support which the parents do not owe to all, which are quite specific to the relationship to the child, but to which their children have no right, and what makes them good parents) (O'Neill 1996:151–152).

7. If one acts against the moral law, the action is morally wrong and morally unworthy. If one's act is universalizable, but not done for the sake of the moral law, it is morally right but morally non-worthy.

8. "Contemporary theorists of justice" says Susan Okin, "with few exceptions, have paid little or no attention to the question of moral development—of how we are to *become* just. Most of them seem to think, to adapt slightly Hobbes' notable phrase, that just men springs like mushrooms from the earth" (Okin 1989:21).

9. Bennett's cases could also be given a different gloss by seeing Huck's and Himmler's sympathies as principles. The conflict would then be between two different principles rather than sympathies and principles. But it nevertheless does not alter the point I am trying to make, that our moral attitudes—be they principles or sympathies—must be open for reconsideration.

10. One of Gilligan's purposes is to include a moral perspective she believes is ignored in traditional theories, the perspective of care. This perspective is found by listening to women and girls' moral reflections, and on this ground she criticizes the claimed neutrality and universality of traditional moral theories. In this her endeavor bears resemblance with feminists in other fields, for instance Sandra Harding's who in *The Science Question in Feminism* (1986) disputes the objectivity of science, and argues that it is gender biased. Gilligan may therefore be understood as participating in an interdisciplinary, critical movement, the common aim of which is to call attention to limitations and inadequacies in established "paradigms" by exposing who and what have been excluded.

11. Which include deontological, liberal as well as utilitarian theories.

CHAPTER SIX

~

Care and Justice

Unlike many other ethical theories, the ethics of care does not have conflict solving as a major focus. Its chief concern is the prevention of conflicts. This is one reason why it does not give strict normative commands on who ought to live or die in life–threatening and dramatic situations, but rather suggests ways of acting vis–à–vis each other on a daily basis precisely to prevent harm and promote growth and flourishing. Stepping back from the dramatic, tragic and often hypothetical situation the ethics of care speaks to the ordinary situations, a feature that makes it an ethical theory in touch with real life.

However, despite its necessity and legitimacy, an ethical theory should also give some form of guidance for dealing with conflicts. A virtually unavoidable consequence of being in a relationship is the risk of falling out and disagreeing. In this chapter I want to explore what an ethics of care can offer in these situations. In addition to showing how the ethics of care deals with the clash of interests, I want also to highlight two other aspects of the theory. The first concerns the concept of mature care. Although the idea of mature care, i.e., capacity to balance interests of self and others, is compelling, we still need to know how to go about it in practice. What if my interests, for instance, are incompatible with yours? The second aspect concerns care and justice in relation to conflict handling and conflict solving. Indeed, how is care related to justice? I believe that the idea of mature care holds the key to reconciling care and justice while framing a nascent conflict–solving model. Were it to be philosophically refined, it would certainly be of benefit to the ethics of care (Pettersen 2006c: 156–157).

This view differs from other interpretations of her theory, which see only a conflict in the relationship between care and justice (Flanagan and Jackson 1993; Blum 1994; Vetlesen 1994:152; 1996:149–153). My argument does not wholly reject the possibility of a dichotomous interpretation of Gilligan's view of care and justice. I argue that such an interpretation is indeed important, but that it is an incomplete reading of Gilligan since she demonstrably makes an effort to overcome the antagonism between the two moral orientations. The move beyond a dichotomous approach in Gilligan's theory was mentioned in the preceding chapter; in the following this approach will be further explored, to help elaborate some of the reconciliatory potential I see in her ethics of care.[1]

Gilligan's Ambiguity

There is an ambiguity in Gilligan's writing as to the relationship between care and justice, and this ambiguity is the point of departure for my claim that there is a potential for reconciliation. In *In a Different Voice* (1982) it is difficult to understand how Gilligan comprehends the relationship between care and justice. Care and justice are sometimes depicted as diametrically opposed, as when she discusses Jake and Amy's response to Heinz's dilemma, and sometimes as fusible, as when she discusses her informants' reflections on abortion. In *Mapping the Moral Domain* (1988) and in "Moral Orientation and Moral Development" (1987) Gilligan and her co–writers present care and justice as two almost incompatible moral approaches. In later works, such as *Making Connections* (1990), *Meeting at the Crossroad* (1992), and in *Between Voices and Silence* (1995), care and justice are represented as able to converge. Since these later works are not on ethics, but on moral psychology, ethicists rarely refer to them. Those works mainly discuss psychological case studies of adolescent American girls. Nevertheless, I find them important to the discussion of the normative potential in Gilligan's ethic of care, as on the relationship between care and justice. The reason is that in the discussions of real life dilemmas, as experienced by the young female informants, the relationship between care and justice plays a prominent role. The ability to reconcile care and justice is integrated into her theory of moral development as presented in her earlier works and gives the model greater distinctness. Particularly relevant is the illumination of care on level three where components from the tradition of justice are assimilated in mature care. Second, the morally mature agent is portrayed as a person able to surpass the dichotomous and antagonistic comprehension of care and justice. Antagonism between these two moral ideals is nevertheless a necessary stage in the developmental process towards moral maturity, but it is to all intents and purposes finally resolved. It is the normative potential for reconciling care and justice I find inherent in her model of psychological development and maturity I want to elaborate in this chapter. However, before commencing, some terminological clarifications are required.

Conflict and Moral Dilemma—Terminological Clarifications

In the works of Gilligan, "moral dilemma" seems to correspond to the quotidian understanding of the term. In everyday language, it is commonly understood that a person faces a moral dilemma if she has to choose between strong moral requirements that cannot both be adopted at once (Sinnot–Armstrong 1988:5). Furthermore, it is customary to use "moral dilemma" and "moral conflict" as interchangeable terms, which is what Gilligan does in her texts.[2] My discussion nevertheless requires a more accurate terminology. I want to use here some definitions taken from Walter Sinnot–Armstrong's *Moral Dilemmas* (1988).[3]

Sinnot–Armstrong distinguishes between a "moral conflict" and a "moral dilemma"; the former is a broader term than the latter. He identifies three types of moral conflicts: First, there is the situation where one moral ideal conflicts with another moral ideal. In our context, it could be a conflict between the ideal of care and the ideal of justice. The second type of moral conflict occurs when there is a contradiction between two moral requirements. A relevant example in our context is when the injunction to care for self and others is conflicting. Thirdly, there can be a moral conflict between a moral ideal and a moral requirement. The ideal of not hurting any of the involved, and the requirement to care for one person in particular illustrates this kind of moral conflict. Moral dilemmas arise when moral requirements conflict and neither is overridden in any moral relevant way (Sinnot–Armstrong 1988:21). More precisely, according to Sinnot–Armstrong, a moral dilemma can be described as any situation where at the same time the following features are present:

1) There is a moral requirement for an agent to adopt each of two alternatives.
2) Neither moral requirement is overridden in any morally relevant way.
3) The agent cannot adopt both alternatives together, and
4) The agent can adopt each alternative separately. (Sinnot–Armstrong 1988: 29)[4]

There are several ways of resolving troublesome moral cases depending on the kind of moral theory applied in the case in question. Given a "monistic position" that morality can be reduced to a single principle—such as the maximization of a particular value—it is possible to find correct solutions to particular problems. Given a "pluralistic position" i.e. that there is more than one basic principle, it is possible to rank the principles lexically. By a "lexical ranking", one principle always takes precedence over another (Sinnot–Armstrong 1988:30–33). The monistic and the lexical/pluralistic–structured theories are often followed by procedures setting out how to apply the principles, and the agent should be able to deduce from abstract moral principle(s) the right solution for the case in question. If the principles are regarded as "prima facie", one must judge each principle's weight in relation to the weight of other principles in the particular situation. "Moral disagreement" is taken to mean a situation where two or more persons arrive at different moral solutions to a particular problem. "Moral conflict" and "moral dilemma" depart from "moral disagreement" because the two former concepts are related to one agent, while moral disagreements appear among two or more agents. Moral disagreements may be hard to resolve. Nevertheless, Beauchamp outlines some attainable strategies: To obtain objective information, to provide definitional clarity, reaching agreements on a common framework of moral principles, and to analyze the arguments (Beauchamp 1991:64–68).

The Species of Conflict Between Care and Justice

The conflict between care and justice is a topic studied in various fields, from literature, drama and films, to theology, moral philosophy, moral psychology and political science. It has been an essential issue in feminist ethics as displayed in Virginia Held' s (ed.) book *Justice and Care* published in 1995. The conflict between justice and care can take place within as well as between different social spheres, as, for instance, between individuals or within a collective, and, indeed, something we experience in our own life. Also, it is often the cause of media exposés. We can take a real case as an illustration. The Norwegian media wrote about the misery of a three–year–old boy who had spent his entire life as a refugee in a Norwegian church because his parents had entered the country illegally, the authorities wanted to throw them out, and church asylum was the only means open to them. Despite the media's focus, the little boy and his family were not granted asylum because, it was said, it would violate the principle of fair and equal treatment. The boy's defense, on the other hand, appealed to our benevolence and our responsibility to care, to our compassion as well as our duty to prevent harm. Here, there was a *conflict* between two moral ideals, as well as *disagreement* between the boy's champions and the government. However, the ideal of care, it should be noted, is not necessarily linked to individuals, nor is justice to institutions. On behalf of a group or a population's welfare, authorities can violate the principle of fair and equal treatment. When a privilege for some means a burden for others, the emburdened sometimes characterize the arrangement as unjustifiable differential treatment. For example, disagreement on the application of positive discrimination when awarding jobs and scholarships to benefit certain groups or minorities, can be understood as a conflict between two ideals; the fair and equal treatment and care for the flourishing of a particular group. The conflict between care and justice can apply between groups too. This is a well-known conflict for utilitarians; if one for the sake of maximizing overall welfare burdens a group of people it can be portrayed as a conflict between care (or, perhaps better, utility understood as benevolence) and justice. We recognize such conflicts in political debates over the distribution of scarce public resources.[5]

Interpersonal moral conflicts are what Gilligan focuses in her discussion. The participants in the conflict are individuals. Most often, the conflicts she highlights can be described as *loyalty conflicts* between taking care of others and taking care of oneself. But her discussion of conflicts can be narrowed down even more since it is based on her studies of American girls in adolescence. One could ask whether this narrow scope has any relevance for moral theory and the philosophical discussion concerning the relationship between care and justice. Despite the limitations of Gilligan's studies, I believe they have a greater potential that is of relevance to ethics and philosophy of care and justice. The heart of the conflicts she discusses is how to care for others as well as oneself when interests are conflicting with each other. This is, I think, the essence of most ethical dilemmas. For governments and politicians, for nurses and teachers and for parents and friends the roots of the predicament are diverging responsibilities and interests.[6]

However, finding solutions may be impossible if one sees moral conflicts and disagreements as arising from two competing, antagonistic notions of morality. The agents involved will have different ideas as to what is ethically relevant. In my reading, a binary approach to morality can be traced in Gilligan's theory, but it represents only one stage in her theory of development towards maturity. Overcoming the dualistic approach to care and justice is essential to attain moral maturity and to solve dilemmas. Nevertheless, interpreting the relationship between care and justice in Gilligan's theory as antagonistic is rather common (Nunner–Winkler 1993:143; Flanagan and

Jackson 1993:71; Vetlesen 1994:152; 1996:149–153). Such binary and in-commensurable readings may be because almost all debates focus on Heinz's dilemma, and, in particular, on the response of two of her informants, Jake and Amy, in *In a Different Voice* (Gilligan 1982:125–31). These remarks are probably the most read pages of her most read book. Gilligan herself, it should be noted, has also given that response weight. For example she maintains that "Amy's judgments contain the insights central to an ethics of care, just as Jake's judgments reflect the logic of the justice approach" (Gilligan 1982:30). In her discussion about Jake and Amy's responses, the differences between the two perspectives are emphasized. Let me present this established understanding of Gilligan's view of care, justice and the relationship between them before suggesting another reading.

Care and Justice: "Traditional Readings"

Jake can be understood as regarding Heinz's dilemma as a situation where Heinz has to choose between two moral requirements: saving a life or respecting someone else's property. Jake takes Heinz's situation to be such that Heinz cannot fulfill both requirements, only one of them. Jake solves Heinz's problem quite easily by overriding one of the moral requirements. He justi-fies his maneuver by referring to what is taken to be a morally relevant dis-parity between the two cases: a human life is worth more than property, Heinz cannot get his wife back if she dies, and since his wife is unique, the loss cannot be compensated. Furthermore, Gilligan describes Jake as ab-stracting the dilemma from the interpersonal situation, and, in the logic of fairness, he finds an "objective" way of deciding how to act. From the per-spective of justice, according to Gilligan, the moral dilemma consists of con-flicting requirements, but the right thing to do can be deduced if one is fa-miliar with the different principles involved and their order of ranking. The main difficulty consists in determining what actions and conducts are right or wrong according to the relevant norms and principles, and how to justify one's ranking of those principles (Gilligan 1982: 25–32).

Applying Sinnot–Armstrong's criteria of what constitutes a moral dilemma (Sinnot–Armstrong 1988:29), Heinz's dilemma is not, from the per-spective of Jake, a real dilemma because the second criterion, i.e., that "nei-ther moral requirement is overridden in any morally relevant way", does not hold true for Heinz, as Jake sees it. Jake starts out from a set of premises, and deduces a way of resolving the issue. Since he assumes agreement on the premises for his reasoning, he also expects agreement on the conclusion he draws. The justice perspective, as applied by Jake, can be interpreted as a universalistic moral approach. The right thing to do can be deduced if one is familiar with the relevant principles and their relative importance. Morality is a matter of rationality. Since Jake holds a monistic position that allows a lexical ranking of the requirements, he finds a solution for Heinz.

To Amy there is no such straightforward solution to Heinz's problem, since what characterizes a moral dilemma within the morality of care is how to care for everybody at the same time. From Amy's perspective, the difficulty arises not from the druggist's assertion of rights, but from his failure of response toward Heinz. The players in the dilemmas are arrayed not as opponents in a contest of rights, but as members of a network of relationships on whose continuation they all depend (Gilligan 1982:30). In Amy's approach to Heinz's dilemma, the moral ideal is to care. The moral conflict arises because this ideal gives rise to several different and, in this context, incompatible requirements, i.e. not to hurt the wife nor the druggist nor their mutual relationship. If only one part is hurt, the moral requirement is not fulfilled and the moral ideal violated. From Amy's point of view, i.e. the perspective of care, Heinz's dilemma creates two types of moral conflicts in Sinnot–Armstrong's terms. First, there is a conflict between the ideal of care and the requirements that can be worked out from that principle. Since the ideal calls for care and concern for all parties it is violated here as not all requirements can be fulfilled at the same time. Also, since several persons are involved, there is a conflict between different, conflicting requirements. For Amy, Heinz's problem is a real dilemma since neither moral requirement can be overridden in any morally relevant way. Amy, in order to find a solution, cannot make use of deduction as Jake did. This is not because she, or other "care–thinkers" for that matter, does not have any normative guidelines to rely on.[7] It is due to the fact that what guides the holder of the dilemma, i.e. the normative injunction not to hurt, does not allow for easy deductions because there is no pre–established lexical ranking to rely on, and to decide how the requirement should be ranked in a particular situation requires extensive contextual knowledge. Therefore, Amy, as the holder of the dilemma, responds by seeking more contextual information in order to be able to determine the degree of the other's vulnerability—and consequently the effect of the different ways of proceeding. This shows why detailed contextual knowledge is important before an agent makes a decision within an ethics of care. The carer needs idiosyncratic information in order to determine the degree of hurt to those involved in the situation.[8] This approach differs from the way a dilemma is perceived within the conventional view of justice (i.e. as it is portrayed in Gilligan), as the resolution of a dilemma first and foremost is a matter of justification. The difficulty consists in determining what actions and conducts are right or wrong according to some relevant norms and principles, fairness in particular (Lyons 1990:44). Within the care perspective, however, determining what is morally right and wrong is not first and foremost a matter of consulting a set of rules; the focal point is the effect on those involved.

What this discussion reveals is that in the two moral perspectives, moral problems are perceived differently. Therefore, presumably, care and justice are most often comprehended as two contrary moral perspectives. Two important questions seem nevertheless to have been left out of the discussion, by Gilligan in her early works, as well as by most of the participants in the subsequent debate over Heinz's dilemma. And the questions are: Is it possible for Amy to find a solution to the dilemma within the perspective of care? Would that solution differ, and if so, would Jake and Amy be able to bridge the gap? If so, it would illustrate that care and justice are reconcilable, since Jake and Amy's disagreement would be a conflict between two moral ideals, justice and care. I proceed, not by addressing these questions directly, but by exploring what Gilligan says about how the relationship between two moral perspectives should be understood.

When care and justice are understood as two perspectives rooted in two different moral ideals, not only would their holders perceive moral problems differently, as did Jake and Amy, but they would apparently disagree on moral terms. Gilligan illustrates the relationship between care and justice by drawing attention to the ambiguous figures used in Gestalt psychology, particularly the figure that can be perceived both as a rabbit and a duck (Gilligan 1987:19,30; Gilligan et al. 1988:8,9,117). Gilligan takes the rabbit–duck metaphor as an analogy of how the same setting can be organized in at least two ways and how one way of seeing it can make the other disappear (Gilligan et al. 1988:xvii,117). Each orientation is associated with a different problem–solving strategy, suggesting that each moral orientation facilitates different kinds of reasoning. Care and justice are said to constitute different ways of organizing a problem, different ways of thinking about what is happening and what to do. The rabbit–duck metaphor implies that the two moral approaches cause a shift in conceptions of what is relevant to the moral domain, leading to different notions of morality and different forms of moral reasoning (Gilligan et al. 1988:119). The metaphor can sustain a reading of Gilligan as positing care and justice as antagonistic moral approaches, a reading represented by Bartlett (1992), Flanagan and Jackson (1993), Blum (1994:240–241) Puka (1994:426–427), and Vetlesen (1994:152).

However, the rabbit–duck metaphor can also be interpreted as if the two moral perspectives, justice and care, constitutes alternative moral approaches based on different cognitive capacities (Ruddick 1995:2003–205). There are passages in Gilligan's writings that defy an antagonistic, dichotomous reading of the relationship between the moral ideal of care and justice. For in-stance, she says it is important to stress that the two are not opposites (Gilligan et al. 1988:xxi) and should not to be understood as two opposites to where caring is perceived as unjust and justice uncaring. However, nor can they be construed in terms of one another. Gilligan says that the effort to construct one orientation in the terms of the other misses the reorgani-zation of relationship that occurs with the shift in perspective. To argue whether morality is really a matter of justice or of care is like arguing whether the ambiguous rabbit–duck figure is really a rabbit or a duck (Gilli-gan et al. 1988:128). She claims that one person can take up both per-spectives, and can solve problems in at least two different ways. Therefore, the choice of moral standpoint, whether implicit or explicit, becomes an important feature of moral decision–making and research on moral devel-opment (Gilligan et al. 1988:xxvii–xviii; Gilligan 1987:27,30,31). The rea-son why people are able to adopt at least two apparently contrary moral standpoints is, she says, that inequality and equality, and attachment and detachment are experienced by both sexes (Gilligan et al. 1988:5,83). They are inherent in the experience of the relationship between parent and child, and give rise to an ethics of justice as well as an ethics of care (Gilligan 1982:62,63; 1987:28,29).

Now how are we to understand Gilligan on the relations between care and justice? First, in Gilligan's work there is no clear–cut evidence for the traditional reading of the relation between care and justice. Second, while passages in her works that concern the issue may be comprehended as evi-dence of ambiguity on the matter, they can also be comprehended as ex-pressing a process of development in her thinking. It appears that she has moved from a rather binary view of care and justice (Gilligan 1979) to-wards an understanding that admits the possibility of convergence (Gilli-gan 1993; Gilligan et al. 1995). As I see it, putting an antagonistic inter-pretation on the relationship between care and justice is out of tune with the anti–dichotomous style found in Gilligan to which I have drawn at-tention. Finally, there is the analogy of the rabbit–duck metaphor with Jake and Amy's moral stances: Where Jake sees a rabbit Amy sees a duck. But Gilligan says it is possible for them to exchange perspectives. Amy should therefore be able to adopt Jake's perspective, just as he should be able to take on Amy's. It is thus possible to shift between the perspective of justice and the perspective of care. Grasping this point is crucial to a comprehen-sive understanding of Gilligan's position on care and justice. It overcomes the dichotomous, antagonistic comprehension of care and justice and gives way to the possibility that disagreement may be solved. Before elaborating further on this possibility, I want to outline certain general thoughts on the possible relationship between care and justice in order to further substantiate my claim that traditional readings of Gilligan on this matter fall short.

Care and Justice: Some Possible Relations

First, and generally speaking, one can claim that care and justice are "mutually exclusive", by which I mean that by holding one of them, conceived as the right approach, one rejects the other as false. Care and justice are thus held to be competitive and conflicting moral approaches in such a way that if one regards, say, care as the right moral perspective, then justice is conceived as a wrong moral approach. Seeing care and justice as mutually exclusive means that they are exhaustive in relation to scope, i.e. that all moral cases can be approached from either the perspective of care or the perspective of justice. It also implies that the two moralities are self–contained, taken to mean that its proponents take each theory as possessing all the theoretical features required to function independently as an adequate moral approach. On this view, one of the three types of moral conflicts mentioned above—the conflict between two moral ideals such as care and justice—would not arise, because one of the ideals would have been already rejected. Gilligan, however, does not advocate this position. On the contrary. As we have seen, there are passages where Gilligan states that each position leaves out something that is seen in the others. Neither care, nor justice can therefore be self–contained and exhaustive. Further, she does not claim the justice orientation to be a wrong moral approach, only insufficient. I take these factors as evidence that Gilligan does not hold the position that care and justice are mutually exclusive.[9]

A second way of understanding the relationship between care and justice is to think of them as "compatible", i.e., able to coexist separately without conflict. This means that some cases are to be approached from the perspective of care, and some from the perspective of justice. The moral domain must then be divided between the two approaches, which could be done by applying the perspective of justice in the public sphere, for instance, and letting the perspective of care cover the private domain. If the demarcation between the private and the public spheres was clear and uncontroversial, there would be neither conflict nor competition between the two approaches. However, there will always be cases where such a division is problematic causing controversy and consternation as to whether care or justice should more readily be applied. This kind dispute, it should be noted, is not a moral conflict between the ideal of care and the ideal of justice. Rather, it is a problem of demarcation, of whether a particular case belongs to the public or the private sphere, or, conversely, where the demarcation line between the two spheres should go. Once such differences are settled, it will be clear how to approach the case.[10] Since Gilligan is concerned about and has highlighted the antagonism and tension between the two perspectives, she cannot reasonably be said to hold the position that they are compatible, that they can coexist without causing conflict. This antagonism between care and justice cannot be overlooked, nor can it be smoothened out by a compartmentalizing strategy. Nor is it in accordance with Gilligan to hold that some cases should be approached from the perspective of justice, and others from the perspective of care. A case can be approached from both perspectives, as the rabbit–duck metaphor is meant to illustrate. Also, Gilligan explicitly rejects a separation of spheres into public and private in regard to the application of care (Gilligan 1993:209). Care transcends the distinction between the private and the public.

As a third possibility we could regard the relationship between care and justice as "incommensurable", i.e., the two orientations are not capable of comparison or mutual ranking because they lack the necessary common premises for such an evaluative comparison to be made.[11] From this point of view, care and justice are two different approaches to moral life, so that all cases can be legitimately approached from the perspective of justice or from the perspective of care. Both perspectives can be applied to the same case, but different aspects will be revealed when doing so, and they will be emphasized and weighted differently. What I have termed the "traditional reading" of care and justice can be comprehended as an expression of this position. Despite the support in favor of reading care and justice as incommensurable, as shown above, there are several weaknesses with this view. These weaknesses relate to the theoretical position as such, to the agent's situation and to the interpretation of Gilligan's theory.

Comprehending care and justice as incompatible is a position that contains a theoretical inconsistency; it allows a single troublesome case to have two different, yet incompatible, answers. Furthermore, such a position creates difficulties for the agent: Due to the tension between the disparate moral ideals the two approaches will, more often than not, give rise to different solutions to a particular case. Comprehending care and justice as incommensurable betokens numerous moral conflicts for the agent. Which values, care or justice, ought to take precedence? A tendency towards ethical relativism can be found in Gilligan's theory, and she uses the dilemma posed by Sartre about whether a young man should join the resistance or stay with his mother to illustrate this "equivocal view on morality" (Gilligan et al. 1988:117). At the same time, she appears also to reject ethical relativism (Gilligan 1988). What once again seems to be an inconsistency in her theory can, again, be understood as an attempt to go beyond dichotomized reasoning: Gilligan neither advocates ethical relativism nor rejects it, but instead ascribes to it a role in moral development. More precisely, she suggests that moral relativism might represent "a necessary transitional step in the progression from conventional moral ideology to a principled humanistic ethics" (Gilligan 1988:145). For adolescents, relativism may embody a protest against conventional morality. A principled, formal conventional morality may generate such a reaction as the agent often experiences the application of a formal morality as conflicting with the actuality of moral experience. In fact, Gilligan sketches three phases in the epistemological development of the moral agent; from an innocent belief in objective moral truth and justification, to knowledge of contextual relativism, and finally to the discovery of ethical responsibility (Gilligan 1988:152). In other words, both the strictly, formally constructed principle–driven morality as well as the "anything goes" attitude must be transcended. The impediment against understanding Gilligan's theory on how the development of mature care takes place and how to solve moral problems that lurks behind the incommensurable position is my third objection against traditional readings of Gilligan on the relationship between care and justice.

In light of these objections, I suggest a fourth possibility: Care and justice are "reconcilable". By "reconcilable", I mean that the two moral approaches can be brought together in ways that put an end to the conflict between them.[12] The latter position rejects the possibility that the tension between care and justice can be resolved, and that solutions can be found to conflicts and controversies. If reconciliation of care and justice is regarded as an option, it becomes possible to resolve the dilemma between the ideal of care and the ideal of justice. By applying this view, the potential relativism inherent in the third position (incommensurability) can be surpassed without strict lexical ranking or straightforward deduction. *Judgment* is granted space. The possibility for applying judgment is an intermediate position between a relativistic and a procedural approach to morality. It attends to the contextual sensitivity, which is an important feature of this ethics of care. In the following, I discuss further the relationship between care and justice.

Care and Justice as Reconcilable

The quandary in a dilemma concerns, from the perspective of care, as the reader may recall, the imperative to avoiding hurting. "Hurt" is understood in a broad sense; it includes emotional and psychological harm on connected selves. However, when no option is available that can be said to be in the best interest of all concerned, one has to select who is going to be hurt (Gilligan 1982:138–142). As one of Gilligan's informants says, "If there could be a happy medium, it would be fine, but there isn't. It is either hurting someone on this side or hurting myself" (Gilligan 1982:80). From the expanded principle of not hurting, however, the agent cannot determine who should be the injured party, since no procedures for making such a choice are given. The question then is whether Gilligan's theory contains a possible way out of this.

To show that Gilligan's theory actually does contain a potential way out of this type of dilemma, I suggest understanding her approach to moral dilemmas as part of a broader discussion, that of moral development. In her discussion on abortion decisions (Gilligan and Field Belenky 1980; Gilligan 1982) and other real–life conflicts (Gilligan et al. 1990), moral dilemmas are perceived as a problem related to the transition from level one to level two, i.e. related to choosing between self–interest and other–interest in circumstances in which both cannot be fulfilled. At this point in the development process, a specific conflict arises over the issue of hurting. One is confronted with the seemingly unbearable and immoral task of choosing a "victim" (Gilligan 1982:80).

This problem of selection is further complicated because of its linkage to culturally defined images of and expectations to gender roles. Gilligan is concerned with how traditional ideas about women's roles interfere with the process of decision–making.

> The "good woman" masks assertion in evasion, denying responsibility by claiming only to meet the needs of others, while the "bad woman" foregoes or renounces the commitments that bind her in self–deception and betrayal. It is precisely this dilemma—the conflict between compassion and autonomy, between virtue and power—which the feminine voice struggles to resolve in its effort to reclaim the self and to solve the moral problem in such a way that no one is hurt. (Gilligan 1982:71)

In *Making Connection* (Gilligan et al. 1990:8), good woman is defined as "the willingness to take care of, or to take on the cares of others, a willingness often to sacrifice oneself for others in the hope that if one cared for others one would be loved and cared for by them". This definition corresponds with the second level set out in her theory of moral development that she terms "goodness", a goodness that is characterized by selflessness and self–sacrifice. "Bad woman" corresponds with her first developmental level, selfishness and self–care. The moral tension in most of the real–life dilemmas she addresses occurs when taking care of one's own interests is perceived as jeopardizing one's obligation to take care of related others.

Using Sinnot–Armstrong's definition of moral dilemmas, all of his four re-quired elements are present in these dilemmas: 1) there is a conflict between two moral requirements; 2) neither is overridden in any morally relevant sense; 3) the agent cannot adopt both; only 4) one or the other. Adopting only one, however, violates the normative injunction not to hurt those in-volved. Moral conflicts, as construed from the perspective of care, correlate fully with Sinnot–Armstrong's definition of a moral dilemma.[13] This means that the dilemma in question cannot be dissolved within the existing theo-retical framework. That framework harbors a contradiction since it requires the agent to adopt two incompatible alternatives. As I see it, generally speak-ing, such a situation calls for a revision or expansion of the moral theory in question. Gilligan makes this move in fact in as much as she is introducing a new perspective to the dilemma as a possible way out. More precisely, her third developmental level represents this new perspective. The morally ma-ture agent at this level understands care as the ability to take care of the in-terests of the self as well as others, and the ability to do so requires that ele-ments from the ethics of justice are integrated, especially the concept of rights. The moral judgment of a morally mature person includes the concept of rights which underlies the traditional conception of justice, i.e., that self and others have the same basic rights. This has a major impact on the com-prehension of care: Care is no longer conceived as a paralyzing injunction only to meet the needs of others, it is expanded to a mature concept of care that allows for attending to self as well as others. A balance between relations and autonomy, between connection and integrity is achieved. This balance enables the agent to be "active" in the relationship, to make decisions that take all the affected parties into account.

To overcome the dilemma caused by having to choose between self–concern and other–concern the key lies in the transition to level three. Gilli-gan calls level three "truth", by which she means "the psychological truth that relationships imply the presence of both self and others" (Gilligan et al. 1990:9; Gilligan 1982:149). This developmental move is regarded as a sign of moral maturity. Moral maturity consists, among other things, recognizing that neglecting one's own interests in a relationship, is a strategy destined to fail (Gilligan et al. 1990:9). The new approach to moral problems, which emerges at level three, is an approach within the care perspective. The read-ing moral dilemmas as problems related to relationships remains the same. As does the perception of the morality of care as resting on an understanding of relationships that entails response to another person on her own terms and contexts—aiming at promoting, flourishing and preventing harm. The most advantageous solution to moral dilemmas is to carry through the activity of caring in such a way that both self and others are cared for, and to restore or sustain the relationship between the implicated (Lyons 1990:42). With the new perspective of level three, the legitimacy of one's own needs is recognized, as is that of the needs of others. The agent is granted a way of responding to herself as well as to others. One's own concerns and desires are adjusted by concern for others (Lyons 1990: 52,53). This could not have taken place without transcending a binary view of care and justice. A carer's ability to find a solution to a dilemma depends on their ability to supplement the altruistic and dualistic care perspective by recognizing and integrating some central values inherent in the tradition of justice. Actually, it is the concepts of justice and rights that give Gilligan's women the chance to find solutions (Michaeli 1995:124). The internalization of the concept of justice and of right also, presumably, means that the caring agent adopts a fresh perspective on the two former developmental levels.[14] From level three, the self–interest of level one is perceived not as necessarily morally wrong, and level two's caring for others not as necessarily resulting in self–sacrifice. The "egoism" of level one can now be understood as having many nuances. It can be graded from the complete and unconstrained assertion of one's own interests to the protection of legitimate self–interests. As to other–concern of level two, a similar gradation can be found. Taking the interests of others into consideration is very different from the complete self–sacrifice found at this level. Caring for the self and caring for the other have many aspects, and if the moral agent lacks the required maturity, an intermediate position between too much and too little concern for self and others cannot be found. When interests clash, the mature agent possesses the ability to weigh and balance considerations in a way that takes account of both care and justice–related values. Therefore, by overcoming the historic dichotomy that keeps care and justice apart, self–interest and other–interest are married.

Deliberation on Moral Dilemmas

Now, one thing is to try and make room for both self– and other–interest, quite another is how to accomplish it when faced with a moral choice. Gilligan does not say exactly how we should act. But we should nevertheless not consider that a failure. It leaves room for contextual sensitivity and judgment in relation to moral choices. Nor is the agent left completely in the dark, as the expanded principle of not hurting directs her to consider the interests of self and others, to avoid hurting self or other and to promote well–being.

Moral dilemmas have no straightforward solution. They are nevertheless part of moral life, and in handling them the moral agent should aim at balancing the interests involved. The ability to do so is the result of psychological growth, a sign of moral maturity. Instead of giving exact directives on how to approach morally tricky cases, Gilligan implies that psychological development towards moral maturity confers on the agent the requisite moral problem–solving abilities. She sets out the kinds of abilities required of an agent for handling moral dilemmas; a self with a consciousness of its connectedness with other people through relationships, and an awareness of independence, rights, integrity and autonomy. Gilligan places more trust in the mature agent 's ability to tackle a difficult situation by ways of judgment than on the ability to deduce a pre–given solution from an abstract principle. In doing so, her ethics of care, sways the agent's moral reflections from principle to context when compared with traditional moral theories. The person facing the dilemma aims at resolving it by transcending the apparently contradictory nature of the values of care and justice by granting legitimacy to both values rather than rejecting one of them. Reasoning in this way is not to be understood as a method in the sense that the agent systematically follows a given procedure in order to arrive at a solution. It is better comprehended as an attitude towards moral dilemmas: The agent recognizes that important insights are available from both positions. Such an attitude, characterized by openness, marks the agent's moral problem–solving approach. It may mean a resolution by combining elements from both moral perspectives. It opens up for new solutions to problems that otherwise would remain unresolved. From a moral perspective where the focus on context is relatively secondary and the principles more deductible, the pondering and searching required of the morally mature agent may be difficult to grasp because reasoning is not based on a binary conception of moral dilemmas, nor is it a mode of thinking that can be described as a process of deduction. It is, as said, an instance of dialectical deliberation.[15] What characterizes the reasoning of the mature moral agent is the attempt to overcome dichotomizing moral choices. A synthesis of care and justice may be the result from a process of deliberation, and may enable the dilemma to be resolved. The idea of mature care bridges the gap between considerations rooted in care and justice.

When Gilligan comments on the manner reasoning takes place on level three, she perspectivizes the dichotomous approach. What characterizes level three is not the conventional "either/or logic" of Western thinking, she says. Moral maturity consists in the ability to think "both/and". It is a type of thinking "which flows back and forth connecting self and other, mind and body past and present, consciousness and culture" (Gilligan et al. 1990:19). It is related to the developmental process of the self and results not in an isolated, and separate self, nor a self without boundaries between self and others, but in a self conscious of its connectedness with other people through relationships, as well as of its independence and autonomy.

Communication and Dialogue

Despite emphasizing that the absence of detailed procedures that set out how to act can be conversely understood as putting more faith in agents' judgments, a more detailed explanation may be required when it comes to what the balancing of self and other actually requires. How does one choose between self– and other–interest when a "happy medium" seems impossible to find? One answer lies in communication and dialogue.

On several occasions, Gilligan emphasizes the connection between the ability to resolve moral dilemmas and the need for communication. In her discussion of Jake and Amy's response to Heinz's dilemma, she interprets Amy as relying on personal communication in order to find a way out. She contrasts Amy's approach with Jake's who puts his confidence in what he believes are shared conventions of logic to deduce the solution to the dilemma (Gilligan 1982:29). In *Making Connections* Gilligan and Bernstein highlight the relationship between unfairness and not listening. In their study, they discover that informants linked the two concepts closely together. Not listening was perceived as "unfair". Sometimes they were defined in terms of one another; fairness as listening, listening as fairness (Bernstein and Gilligan 1990:155).

Listening to people is not simply a way of being nice or polite, it enables decision–making. The reason is that decision–making within an ethics of care is based on responsiveness towards needs. Not listening to others would confound the possibility of making a choice. Approaching moral problems as problems of relationships leads to an overriding concern with listening and responding. This concern is not restricted to private relationships only; it covers most kinds of human relationships. According to Gilligan's co–writers, Lyons, Salonstall and Hanmer the care thinker's focus on communication and dialogue is reflected in ideas about leadership. The leadership mode can be either interdependent in relation to others, or independent. All the things people have said are taken into account by the interdependent leader before deciding. It means considering individuals in their own contexts and situations. The required skills of such a leader are the ability to listen, exercise patience and to draw ideas and information from people. Lyons et al. sets up the independent leader as a contrast. In order to move forward, this leader makes decisions regardless of whether everybody has been consulted. Decision–making rests on sets of standards and principles. The required skills, she says, are mainly to be organized, efficient and persuasive (Lyons et al. 1990:202–203). The two types of leadership render some features also emphasized in the concept of autonomy discussed above. The traditional –independent—leader will often be autonomous in the sense of having sovereignty over a dominion. The interdependent leader is more likely to embody, on the other hand, a (feministic) concept of autonomy with its greater allegiance to the interplay between self determination and relational considerations is accentuated.

Fulfilling the requirement not to hurt requires idiosyncratic knowledge attainable through communication and dialogue. It is not sufficient for agents to be able to deduce from abstract principles only, or to put themselves in the other's situation. Bearing Gilligan's psychological approach to morality in mind, the importance given to conversing and listening is hardly any surprise. Her ideas about an ethics of care arise from listening to the voices of women. By reading her works, one also perceives an increased accentuation and awareness of the importance of other voices. In *In a Different Voice*, Gilligan is mainly concerned with the silence of women's voices in ethics but in later works (such as Gilligan and Brown 1992; Gilligan et al. 1995), Gilligan et al. emphasize how culture, race, class and age may affect whether voices are silenced or heard. This inclusive development and the accent on communication can be interpreted as a move towards discourse ethics where both Seyla Benhabib and Allison Jagger have contributed substantively. Before proceeding along that line, however, I want briefly to point to some quandaries this emphasis may create.

Paradoxically, the method of listening and communication as a way of solving moral problems might in itself create new moral problems for the carer. First, listening to all involved is time consuming. It calls for a demanding intellectual process; to follow the reasoning of another (Lyons et al. 1990:187). In fact, it often puts great strains on the carer (Romain 1992:96). Second, the belief in communication as a manner of resolving moral dilemmas may appear naïve and immature—as did Amy's response to Kohlberg. The reliance on relationships when decisions are to be taken also means continuing dependence and vulnerability—sometimes at the costs of self–realization and freedom (Gilligan 1982:30). This reliance may obstruct the development of autonomy and independence, both necessary for morally mature agency according to many ethical theories, including Gilligan's. Empathic understanding of conflicting perspectives in a situation sufficient for an adequate response renders decision–making difficult. The more diverse the voices one has to listen to, the more difficult the decision–making becomes.

> The difficulty arises when the imperative to listen or care mandates listening to many voices in a situation, which may not be in harmony. In such situations, described by girls at higher grade levels, a new sensitivity to disparate voices or perspectives leads to a new difficulty in judgment and in action as girls struggle to hear and reconcil conflicting perspectives in the determination of a fair or good solution. Lacking a simple standpoint, their efforts to arrive at fair solutions can become painstaking or problematic, often reflecting tension and ambiguity over what a fair solution would be. (Bernstein and Gilligan 1990:159)

Emphasizing listening and dialogue, and the need to include multiple voices, indicates a connection between discourse ethics and the ethics of care, a connection we shall return to. Let us proceed then by looking at other attempts to take account of both care and justice, which emphasize dialog as a way of overcoming the conflict between them. First, we shall revisit Kohlberg, who suggests that the Kantian principle of equal respect for the integrity or dignity of each person lies at the heart of both perspectives.

Care as Justice

Till now, the reconciliation of care and justice I have advocated is based on the attempt to admit of central elements from both perspectives.[16] Another strategy would be to transform care to justice, or justice to care. This can be termed a reductionist strategy, by which is meant an attempt to reduce the perspective of care and justice to a single lowest common denominator. In the article "The Return of Stage 6: Its Principles and Moral Point of View" Kohlberg et al. aim at a refinement of the much–debated stage six set out in Kohlberg's theory of moral development (Kohlberg et al. 1990).[17] I want to focus, however, on their suggestion concerning how to integrate care (benevolence) and justice.[18] Kohlberg and his co-authors' strategy is to establish a principle from which both care and justice can be derived. Both the principle of justice and of benevolence, they assert, can be derived from a higher principle; the respect for persons. This is the Kantian principle of equal respect for the integrity or dignity of each person, which corresponds to the formula of the categorical imperative whereby each person is to be treated as an end in herself (Habermas 1990:242). According to Kohlberg, the idea of respect covers not only the negative imperative not to violate the rights of others, but also the positive responsibility for the needs and welfare of those others (Kohlberg et al. 1990:156). This is required since "justice and benevolence concerns are both necessary dimensions of moral relationships" says Kohlberg, and continues by advising that "coordination of these concerns must be sought in resolving moral problems" (Kohlberg et al. 1990:153).

In addition to the integration in principle of care and justice at stage six, there is another element related to reasoning at this stage relevant to the solution of moral disagreements.[19] It is the attitude of recognizing the necessity of entering into dialog in the face of disagreement about what is right. Dialog actualizes the principle of equal respect for persons, and is necessary for reaching mutually acceptable agreements.[20] When consensus cannot be reached through actual dialogueue, agreements have to be sought through a set of imaginative procedures by which principles can be chosen and interpreted, procedures that give equal consideration to everyone's interests by constructing perspectives from which the relevance of particular factors can be expressed (Kohlberg et al. 1990:163). Kohlberg sets up his own thought experiment for reaching ideal consensus. The actor enters into this thought experiment with three cognitive abilities: sympathy; ideal reciprocal role–taking; and universalizability.[21] The search for ideal consensus, either by means of a thought–experiment or actual dialogueue is to "take the moral point of view" and is characteristic of the moral reasoning at level six. At this level, several fundamental moral values such as life, liberty, equality and mutually beneficial social interaction are integrated in a single moral principle "equal respect for human dignity" (Kohlberg 1990 et al. 179).[22] The principle attends to care as well as to justice.

> From a stage 6 standpoint the autonomous moral actor has to consciously coordinate the two attitudes of justice and benevolence in dealing with real moral problems. [. . .] Benevolence constrains the momentary concern for justice to remain consistent with the promotion of good for all, while justice constrains benevolence not to be inconsistent with promoting respect for the rights of individuals conceived as autonomous agents. (Kohlberg et al. 1990:157–158)

It is interesting to note that Kohlberg and his team and Gilligan and hers in their later works, seem to have several things in common; the need for care *and* justice is recognized by both, as is the observation that a morally mature agent needs to balance care and justice when dealing with real–life dilemmas. Furthermore, they both emphasize dialogueue as a way of finding a solution. But there is a significant difference. Kohlberg and his co-authors hold that morality can be reduced to a single principle: The principle of respect for persons, a principle that does away completely with the incompatibility of care and justice and enables the agent to find "the correct solution" to a moral problem. In keeping with what was said earlier, Kohlberg's position is "monistic", that morality can be reduced to a single principle. His strategy can also be understood as using a form of moral reductionism; his analysis of the relationship of care and justice consists in finding a basic common feature. His approach upholds moreover the traditional moral point of view, which Gilligan opposes.

Seyla Benhabib (1994) criticizes this approach, and presents another model of reaching agreements through dialog: Interactive universalism. According to Seyla Benhabib, universalistic theories, in the Western tradition from Hobbes to Rawls, are "substitutionist" in the sense that the universalism they defend is based on a generalization of the experience of a particular group, that of white adult male, possessing property or at least higher education. As an alternative to this form of universalistic ethical theories, Benhabib presents "interactive universalism". "Interactive universalism" acknowledges a plurality of human living, but without admitting that all of these diversities are morally or politically legitimate. From the point of view of interactive universalism, it is held that normative disputes can be rationally solved, and that justice, reciprocity and universalizability are constitutive elements in the moral point of view (Benhabib 1994:170,171). Interactive universalism is perceived as a concrete dialogue where actual individuals communicate with each other, not a hypothetical thought experiment (Benhabib 1994:91). The concrete other is attended to too because idiosyncratic information is considered relevant, and the generalized other is respected through the procedure that implies the willingness to change perspectives and openness towards other voices (Benhabib 1994:24).

As I see it, Benhabib's model of discourse ethics is a more viable framework through which to reconcile care and justice, as it is more in tune with Gilligan than Kohlberg's reductionist approach. The discursive practice attends to Gilligan's concern for listening to voices that otherwise might not be heard, and its point of departure is particular individuals and their actual experiences. Also, it echoes the feminist traditions of the 1960s and 1970s from where Gilligan departed, where consciousness rising and attempts to remap established perspectives of social structures, science, politics and moral reasoning where important. Alison Jagger (1998:356) draws attention to the fact that several feminist groups from the 1960s until the present have continued to develop the discursive traditions of moral reasoning set out by Plato, Mill, Rawls and Habermas. Jagger has done a great deal to advance the feminist ethics discourse. She presents a cogent argument, in my opinion, for hearing the voice of the poor women of the global south in feminist discussions (Jagger 2004). As Benhabib, she finds traditional models of dialogue too idealistic because they fail to do justice to the structures of powers and resource imbalance.

Another reconciliation requirement is a more refined conception of justice. Without addressing the many theories in the area, I want to draw attention to an article that conceives of some aspects of justice in a manner I take as challenging Gilligan's position.

Justice as Care

In the article "Beyond Either/Or: Justice and Care in the Ethics of Albert Camus", Elizabeth Ann Bartlett (1992) suggests that Camus's ethics of "rebellion" as put forth in La Peste (1947), draws on both care and justice.[23] Important here is the comprehension of justice; claims of justice are not merely based on the resentment of privileges one does not have. In Camus's ethics of rebellion, justice and rights are said to originate from a passionate concern for oneself and for others.

Bartlett draws a general assumption from her reading of Camus: It is often through the compassionate witnessing of the suffering of others, their oppression and injustice meted out to them that we are moved to act for justice (Bartlett 1992:84). This view of justice, says Bartlett, gives acting from justice a different motive than perceived from Gilligan's level two where claiming rights is perceived as selfishness. Claiming rights, for Bartlett, is not synonymous with merely claiming rights for one self. One may claim the rights of others, and the motive for doing so may be care. Therefore, justice can be understood as originating from care, from the notion that other people ought not to be hurt, or should be given an equal chance to flourish. Furthermore, claiming rights only for oneself is, says Bartlett, an act of oppression. Claims that rights must be extended to all similar cases confirm human interrelatedness. In fact, "human connectedness and concerns lie implicit in every rights claim" (Bartlett 1992:85).

Barlett's interpretation of justice not only differs from Gilligan's perception of the ontology beyond the tradition of justice, but also her claim that the right thing to do in this tradition is derived from an abstract, impersonal point of view. For Camus, says Bartlett, justice is embedded in particular persons, their passions, their friendships, and their concrete realities.

Isn't the point of fighting the plague (read: injustice) the fact that we value each other that we care? Yet if we get so caught up in our struggle, so consumed by "justice" at all costs, that we do not longer care, then we simply perpetuate oppression [. . .]. (Bartlett 1992:87)

Comprehending justice in this way can also prepare the way for reconciliation. The motive for Camus's justice is, in Bartlett's reading, concern for others. Also, it originates from a concern for the concrete others. Camus's justice is apparently in line with vital aspects of Gilligan's concept of care. However, his strategy for resolving the incompatibility of justice and care is also reductionist: Both perspectives are explained by referring to a common core, a deep concern for human dignity. Although this concern is fundamental within, as well as shared by an ethics of justice and an ethics of care, perceiving or solving dilemmas by way of reduction does not adequately account for Gilligan's endeavor. A reductive strategy would require, in order to find the common denominator, an intolerable abstraction from context. True, sometimes the affected parties' recognition of a common interest may be the first step towards the resolution of a conflict, but additional steps are required. Aiming at finding the best solution to a particular dilemma—a solution that attends to the particular interests of both (or all) the affected— Gilligan takes advantage of agents' ability to look at situations from different angles instead of reducing the interests of the one to the other. Such an approach towards moral dilemmas can be comprehended as a search for finding a third way.

Finding a "Third Way"

At this point, it might help to illustrate such a "third way" with an example of a morally difficult predicament. Let us therefore consider Amy's dilemma one more time. How is she to find a solution for Heinz? First, she reflects on possible consequences to those who would be affected if Heinz chose stealing the medicine from the druggist as a feasible way forward. She then weighs these consequences for each of the parties involved: If he stole the drug, he might save his wife. That is a good thing, but by stealing he might also end up in jail, Amy says, and if he does, his wife might get sicker again. Further, in jail Heinz would be unable to get hold of more of the drug for his wife, and this is not good (Gilligan 1982:28). Given these reflections she finds that stealing is not a good solution as stealing violates the ideal of care; that no one should be hurt. If stealing were the only possible alternative, Heinz would be stuck with a *dilemma* since there is no way of adopting the different requirements without violating the ideal of care. However, in order to avoid such a predicament, Amy has, as I see it, two ways out. First, she could seek more contextual knowledge of the situation, such as how critical the situation is for Heinz's wife, the likelihood of him being imprisoned, and so forth. Such knowledge would help Amy prioritize. Second, she could seek out a new course of action, which is exactly what she proposes: They should try to find "some other way", she says, and suggests that Heinz could "borrow the money or make a loan or something" (Gilligan 1982:28). To borrow money or to take a loan are alternatives that attend to values of both moral orientations: The druggist's right to payments; the prohibition not to steal; the need to save a life; the injunction to reduce harm for all affected.

Finding a third way relies on access to contextual information rather than strict deduction, on actual communication rather than a thought experiment. It depends on the agent's judgment rather than a pre–established ranking, and the solution is justified by reference to how well all the particular others are cared for, rather than to abstract principles. The third way is an approach to moral challenges not characterized by acting spontaneously out of sympathy or by relying entirely on pre–established principles, but by deliberation on how to prevent hurt and promote flourishing based on general as well as contextual knowledge of the actors.

This approach seeks new solutions to morally difficult cases, and enable in doing so the ability to shift between perspectives to gain the required contextual knowledge. The agents must be morally mature and willing to listen to and acknowledge the soundness of others' reasoning. Given an unprejudiced and tolerant attitude, the agent might be able to integrate elements from the ethics of care as well as from the ethics of justice. In practicing the moral ideal of care, a carer would make an effort to find a way for Heinz to solve his problem so that more than one requirement can be attended to, meeting in the process Sinnot–Armstrong's third criterion of what constitutes a moral dilemma (i.e. that the agent cannot adopt both moral requirements together). To care is also to be concerned about finding a viable solution. It means that Heinz should be considered a person with a particular problem that ought to be solved in such a way that harm is reduced for the actors, rather than applying preexisting formulas when they are not the most advantageous means available.

Therefore, the third way represents not only a way of solving conflicts *within* the perspective of care, as Amy's efforts might be understood, it is an approach that could settle the moral disagreement *between* Jake and Amy, that is, between the two apparently incompatible moral ideals of care and justice. In order to do so, Jake, the representative of the justice perspective, must be willing to reexamine his solution, which relies on a pre–conceived ranking of the requirements. An impediment is that since he already has found a way out, making such an effort may not appear urgent to him. However, as a rational agent he probably realizes that the conventional system of ranking requirements fails to take the possible negative consequences to the affected into account, and that another approach could in fact do so. Thus the druggist's rights; the prohibition against stealing; the injunction to save life; and the responsibility to limit harm to all parties would all be taken into account.

My claim is not that all morally difficult questions can be resolved by a third way approach, but that it may disentangle some. The ethics of care would not put faith in "Grand Narratives"—much less in "anything goes". It holds that even if a moral agent cannot always overcome dilemmas or ambivalence, she can commit herself to strive for the best possible solution as the art of morality means taking upon oneself responsibility for self and others.[24]

Notes

1. In the first part of this chapter I present my interpretation of Gilligan's ethics of care, the relationship between care and justice in particular. My interpretation goes beyond what is actually articulated in her works. In fact, in attempting to fill the gaps I construe a normative position, where Gilligan's theory sometimes serves as no more than a stepping–stone, but obviously the most important one. I term this interpretation a Gilliganian ethics of care. In the second part, I briefly enter upon a broader ethical discussion about care and justice.

2. This may be because her informants use everyday language when talking about the dilemmas. When Gilligan presents their moral experiences and reflections she does so in "their voice", i.e. their everyday language rather than the lexis of moral philosophy, and continues to do so in her own commentary and reflections.

3. My only purpose here is to find useful analytical tools that can aid the examination of Gilligan's position on the relationship between care and justice. I do not provide a detailed discussion of the concepts involved.

4. Since this definition implies a contradiction, i.e. to adopt two moral requirements that cannot both be fulfilled, it is necessary to mention that whether moral dilemmas actually exist or not is a debated topic. If moral theories are, or one believes that they ought to be, constructed as to be consistent in their requirements, one may find that once the difficulty is analyzed and sorted out what at first sight appears to be a dilemma in fact has a "right" answer.

5. Now, one may object that these moral problems are not to be perceived as a conflict between care and justice. For instance, the disagreements on distribution of scarce public recourses can be portrayed as a discussion within the ethics of justice concerning how just allotment of benefits and burdens is to be understood. This reveals that the description of moral problems is depending on the understanding of

the concepts applied. The positions taken concerning the relationship between care and justice is influenced by the comprehensions of "justice" and "care". There are several different conceptions of justice, like "distributive justice", "corrective justice", and "retributive justice"—each discussed to a great extent. I will nevertheless continue to use the comprehension of care and justice as spelled out in the previous chapters.

6. Or as Thomas Nagel phrases it: "The central problem of ethics [is] how the lives, interests and welfare of others make claims on us, and how these claims, of various forms, are to be reconciled within the aims of living our own lives" (Nagel 1986:164).

7. Arguments for this interpretation are given in Chapter 3.

8. This could be perceived as the presence of uncertainty in the agent, as well as the presence of contradictory moral beliefs. It could also be perceived as an agent's unwillingness or inability to provide a firm answer to moral problems (Stern 1990:73–87). For Gilligan, this is what in Kohlberg's studies is perceived as moral immaturity (Gilligan 1982:85), and what she argues might be just the opposite; a sign of that of moral maturity (Gilligan 1988:85).

9. Nel Noddings (1984), however, could be interpreted as representing such a position (Tong 1993:108–182).

10. It presupposes, of course, that one believes that all cases defined as public always ought to be approached from the justice perspective, and that all cases considered to be private always ought to be solved by applying the care perspective. If one doubts this, the point in separating the domains seems to vanish.

11. For a discussion of "incommensurability", see for instance Wong 1989:140–158.

12. I return later to ask whether fusing care and justice can solve all, or only some, of the thorny cases. At this stage, I am content with emphasizing a difference between reconciliation and incommensurability.

13. Which differs from the troublesome cases perceived from the perspective of justice, which, with closer examination, turns out to have a solution.

14. The step from level two to level three is influenced by cultural, social and political variables.

15. An example of this deliberation is given by one of Gilligan's co–writers Lori Stern in the article "Conceptions of Separation and Connection in Female Adolescents" (Stern 1990:73–87). Stern says that it is commonly thought that in female development, girls must follow either the route of separation, or that of connection, and the fact that young women do not dichotomize separation is difficult to understand in psychological terms. However, what eventually is discovered, and what also marks the psychological growth of adolescent girls, is the realization that relationships without independence become just as problematic as independence without relationships, for neither is prior to the other.

16. Others have also aimed at integrating care and justice, for example Bill Puka (1994). Puka suggests how Gilligan's care and Kohlberg's justice could be nurtured

together, by way of adjusting inadequacies in both approaches. He concludes however by arguing for the primacy of the principles of justice theory.

17. This article is an important contribution in what is termed the Kohlberg–Gilligan controversy and interrelates with Bill Puka, Jürgen Habermas and Benhabib's contributions. However, since my task here is to discuss different strategies of integrating care and justice I shall not provide an overview of this debate.

18. Care and benevolence are here used as interchangeable.

19. Although respect for persons can be expressed in moral judgment at earlier stages, its expression takes a principled form at stage six (Kohlberg et al. 1990: 151–182).

20. Kohlberg regards "dialogueue" as the process by which each person offers his/her best reasons for their choices and listens to the reasons of others in the mutual endeavour of solving problems (Kohlberg et al. 1990:160).

21. "Sympathy" is the active interpretation of the attitude of identification and the empathic connection with others. Sympathy is the substantive grounding of the benevolence component of respect for persons, and is related to at least two interrelated dimensions of social understanding: The understanding of persons and the understanding of general facts of the human condition which persons exist and interact (Kohlberg et al. 1990:165) "Ideal reciprocal role–taking" is the adjudicatory dimension of respect for persons that aims at fairness. First, this requires the balancing of interests which is made possible through a process where we first take the perspective of the other in the problematic situation. As a second step towards ideal reciprocal role–taking one assumes that the relevant others are doing the same. Third, it requires a temporary separation of the actual identities of persons from their claims and interests from the point of view of any person implicated in the dilemma. When rational, autonomous moral agents derive what is considered to be a reversible claim, they have come as close as possible to expressing the orientation of what an ideal consensus would take. The operation of "universalizability" comes into play when a reversible claim or choice has been constructed, and this operation imaginatively validates the reversible choice in the context of two interrelated dimensions, say Kohlberg et al. The aim is to find a solution that is ideally acceptable from the point of view of anyone. The operation of universalizability therefore can be regarded as a check on consistency, which includes two dimensions. First, that judgment in this particular situation is right: it could be considered similar of all persons who could be moral actors in these situations. Secondly, the operation of universalizability validates the reversible choice by committing the decision–maker to make similar choices in similar cases (Kohlberg et al. 1990:165–169).

22. Kohlberg's theory of moral development, especially its stage 6, is much debated. Without plumbing the depths of the debate here, I want only to refer very briefly to an assertion of importance to this thesis, i.e. that Kohlberg's theory of justice is male biased, class biased and an expression of "Western moral ideology" (Gilligan 1982; Gilligan et al. 1988:145; Puka 1990:182–223; Nicholson 1993:87–101).

23. "Rebellion" means here an action that simultaneously rejects injustice and oppression and affirms human dignity (Bartlett 1992: 84).

24. This strategy is not unique to a Gilliganian ethics. It bears similarities with Aristotle's account of the virtuous agent, Rawls's reflective equilibrium, the discourse ethics of Habermas and Benhabib, and even with Baumann's (1993:182) way of perceiving moral life.

~

CHAPTER SEVEN

Distributing Mature Care

Balancing the interests of self and others is an important feature of the concept of mature care, but *who* are these others whose interests we are to be
concerned about? Above I said that Gilligan's care ethics first and foremost
is displayed in interpersonal relationships; among those we are connected
with and have a concrete responsibility for. But with whom are we having
these interpersonal relationships, and for whom are we responsible? And
also, *how much* are we supposed to care? As our caring capacity is limited, we
cannot care for all the needy, nor can we accommodate all their needs. But
we need to know how to go about selecting the recipients of our care, and
how to distribute care.

With Whom Are We Related?

With its relational point of departure, the ethics of care is typically preoccupied with our moral responsibility towards our related others. Some critics
wonder whether the carer is therefore in danger of overlooking or disregarding moral challenges outside her immediate relational network. (O'Neill
1996:141; Kuhse 1997:155). The antagonism they posit between our moral
responsibilities for our nearest on the one hand and strangers and distant
others on the other does not stand up to scrutiny. Nor indeed does it follow
from the ethics of care's relational focus. Concern for related others does not
rule out concern for distant others; but this area of the moral domain has
been more or less neglected by traditional ethics and moral philosophy. In

Chapter 10, I hope to demonstrate the strength of the ethics of care also in relation to more distant others. In this chapter, I look rather at our responsibility for our related others under the purview of an ethics of care. This will include a further investigation of the concept of care.

There are similarities to caring for people close to one and people with whom relations are more tenuous. There are differences too, of course. They correspond to my notions of "thick" and "thin" forms of care. They are distinguished by how well we know the person involved and level of (expected) reciprocity. Thin care is what the carer does for people she doesn't know well, when her information about them is general and impersonal. Donating money to Oxfam or helping a disoriented tourist find her way are examples of thin care. Thick care requires a personal relationship between the carer and cared–for, where one's knowledge of the other is detailed and discriminating.

Close relationships are elusive, of course, and subject to gradual and sudden change. I use here for the sake of simplicity an ideal–typical conception of the related others, people with whom we have an established relationship. They include relatives and friends, colleagues and neighbors. Note how the group of related others transcends the traditional private/public dichotomy; the terms include both professional and personal relationships. They also include the stranger (for instance the unknown beggar at the corner) and the distant others (for example the poor child in the global south). The ethics of care is an ethic not only for the intimate relationship in the private sphere, then. Indeed, the ethics of care requires us to develop a sense of moral responsibility for everyone, even though, as we shall see, its implications for the way we provide care vary according to distance. In addition to this, the ethics of care also insists that we take our own interests into account. Remember though that the ethics of care advanced here is neither an altruistic nor a particularistic theory. Balancing between them, i.e., the interests of self and others, is one of the mature carer's primary duties, and required of us whether the care we are giving is thin or thick.

The relational ontology of the ethics of care is based on empirical observation and people's actual experience, not metaphysical speculation or abstract ideas regarding humankind and human nature. Hence, when care ethicists speak about the related others one often envisages the concrete, established relationships the carer is part of. And when the caring agent considers how best to cater to different needs for care, she does so from a relational point of view not a view from nowhere. For instance, a carer cannot decide how to respond to world poverty or a beggar on the corner without also contemplating how her action will affect her related others (Pettersen

2003). In agreement with feminist theory ever since Beauvoir, the ethics of care acknowledges that moral deliberation is situated in a relational context.

Still, there are other challenges with the notion of the "related" others. First, the extent of this group is both unstable and it appears to be subjective. It is unstable because bonds between people are more or less continuously being established and dissolved, strengthened and weakened. And it is subjective if it is up to the carer alone to determine who is to be defined as within the group of related others. Furthermore, those who are near are not necessarily dear.[1] In this chapter I take as given that our near and dear ones make up a stable group, and that there is a correspondence between those we are related to and those we have a duty towards and feel responsible for—as Gilligan seems to do.

In order to elucidate the moral responsibility for the related others I first concentrate on contrasting Gilligan's theory with some other ethical theories.[2] As we will see, her theory has a different focus than theories prioritizing the "generalized anonymous other" as well as those emphasizing the "concrete anonymous other".[3] Also, I consider how the carer selects recipients among those defined as related. Furthermore, I also discuss the motivation for mature care in contrast to other incentives for moral concern, such as the consequentialist apprehension of the best overall consequences and altruism, charity and love of one's neighbor. What characterizes mature care in this respect is the resistance against unrestrained self-sacrifice—regardless of whether such self-sacrifice is ideally required to fulfill the needs of distant strangers or called upon by "the face of the Other". However, rejecting the view that the most distinct mark of care is unselfish concern for others, and rather balancing the concern for self and others does not mean that strict equality is what always is aimed at. Care sometimes requires going beyond equity, but as will be explained with some references to Aristotle's ethics, there is a limit to how far beyond equity the carer can go.

Potential Recipients of Thick Care

The scope of the ethics of care has been discussed since Gilligan's publication of *In a Different Voice* in 1982. Kohlberg says with reference to the scope of "the morality of care" that it "represents merely the spheres of personal decision-making" (Kohlberg 1984:231–232).[4] Gilligan and Wiggins (Gilligan et al. 1988:138) dispute Kohlberg's view in "The Origins of Morality in Early Childhood Relationships", as does Seyla Benhabib in "The Generalized and the Concrete Other. The Kohlberg–Gilligan Controversy and Moral Theory" (Benhabib 1987:159). Gilligan/Wiggins and Benhabib focus on the same pronouncement but from different perspectives. The quarrel Benhabib has with Kohlberg is whether the "personal" is a moral concern. According to Benhabib (1987:159) personal relationships—like friendship and kin-ship—are "personal" issues for Kohlberg as opposed to "moral" issues. Ben-habib argues, however (as does many other feminist philosophers) that the personal is part of the moral domain. Gilligan does not discuss the ques-tion—that personal relationships concern morality is taken for granted—nor does she relate to the debate on the public/domestic distinction—a debate concerning some of the most vital insights of contemporary feminism. In re-lation to Kohlberg's view on scope, only the following is claimed:

> But the "morality of care" represents not merely the spheres of "personal deci-sion–making", as he puts it, but an alternative point of view from which to map the moral domain and reveal "the laws of perspective" (in Piaget's phrase) which describe a relational grounded view on morality. (Gilligan et al. 1988: 138 fn.2)[5]

As the concept of care appears to have different meanings for the partici-pants in the debate, the discussion suffers from obscurity as a result. When discussing the range of the application of care, a common understanding of "care" is necessary. If care is comprehended as "thick care", I partly agree with Kohlberg on scope because thick care is only adequately applicable for decision–making when the carer is familiar with the cared–for, as in "per-sonal decision–making". However, it is not only within personal relation-ships, such as family relations and friendships, that the carer may have idio-syncratic knowledge of the other(s). Relationships established in professional and public contexts may also be of this kind, which is why I previously asserted that Gilligan's concept of care transcends the private/public distinction. In my opinion, thick care concerns the sphere of interpersonal interaction, a sphere that among other things includes per-sonal decision–making.

The scope of thick care is people with whom we have a relationship, not strangers. Let us nevertheless consider closer the group of strangers who are potential recipients of thin care. Strangers can be divided into two cate-gories: the "singular, unknown persons" we pass by incidentally and, the ab-stract "everybody else". This portrayal of strangers is influenced by Ben-habib's distinction between the "generalized" and "concrete other", yet not completely identical. Let me enlarge. The universal everybody else is the same as Benhabib's generalized other; we consider them moral agents by means of abstracting away their concrete identity. The singular, unknown person we face is not identical with Benhabib's concrete other. According to Benhabib the concrete other is, "an individual with a concrete history, identity, and affective–emotional constitution" (Benhabib 1987:163–164). The needy persons we pass on the street are not concrete others in this sense, for us they are individuals *without* a particular identity. They are also strangers. True, we can probably identify, say, the person's race, sex, age and the like. This information is nevertheless morally irrelevant—for the ethics of care as well as for most ethical traditions.

In contrast to the relational aspect of thick care, Benhabib's concepts of the generalized and the concrete other appear to share an essential feature; from the perspective of the moral agent both groups are anonymous. By definition, "strangers" are a group of individuals with whom the agent has no established bonds or connections, and usually no idiosyncratic knowledge. To ground this feature further, in the following I make use of the terms "generalized anonymous other" and the "particular anonymous other". In addition to the two groups of strangers come our "acquaintances": persons with whom we have established a relationship. People in this category are termed the "related other".[6] Care delivery will differ according to different groups of recipients. This is a basic premise of the following discussion. I start by examining differential treatment for the generalized anonymous other and for the related other, and emphasize why differential treatment can be considered morally justifiable.[7]

The Generalized Anonymous Other and the Related Others

In a discussion concerning how we should choose between related others and the generalized anonymous others when there is a conflict of interest, the reflections of one of Gilligan's informants may be illuminating. The informant says: "I feel strongly toward directing actions toward the good of individuals. If everyone did so, logically these actions would be for the good of everyone" (Gilligan et al. 1988:132). Her words bear comparison with a consequentialist version of arguing in favor of the near and dear—as does Gilligan's comment on her informant's response. Gilligan implies that if the norms of care and attention in each idiosyncratic relationship were universalized, everyone would benefit (Gilligan et al. 1988:132). We have seen already consequentialist elements in Gilligan's theory, particularly when we discussed how attempts are made to resolve moral problems by finding a solution in the best interests of all the affected. As we are now deliberating the relationship between the generalized and the related others, it gives us the chance to make a brief comparison of Gilligan's theory and consequentialism.

Consequentialism and the Ethics of Care

Consequentialist ethical theories do allow agents to favor their own concerns, rather than always focusing on producing maximum welfare for everyone (Scheffler 1982:15–17).[8] Therefore, within the consequentialist framework, differential treatment based on thick care can be the morally right thing to do. What settles this matter is a calculation based on empirical and statistical information. Two main arguments have been given for justifying this favoritism. First, since our caring capacity is limited it seems more rational (i.e. efficient) to spend it on family and friends. Due to the benefactor's specialized knowledge of their nearest and dearest, they will also know what is needed and how to attend to the needs. The risk of wasting resources is considered to be smaller when dealing with acquaintances than with strangers (Engelstad et al. 1998:397–401). The second consequentialist consideration for allowing agents to promote their own welfare more than others' is given by an appeal to human nature. People cannot function well if they do not use some time and energy to promote their own well–being.This is not an appeal to immediate consequentialist advantages, but rather to the long–term benefit of having psychologically healthy agents to produce the good efficiently (Scheffler 1982:12).

Both Gilligan's ethics of care and consequentialism allow of differential treatment between the generalized anonymous other and the related others. The two consequentialist considerations appear to be shared. The first consequentialist argument conforms with thick care several important points— that care is "grounded in the specific context of the others" and that care requires "the ability to perceive people in their own terms and to respond to their needs" (Gilligan 1984:77). Responding to people on their own terms cannot be done simply on the basis of a general knowledge of humans and abstract moral principles. Thick care requires in addition contextual knowledge—as is stressed in the first consequentialist consideration. Not only is caring more efficiently exercised vis–à–vis related others than anonymous strangers; Helga Kuhse claims the dispersion of care is also self–defeating. Kuhse demonstrates her point with reference to Charles Dickens's portrayal of the impartial Mrs. Jellyby, "who could see nothing nearer than Africa, neglecting her own children so that she could care better for those in foreign lands" (Kuhse 1997:136).[9] The second consequentialist point, that human thriving is linked to care of both self and others, seems also to be in harmony with Gilligan's ethics of care as her anthropology emphasizes both the necessity and the beneficence of nursing relationships. The consequentialist permission given to agents to pursue their own well–being does not rule out devotion to their nearest and dearest. Despite these resemblances, there are some significant differences between the ethics of care and the consequentialist approach that allows agents to downplay their concern for the generalized anonymous other. A closer examination of the respective motives involved in the two approaches will reveal why this is so.

The motivation for permitting favoritism of the related other differs in the two theories in question. Both consequentialist dispensations are justified in relation to the anticipated result—the best overall outcome. In the ethics of care the best *overall* outcome is not the single, most important reason for permitting differential treatment between related others and the generalized anonymous other. Even if thick care can be defended from the viewpoint of the overall good, the overall good is not decisive for the carer. Furthermore, thick care cannot be performed on impartialist grounds only. Concern for the *particular* others is what motivates thick care—but this does not imply a lack of concern or work for children "in foreign lands". The point is that such concerns, i.e. thin care, must be pursued in addition to the nurturing of connections and relationships. In an ethics of care the related others cannot be replaced or substituted by devotion in line with a theory devoted to the best overall outcome.

Also, within a consequentialist framework caring has instrumental value only, the anticipated consequences are the decisive guide to how to act. If favoring one's nearest and dearest does not enhance the overall good, it is not admissible.[10] In the ethics of care; however, care has intrinsic value; it is good–in–itself. Care, as e.g. health or art, is pursued also for its own sake, not only because of its overall beneficial consequences. Instrumental and intrinsic values are nevertheless not mutually exclusive; an instance or a phenomenon can have both values. Paying attention to consequences is not a prerogative of consequentialist theories. If an ethical theory attends to consequences, it does not necessarily mean that it should be classified as a consequentialist theory. Or to quote Rawls (1971:30): "All ethical doctrines worth our attention take consequences into account in judging rightness. One that did not would simply be irrational, crazy".[11]

One could object that care now seems to be defended in a circular way: caring is upheld as a normative ideal with intrinsic value. In addition, caring is claimed to have beneficial consequences (like promoting human flourishing). In turn, these consequences are, partly the reason why caring is upheld as a normative ideal. This objection is sound. One could, however, reply that demonstrating circularity is not always sufficient cause for complaint. "The caring circle" is a virtuous circle. It tells us that that there is an agreement between our principle(s) and our practices. The fact that the ethics of care aspires to harmony between our principle(s), intuition(s) and practice(s) is a feature that separates this ethics from consequentialist theories. An ethics of care would not recommend Mrs. Jellyby to abrogate responsibility for friends and family for the sake of generalized anonymous others in foreign lands.[12] Therefore, the ethics of care does not immediately violate our intuition of taking care of our close ones—a critique often leveled at consequentialism from feminist quarters. Examples like that put forward by William Godwin, where impartialism requires us to save the archbishop and leave our mother to burn in order to secure the happiness of the many, is precisely what weakens the moral credibility of utilitarianism (Tong 1993:17). Other philosophers like John Rawls (1971), Bernard Williams (1991), Samuel Scheffler (1991) and Thomas Nagel (1991) have criticized consequentialist theories along similar lines, highlighting the problem of how to distribute satisfaction and dissatisfaction and the requirement that people have to do whatever it takes to produce the best overall outcome, and judging the consequentialist requirements as too demanding for the agent (Scheffler 1991:3–4). Embedded in these criticisms is the objection to the consequentialist's unwillingness to favor the near and dear unless doing so contributes to maximizing the happiness and welfare of everybody. The source of these objections lies in the defense of personal integrity, autonomy and individual rights. But pursuing individual "ground projects" at the cost of abandoning one's nearest and dearest is also unlikely in the ethics of care. A one–sided stress on self–interests is just as implausible within the framework of mature care as a one–sided concern for the generalized anonymous other. Personal integrity, autonomy and self–interest are important elements in mature care, but must be balanced and attuned against the concern for others.

Thin Versus Thick Care

Within the framework of deontology, the agent cannot do what is prohibited and must do what is mandatory—even if so doing results in harm to (related) others. If someone chooses not to lie so as to prevent harm, the deontological agent's interests in not violating the moral law obviously trumps the interests of the injured (Davis 1993). More weight is given the avoidance of breaking abstract rules, than to the prevention of hurting others. Not so within the ethics of care. Its relational ontology, its care to avoid causing pain, means that it can protect the interests of related others in ways neither deontology nor utilitarianism can manage. The ethics of care does not require us to maximize the general good, nor to inflict unnecessary harm in order to keep the rules. Although there are important distinctions between deontological and utilitarian theories, and many nuances within each theoretical tradition, they share certain constitutive factors. The ideal of universalizability, for example, is not only shared, it is a core value and requirement of the two theories. From the perspective of deontology as well as utilitarianism it is possible to compel an agent to inflict harm in order to conserve the sanctity of a moral rule. This is impossible to *demand* under an ethics of care, the carer would not be obliged to harm related others in order to act morally. The ethics of care avoids, then, what might be considered morally counterintuitive, sacrificing the related other in order to benefit remote others.

The fact that the ethics of care does not tell us how to balance the near and distant, thin and thick care, can be regarded as a strength. It is up to the agent to judge how much care to give and where to give it. This does not, however, imply that care is distributed randomly; the injunction not to inflict harm is central to moral reasoning based on care (Gilligan 1982:166). But a mother—Mrs. Jellyby or others—who leaves her own children to care for others' is not necessarily a heroine. If the children she leaves depend on her, the moral responsibility for the distant others (whether they are located in faraway countries or the next street) must not outweigh her responsibility for her own children.

Many ethical theories are highly sensitive to the question of generalized moral responsibility for the distant other, but far less attentive to the needs of related others. As a consequence, those ethical theories may inhibit a broader moral commitment. Because our image of the moral agent is inadequate, demands on her seem unrealistic. Traditional theories, such as deontology, tend to espouse unrealistic conceptions of a moral agent's interdependency and autonomy. The relational nature of the agent is neglected. Within the ethics of care, however, the carer is not expected to abandon her responsibility for her related others to reduce suffering elsewhere, or remain faithful to rules. The ethics of care adopts in this sense a more realistic approach to generalized moral responsibility. The relational ontology of the ethics of care is also able to accommodate the fact that responsibility for related others is not constant. In some circumstances, an agent will have extensive duties at home. In others, she will not. Due to the shifting nature of a moral agent's situation, it must be left to the agent to decide when, where and how her limited caring recourses should be distributed.

When Thomas Pogge (1998, 2003) says that citizens in affluent countries have a negative duty towards the victims of hunger—because they participate in an economic scheme that maintains global injustice—we should note that he does not prescribe how each of us should act. But as a minimum we should, according to Pogge, expect a moral agent to reflect on what she, in her situation, can and will do to alleviate global poverty. "In view of their plight, we owe the global poor at least a reflective answer to the question what responsibilities we have with regard to the social conditions that blight their lives" (Pogge: 2003). The reflection Pogge calls for, is not difficult for the ethics of care to accommodate; such deliberation is part of caring. A caring agent needs constantly to balance care giving between potential recipients of care. We, as carers, must reflect on how best to serve our own interests and those of others. Moral priorities, also between thin and thick care, cannot be left to an abstract principle, they must be assumed by the moral agent herself.

The Particular Anonymous Other And The Related Others

Not only is the concern for the anonymous generalized other toned down when thick care is given a prominent role, but the unknown, needy person we accidentally face is more or less moral periphery too. This distinguishes the main scope of Gilligan's ethics, not only from consequentialism, but also from other care approaches. In the following, comparing Gilligan's thick care with the Norwegian philosopher and nurse Kari Martinsen's concept of care, as well as with Løgstrup's and Levinas' ethics of proximity, will help make some problems as well as possibilities with Gilligan's ethics of care more clear. Before starting, it should be noted that Martinsen belongs to a different theoretical tradition than the Gilligan's Anglo–American. She is influenced by Scandinavian nursing debates and by phenomenology. Of particular importance for Martinsen's thinking are the writings of the Danish theologian Knud E. Løgstrup who emphasizes that our moral responsibility is "given". Løgstrup (1999) says that our moral responsibility is not something we can choose to take on or leave alone, and he underscores the duty of the moral agents to take upon themselves responsibility for the other. It does not mean that the agent shall take over the duties and responsibilities of the other, but the duty exists irrespectively of the relationship between the individuals, it is "implied by the very fact that a person belongs to the world in which the other person has her life, and therefore holds something of that person's life in her hands" (Løgstrup 1997:83). It is nevertheless Martinsen's concept of care I want to focus on here, and in her book *Omsorg, sykepleie og medisin*

(1989:72–74) she distinguishes between different types of care: 1) care founded on balanced reciprocity; 2) care–work; 3) spontaneous care. She also mentions 4) personal services, which may or may not have anything to do with care.[13]

Professional Care–Work and Mature Care

Several theories of care are based on care–work. Kari Martinsen's is a case in point. Gilligan's scope is broader, concerning interpersonal interaction with our related others. In fact, Gilligan does not address the question of professional ethics. There is nevertheless no reason why her theory, based on concern for particular others, might not be applicable to care–work. A care–worker interacts with particular others, has contextual knowledge of the cared–for and aims at relieving hurt and promotes their flourishing. I have argued that the concept of mature care transcends the sphere of private decision; it regards interpersonal interaction, and therefore it transcends the traditional demarcation between the private, the public and the professional. But even though Gilligan's theory is applicable to the domain of care–work, it departs markedly from Martinsen's. The reason is first and foremost that Martinsen's care motive is of a different nature from that of mature care.

Professional care–work, according to Martinsen, is based on "generalized reciprocity". This is different from "balanced reciprocity" which according to Martinsen is what ideally obtains between equal partners in friendships and marriage. Professional care–work has no "balanced reciprocity" as the carer does not and cannot expect or anticipate anything in return. In care–work, we care for others, not each other, says Martinsen (1989:16,72). Care–work is characterized as altruistic; it is a "gift", precisely because the care will probably not be returned. Care is motivated and activated by the needs of the other. In many respects it corresponds to Gilligan's description of unselfish care in her theory of moral development (level two). According to Gilligan, transcending unselfishness at this stage is necessary to reach the mature care stage. The concept of mature care, where self–sacrifice is toned down, has several advantages over a concept of care where altruism is dominant.

One might object that Martinsen centers her conception of care on professional care–work, while Gilligan's three concepts are based on studies of decision–making by ordinary people. The basic premise of the caring professions is to care for others. Putting the interests of the other (i.e. the client or patient or student) first is part of the job. Martinsen is therefore right to that extent; in professional care–work the main focus is of course the other. The nurse's center of attention is the patient; she cannot expect the same of her patient either in degree or focus. Mature care is not the same as allocating care equally. Both the type and amount of care depend on the situation. Sometimes an unequal distribution is appropriate; ensuring equality of care could even be harmful. Some situations require unconditional care, i.e., with no strings attached.

The point however is that caring should not and cannot be boundless. Setting limits is therefore inherent to any concept of mature care. Where exactly they should be set will vary with the circumstances, and this is something the mature agent must consider in each situation. But accepting constraints on the distribution of care does not imply that the altruistic component of care disappears. Mature care presupposes altruism and good will towards the other. The altruistic aspect, however, is not the only or even the decisive element. The reason for controlling the altruistic dimension is that unchecked it can lead to self–sacrifice. A willingness to sacrifice all personal wants and needs (and those of related others) could result in serious harm to oneself and others. This is a major objection against basing professional care–work on an altruistic conception of care, and an important reason to adopt the concept of mature care instead.

There are further objections to altruistic care, of both a theoretical and practical nature. There is, for instance, the problem of identifying what counts as an altruistic motive. True, strong altruistic callings may motivate some care–workers, but different types of motivation might also lead people to choose caring occupations. Motivating factors could be vocation, self–realization, instrumental reasons and compensation factors (Henriksen and Vetlesen 1997:94–99). Another problem with the altruistic concept of care, then, is that it is very difficult to distinguish between the different reasons underlying the wish to care, and hence determine if a care–worker's motivation may be termed altruistic or not. People's reasons for embarking on a career in a caring profession will clearly vary. Some will be worthy, others less commendable. But that fact need not on its own make the person a less capable or skilled care–worker.[14] And there is no guarantee that a strong sense of vocation will remain strong forever. There may be financial considerations, not least as the person's children grow, either to remain in the job or look for a better paid one. An instrumental reason may transmute into altruism as a result of witnessing the suffering of others. (Advocates of psychological egoism would deny the existence of the altruistic motive altogether.) Even if the altruistic care–worker knows that an immediate return of care by the recipient of care is uncertain, there may linger expectations for some future return: The efforts put in for caring may be retrieved in the long run.[15] If not returned by the recipient herself, then possibly by others.[16] Furthermore, care does not have to be what the carer wants in return: Social recognition and moral praise can motivate care—as can money.

These objections see altruistic care as issuing from emotional instability or plain whimsy. I suggest, however that we treat care as a virtue. Care is characterized by, among other things, constancy; it is not pulled off course by variations in everyday life or mood swings, nor by what is returned or not returned. An ethical approach, however, is exactly what has inspired the development of the concept of mature care. Mature care is considered to be a developed disposition; it is a mean between two vices. The excessive extreme can be comprehended as selflessness, the deficient selfishness. As a virtue, mature care is not the opposite of vice; it is not the other side of selfish or selfless acts or emotions. Mature care is characterized by its intermediate position, it is the mean between too little and too much concern for others (or for oneself). In care–work, selfishness is likely to correlate with indifference to and ignorance of the patients in one's care. It can result in harm. Self-sacrifice, at the other extreme, (apparently caring too much for others) encourages a paternalistic approach, and increases the danger of violating the patient's autonomy. From the point of view of virtue ethics, mature care is also an ability to share care proportionately. Care–workers are paid to do this in practice. In professional care–work, caring is the significant qualification. This is the essential skill, not altruistic motivation. Interestingly, other occupations involving dealings with others avoid overemphasizing altruism. Teachers, scientists, police and political workers could all base their motivation on altruism, but tend rather to keep quiet about 'noble motives', preferring instead to market their public utility and unique professional skills.

In professional care–work such as nursing, altruism is emphasized, and it its worth asking why. There are of course historical links between caring, Christian ethics, hospital traditions and charity. History as related to care–work is gendered. Women have almost always been the carers, whether in the family, workplace or voluntary association. Women are culturally preconditioned to sacrifice themselves altruistically. So when care–work like nursing is associated with altruism, while male dominated occupations like the fire service are not, it is probably an expression of gendered history and culture.

Moral philosophers have been preoccupied with whether an act is morally less valuable if it is based on altruistic inclinations. Kant says acts motivated by such emotions cannot be classified as morally good. Only acts based on duty are moral. Gilligan and many feminist ethicists have criticized Kant for excluding ethical challenges, experiences and expedients customarily associated with women. When nurses expend energy on portraying their occupation in terms of traditional female values such as compassion, sympathy and benevolence, some feminists think they are attempting to give these values a boost. Insisting on a role for other–regarding emotions in moral evaluations helps to redress the historical devaluation of emotions and women's care–work. But one thing is to discuss how far the moral status of the agent's motivations and emotions impinge on their ability to deliver care, quite another to expect professional care–workers to act altruistically. The transference of the altruistic element from one domain to another, that is from personal motivation to professional occupation; makes the care–workers vulnerable to manipulation and exploitation. In "Sexual Harassment and the Genderization of Work", Kjersti Ericsson (1998) draws attention to the fact that caring qualifications can be seen as a traditional feminine skill, which in caring professions might tempt employers to exploit personnel in several ways—for instance by making them do more than is specified in the terms and conditions of the job, or by keeping the salary down. Cultural expectations of women as the primary care–givers goes hand in hand with criticism if she fails on these terms to deliver. It doesn't matter if her reasons for holding back are inspired by gender critique. In her empirical research Gilligan highlights the obstacles facing women's attempt who try to substitute mature care for altruistic care:

> The notion that virtue for women lies in self–sacrifice has complicated the course of women's development by pitting the moral issue of goodness against the adult questions of responsibility and choice. In addition, the ethics of self–sacrifice is directly in conflict with the concepts of rights that has, in this past century, supported women's claim to a fair share of social justice. (Gilligan 1992:132)

Gilligan discusses two problems, one psychological the other practical. The first is to set limits. The second follows this. By not claiming their rights, women risk exploitation. The ideal of altruism contains a cultural and a psychological imperative for many women. It is sanctified by women's professions and is concealed in structures of power that disfavor women. Although altruism is historically biased towards women, the problems it causes affect both sexes. For instance, an employer may seek to influence the care–worker by appealing to her sense of altruism. Patients may appeal to brotherly or sisterly love when they want something done. Power games like these are not confined to the workplace, of course.

If we could transform altruistic care into mature care, some of these problems could be overcome. First, there is no demand on the agent to be selfless. In professional care, as in our relationships with our nearest and dearest (the parent–child dyad for instance), this point is particularly relevant. The con-

cept of mature care implies that an agent must uphold integrity and autonomy, as well as supporting the patient's attempt to do so. Second, due to the
conventional gender division of labor and conventional gender–related expectations regarding showing consideration, women have good reasons for
being cautious with the altruistic concept of care (Blum et al. 1976). Mature
care, as I see it, avoids linking traditional expectations of women's willingness to sacrifice themselves with care. Thirdly, on a theoretical level, the difficulty ascertaining the presence or degree of altruistic motivation evapo-
rates. Applying the concept of mature care such refinement is unnecessary as
it presupposes a balance between egoism and altruism.

The concept of mature care appears to resemble the concept of care Martinsen terms balanced reciprocity as both concepts seem to presuppose that
the caregiver and the recipient are equal. But as a matter of fact, this is not
always the case. Sometimes relationships are asymmetric; there exists an inequality in power and resources. For Martinsen this does not constitute a
problem, as her altruistic concept of care does not *require* a balance: the carer
can render more than what is returned. Balanced reciprocity is meant to depict situations where caring takes place between equals; her other concepts
accommodate for unequal relationships. Un–equals can be the recipients of
care in Martinsen's theory. The prominence given to balancing the interests
of the carer and the cared–for in the concept of mature care, creates a problem: It becomes difficult to deal with asymmetric relationships. The question
is whether the concept of mature care, can cover asymmetric relationships.
It is, I admit, difficult since in mature care the *balance* is constantly accentuated. It would nevertheless be counterintuitive if mature care were not to be
carried out in relationships where inequality exists. Is it possible to accommodate unequal relationship within mature care, a concept of care based on
reciprocity? I turn to Aristotle here because he can help us conceptualize the
limits of caring and the concept of mature care for when we explore the
virtue of friendship and relate it to the concept of mature care.

Mature Care and the Aristotelian Virtue of Friendship

Some virtues are primarily concerned with our emotions; temperance with
desires, courage with fears and mildness with anger. Other virtues, like mag-
nificence and generosity, deal mainly with a reasoned–based emotional response such as giving and spending. In both cases these virtues primarily concern the person's attitude toward her own emotions and behavior, and these
essential features of Aristotle's concept of virtue are distinguishable in the
concept of care advanced here, particular as discussed in Chapter 4. Friend-

ship and justice are virtues essentially to do the relationship of self and others. They are relational virtues, as is caring. However, friendship and justice involve different types of relationships. Friendship is relationship with a concrete and particular other; justice deals with our relationship towards the generalized others. Thick care and friendship seem to overlap both in scope and focus. Let us examine this.

'Friendship' for Aristotle is a far wider concept than is the rule in contemporary thinking. It covers a variety of different relationships—from various familial ties to what Aristotle calls "friendship in community".[17] There are three species of friendship, depending on the type of attachment between the persons; pleasure can be a source of friendships; advantage is another possibility; and the recognition of the other person's moral goodness the third option (NE 1155b15–20).[18] Some friendships rest on equality, others on inequality (NE 1162a349).

Aristotle pays substantial notice to friendship. He also appreciates the varieties of friendship: Rich people need friends as do people in poverty, young as well as old. Further, parents and children can be friends, as can husbands and wives etc. By exploring the variety of attachments between different individuals, Aristotle shows how friendship can occur under different circumstances. His focus on the variety of relationships is relevant to our comprehension of care, since care may equally be present in different types of relationship such as intimate family relations and relations between colleagues, students, neighbors, etc. Care may therefore exhibit a range of distinctive characteristics depending on the contextual situation that obtains at the moment. It appears in different situations and can be expressed in various ways. Obviously, caring for your neighbor will differ from caring for your lover. Variety then, is also an important feature of care.

Even if the appearance of care varies according to different types of relationships and circumstances, we must not let accidental variations obliterate the common factors. Identifying them in the different types of caring will promote a better understanding of care. Let us see what Aristotle has to say concerning the shared aspect of friendship. According to him, there are some necessary conditions for friendship (NE 1155b30–35):

1) One must wish the other's good for his own sake. (Which means that wishing the welfare of the other is not a means to secure one's own good.)
2) "Goodwill is to wish good for the other's sake, but the other does not wish well in return, and he might also be unaware of this. (NE 1155630-1156a5).[19]
3) To be friends both parties must be aware of the reciprocated goodwill.

The first condition requires the agent to wish the other good regardless of the consequences to herself. By emphasizing the altruistic aspect, it prevents self-ish motivation governing this particular relationship. Wishing the other well only because you stand to gain from it is invalid as a basis on which to build this type of friendship. Hence, condition two prevents exploitive and abusive relationships, and this is essential in a caring relationship too.

Condition one—goodwill towards the other—is necessary, but still not sufficient. "Goodwill", says Aristotle, occurs when the other does not return our wish of goodwill (NE 1155b30–1156a5). Two additional criteria must be met: 2) Your wishing the good of others must be reciprocated, and 3) the goodwill of both must be accepted by both. Reciprocity is a central condition of both criteria. We may wonder why it is necessary to demand reciprocity when the first criteria is already met, i.e. we express our goodwill towards the other. Is it not inconsistent to demand unselfishness of ourselves, and then ask the other to reciprocate in like manner? First, the second and third conditions guarantee a close relationship. It is indeed possible to have goodwill for distant others, but this alone does not constitute friendship—or a caring *relationship*. A functional relationship requires fulfillment of criteria two and three. They reduce the possibility of a lackluster relationship turning into a hurtful relationship. Put differently, criteria two and three help us steer a middle course between the caring relationship's Scylla and Charybdis—paternalism and self–sacrifice. Let me enlarge.

Goodwill for the other is not enough to make a relationship work. Egoism can turn a relationship into a burden; the same holds true for altruism. Too much goodwill or care can become a problem for the carer as well as the cared–for. Condition two (reciprocity), prevents situations in which only one part has goodwill for the other, increasing the likelihood of power games and subjection. The generous one becomes the vulnerable one; she risks exploitation and reduced autonomy. She is likely to sacrifice herself if goodwill is not mutual.

If one instead, as Aristotle insists by his second condition, requires reciprocal goodwill, giving and receiving cannot go in one direction. With mutual goodwill, neither will neglect their own interests. If *both* wish each other well, self–sacrifice and selfishness in their extreme form are out of the question—nobody would expect or want boundlessness from the other. The second criteria, I believe, urges us to find a middle way between too much and too little concern for self and other. In order to perform mature care, to establish and maintain a flourishing relationship, balance is required. Actually, the second condition (concerning reciprocity) brings justice (as fairness) into the relationship. To be sure, Aristotle says that as long as one remains friends, justice is not required. But this is not so because justice is unimportant between friends, but because justice is already present in the foundation of a good friendship.

Awareness is needed to enable us to tackle a relational challenge. Finding the border between the interests of self and others, between identifying with and separating oneself from the other person (a challenge also Gilligan is preoccupied with). If we fail to distinguish between our own perspective and that of others, paternalism will again threaten the relationship. Goodwill shared by friends for each other lies in their caring for each other. But if the goodwill of the one is not acknowledge by the other, one's intentions may be irreproachable, but good intentions do not guarantee success. Conditions two and three ensure that both parties control what happens in the relationship, they can be understood as a request for consent.

Together these conditions imply that friendship is a special sort of attitude, a mutual and recognized attitude between two or more person. Friendship is considered to be a virtue. Our attitude towards self and others, and of others to us, is decisive for a sound relationship to develop. A sound relationship means the ability to close the gap between egoism or altruism. As altruism and egoism are considered excessive, they should also be regarded as a vice. What Aristotle terms friendship between equals is the ideal, because the relationship strikes a balance between the interests of both. A sense of the right balance comes through experience. Aristotle shows us the way, and gives us guidelines to rely on. Friendship of character, where the three conditions are present in both parties, is an archetype of relationship. It is based on mutual recognition, and such friends are, according to Aristotle, equal.[20]

In our context it is noteworthy that Aristotle presumes that these three conditions obtain in unequal friendships too. These relationships can be unequal in at least two ways, in terms of what is exchanged and in terms of possessions. As examples of unequal relationships, Aristotle mentions those between father and son, humans and Gods, and husband and wife. In the case of parents and Gods, Aristotle says: "For no one could ever make a return corresponding to their worth, but someone who attends to them as far as he is able seems to be a decent person" (NE 1163b17–16). He expects friendships between personages of unequal standing in that he accentuates that what is reciprocated does not have to be similar, nor of the same worth. If we are benefited in virtue or money we should, according to Aristotle, return what we can—for instance honor and respect. Reciprocity is present also in asymmetric relationships. The difference lies in what constitutes an appropriate exchange. It is in asymmetric relationships the necessity of the two last conditions is most clearly displayed—they prevent exploiting the unevenness. In relationships where virtues are not fully developed, the conditions are guidelines for conduct. Friendship among young people is an example. Virtues are not fully developed in the young, and will necessarily fail sometimes to find the right balance. Therefore they need guidance until they obtain the virtue of friendship. Hopefully this examination of Aristotle's analysis of friendship from the *Nicomachean Ethics* helps us understand mature care as both symmetric and asymmetric care.

Symmetric and Asymmetric Care

"Symmetric care" is care that takes place in relationships between persons who consider themselves as equals, where receiving and giving is reciprocal and recognized, and where the role of recipient alternates with the role of the care giver. In equal relationships, at least in the long run, there is no one–sided dependency; none of the parties are in sum more vulnerable or influential than the other. Symmetric caring is based on mutual goodwill, i.e., an attempt to balance between the concern for self and concern for the other. Equal relationships where symmetric care are carried out can take place in private as well as public life. A prototype of private symmetric relationships is close friendships, while teamwork between colleagues can be an example of public equal relationships. The distinction between private and public relationships is nevertheless insignificant. More essential is the point that the relationship is between particular equal others. Symmetric care resembles Martinsen's "balanced reciprocity", and has parallels with Aristotle's friendship of character in *Nicomachean Ethics*.

"Asymmetric care" takes place in relationships where one part is superior in power, resources, competence etc. and where this superiority influences the exercise of caring. Relationships between parent and child and between nurse and patient are examples of unequal relationships. Asymmetric care, like symmetric care, is concerned with the prevention or reparation of harm as well as with thriving and flourishing. Unlike symmetric care, balanced reciprocity is not an essential feature of asymmetric care because the carer probably will not get care in return. In contrast to symmetric care, desiring the welfare of the other does not need to be mutual or recognized in asymmetric care. The child or the patient does not take care of the parent or the nurse. True, both parties in the relationship may, and sometimes will, wish each other well as when a child wishes its parents well. Further, as Aristotle mentions, "reciprocity" may be present even when what is given and received is not of the same kind, or even the same worth. In return for care, the nurse and the parent may receive, say, gratitude, admiration and even love. Even if it is not done explicitly, the person's growth and well–being will be considered as a reward, as in the case of infants. If the patient is very sick, the alleviation of pain might be a reward for caring.

What allows for asymmetric care within the notion of mature care is, first, that the agent's maturity enables her to see and understand the asymmetry Aristotle draws attention to—that what is given and received in an asymmetric relationship is not of the same kind, or even of the same worth. Sometimes reciprocity is impossible. The patient may be unconscious or unable or unwilling to respond. This does not mean that the carer should refrain from caring, but that there is no caring *relationship between* them (Noddings 1984:181). When this is the case, the carer must proceed to care without specific information on the person concerned. Care is no longer motivated by reciprocity, but an ideal of care, in the sense suggested by Noddings (1994:5, 8,82). When a carer gives care to a nonresponding person, the carer performs thin care. But thin care must aspire to be mature care, to balance the interests of self with those of others. This might seem a calculating and callous way of depicting mature care, but it is nevertheless necessary to avoid the risk of being exploited or exploiting others. Lack of mature care often goes with a paternalistic approach, an unequal, one way relationship between empowered and disempowered, bosses and underlings. Self–sacrifice is also likely in the absence of mature care, which basically impinges on the benefactor.[21] How to promote mature care is the topic of the next chapter.

Notes

1. Usually, "the related others" connotes a friendly approach, and this assumption probably also underlies Gilligan's use of the word. However, the carer might be related to someone for whom they feel nothing, or possibly even antipathy. An example would be a parent who feels nothing but resentment towards her own child, an issue with which I deal later, in Chapter 9, when discussing Robert Goodins's vulnerability model. Previously, in Chapter 4, I have discussed Nel Noddings' attempt to solve this challenge vulnerability model. Previously, in Chapter 4, I have discussed Nel Noddings' attempt to solve this challenge.

2. I.e., some versions of consequentialism, other representatives of an ethics of care (Kari Martinsen) and what might be described as an ethics of proximity (K.E. Løgstrup and E. Levinas). Also I will touch upon Aristotelian virtue ethics. As several other ethical theories are involved in the following discussion it is important to note that I neither intend to describe them exhaustively, nor provide a complete comparison between them and the ethics of care. They are mentioned in order to map the ethical landscape, and this is necessary to enable a discussion of where the ethics of care I advance belongs.

3. I explain these terms below.

4. It is debatable whether Kohlberg's position is as crystal–clear as it seems to be in this citation, as he and his co-workers revised their theory several times in response to criticism from, among others, Gilligan (Kohlberg et al. 1983; Kohlberg and Colby 1987; Kohlberg et al. 1990).

5. It is questionable what is meant by "an alternative point of view". I have nevertheless discussed how I interpret the relation between the traditional moral point of view and Gilligan's theory in Chapter 5.

6. The "generalized anonymous other", then, corresponds to Benhabib's "generalized other"; I have simply added the word "anonymous" to highlight the lack of idiosyncratic knowledge. The "concrete anonymous other" does not correspond with Benhabib's "concrete other", nor does the "related other"—even if they overlap.

7. It should be noted that these categories merge into each other. One particular person can move from one category to another, and there may also be "borderline cases"—i.e., it is difficult to determine whether a person is to be regarded as a related other or not, but this problem will be left aside here.

8. "Consequentialism" is understood here as the commitment to the principle which says that the right thing to do is to choose the action that will produce the best consequences altogether.

9. Also Robert Goodin refers to Mrs. Jellyby in Dickens' *Bleak House* in a similar discussion, and calls Mrs. Jellyby's inclinations "telescopic philanthropy" (Goodin 1985:23).

10. At this point, it should be made clear that my account of consequentialism is a simplification, but a sophisticated presentation of these theories is what I am aiming at. I am interested in a certain feature of this ethical tradition: The impartialist claim understood as incompatible with giving related others preferential treatment and therefore at odds with Gilligan's thick care. This comprehension of imperialism is based on a certain reception of consequentialism favored by certain philosophers on which Robert E. Goodin provides an overview in Chapter 1 of his book *Protecting the Vulnerable: A Reanalysis of Our Social Responsibilities* (1985). Among them are Bernard Williams who holds that "the moral point of view" as conceived by utilitarians and Kantians alike is "characterized by its impartiality and its indifference to any particular relations to particular persons" (Williams 1981:2, cited in Goodin 1985:7).

11. If the ethics of care is comprehended as a virtue ethics one cannot disconnect the intrinsic and extrinsic value of care. Nor can the caring agent's character be detached from the act of caring.

12. This, however, is not to say that the protagonists of care would allow violations of the negative duties towards the generalized, anonymous other in order to allow related others to flourish.

13. Martinsen's types of care are presented here in a different sequence than she does in her book. It should be noted that the subsequent discussion is not meant to be exhaustive as to Martinsen's theory of care.

14. In the regulation for the Norwegian Nurse education, decided in 2004, the concept "barmhjertighet" was introduced as an ethical ideal for nursing. "Barmhjertighet" can be translated as "compassion" or "pity". It is the term used in the story of the Good Samaritan (i.e. "Den barmhjertige Samaritan").

15. Also, the thought that the world enlarged might be a better place to live in if everybody practiced caring can be regarded as an expectation of a return.

16. The "uncertainty argument" can be used to support as well as to undermine a position. However, my criticism here is an objection in principle, related to the problems of using impermeable arguments.

17. Aristotle mentions fellow–voyagers, fellow–soldiers, members of religious societies and dining clubs as examples of friendship in communities (NE 1159a25–1160a20).

18. It is debated if the friendship of character is the only proper form of friendship, or whether all three types are essential to a good life. John M. Cooper (1980) holds the latter position. Also, one can discuss the role of self–interest in the different friendships, whether or not only perfectly good men can form friendships of character etc. (Annas 1993:249–262; Cooper 1980), but these issues will not be pursued here since they are not relevant for my purpose. "Goodwill" is to wish good for the other's sake, but the other does not wish well in return, and he might also be unaware of this (NE 1155b30–1156a5).

19. In friendship among young people, who still lack maturity of vision, the relevance of conditions two and three is obvious. The young lack the ability to strike the right balance. Aristotle's guidelines can be of help here.

20. It should be mentioned that while Martinsen's "balanced reciprocity", corresponds with "symmetric care", but not with "asymmetric care". Nor are "care–work" and "spontaneous care" quite the same as asymmetric care since Martinsen focuses on paid care or the immediate care of strangers; asymmetric care concerns inequality between the carer and the related others.

~

CHAPTER EIGHT

Conditional Care

In every situation the mature caring response is restricted by the requirement neither to sacrifice oneself utterly, nor act completely selfishly. Nor should the carer forfeit the interests of the related other, or neglect the needy outside her own circle of related others. Mature care includes asymmetric relationships, and will potentially encourage the development of trust, support and growth in personal relationships. It renders unfair exploitation and oppression less likely, or as one of Gilligan's co–writers says, "relationships can best be maintained and sustained by considering others in their specific contexts and not always invoking strict equality" (Lyons 1988:349). Indeed, mature care requires accomplishment in the art of balancing.

However, as the carer's recourses are limited, and the needs of others appear to be unlimited, the carer must choose *whom to care for* and *how to respond* in a particular situation. The carer must make choices, among related others, among generalized others, among anonymous strangers and sometimes between these groups. Also, the carer must determine how to respond in each situation. Two related others with apparently similar needs may be given differential treatment by the carer (e.g. a mother's response to her children's need for comfort in their fear of darkness). What is more, two different caregivers (e.g. a mother and father) may respond differently towards a person's specific needs (their son's need for consolation). Caring will vary according to the receiver's needs, what the carer is able to give, what the carer knows about the other and so forth. Such contextual sensitivity is important (Gilligan 1988; Gilligan et al. 1988 132). The other should not, however, determine the response alone. Mature care means to balance the response between selfless-ness and selfishness, but is also dependent on the carer's reading of the par-ticular circumstances involved. The choice of recipients, and the appropriate caring response will therefore depend upon the context. In this chapter, some relevant circumstances affecting the type of response given and choice of care–recipient will be considered. A mature carer is prepared to go beyond ex-act equivalence. But, as emphasized in relation to an altruistically based con-cept of care, there is a limit to how far the mature carer would be willing to go. This limit will be explored in the next sections.

Spontaneous Care—Samaritanism

"Spontaneous care" is to spend time helping people one meets by coinci-dence, people "carrying a heavy burden" (Martinsen 1989:74). They could be strangers just as well as one's neighbors. "Spontaneous care" can be un-derstood as Samaritan behavior, acts based on the ideal of providing uncon-strained help to those in need regardless of the circumstances and without expecting reward or recognition. In the book Øyet og kallet Martinsen (2000:16–21) discusses the story of the Good Samaritan (Luke 10, 25–37), which she considers a "ground story" for the ethics of care.[1] In my opinion, this story cannot function as a paradigmatic example for the ethics of care. Let me enlarge.

The parable expresses two features often associated with care, an altruis-tic motive and a spontaneous action. Above, I addressed several problems arising from regarding pure altruism as the (dominating) motive for care, ob-jections that remain valid for the story of the Good Samaritan. The source of these objections is the concept of mature care which requires deliberation between the interests of self and others: There is a limit to how much help one person can give and expect to get.

If a carer devotes herself to the first needy individual to appear, the carer might neglect others who are suffering more. Samaritanism seems to dis-criminate against other people in need, those for whatever reason happened not to be first in line. Another consequence of Samaritanism is an increased risk of spending all of one's resources on one person—who may not even be the most needy. In other terminology, directing scarce resources in one di-rection only suggests inefficient and incompetent resource management. If an unlimited amount of time and resources were available, Samaritan distri-bution would probably harm no one. As this hardly ever obtains, the carer needs to reflect on her priorities with the resources available to her. This is not to say that a carer should never practice Samaritanism, in some situations

it may be an appropriate way to distribute care. As argued, there is no rigorous rule within the ethics of care on how to distribute care, only an imperative to consider one's response seriously, and how best to distribute care given
the circumstances.

In addition to the possible harm caused by ignoring the most needy, and
the risk of squandering everything on the first in line, spontaneous care can
also inflict the "harm of discrimination" (Ariansen 2000:174–175). No decisive arguments are given for prioritizing the first person in the queue, and
Samaritanism seems to discriminate against people who for different reasons
are not first in line. Unjustified differential treatment is an infringement on
a person's rights and reasonable expectations, and Samaritanism could actually inflict harm twice, first by failing to provide the required care, and second by treating her unfairly.

Moreover, a Samaritan distribution of care could even encourage ruth-
lessness and uncaring behavior. Is it the most needy, poorest or sickest who
are first in line? Or is it the most self–asserting, cynical and affluent? Those
at the back of the queue may be too weak, polite—or self–sacrificing—to assert their needs. Perhaps the last are the most altruistic, willing to sacrifice
their own interests for the sake of the others. The distribution principle behind Samaritanism is "first come, first served", a principle that encourages
neither care nor love of one's neighbors.

Basing the ethics of care on the parable of the Good Samaritan is, I have
argued, problematic. Many of the problems could nevertheless be solved by
attending to the core value of the ethics of care as expressed by the idea of
mature care. Mature care allows for deliberation and gives due weight to the
interests and responsibilities of related others, as of our self.

Charity and Love of One's Neighbor

By anchoring the ethics of care in connections and networks, Gilligan clearly
departs not only from ethical traditions that focus on the generalized, anonymous other, like consequentialism and deontology, but also from Christian
ethics and its theoretical successors. Within the Christian tradition the
virtue of charity implies doing good for "sinners and enemies" as well as for
family and friends.[2] Charitable acts are not biased, nor a result of preferential
treatment. Thomas Aquinas explains why the needs of the concrete, anonymous other sometimes must override considerations of one's nearest and
dearest: Strangers may, in particular cases have greater claim on care because
of greater need. The obligation to do good first to those closest to us, he says,
only holds when all other things are equal. In a situation where one person

is closer to us but another more in need, there is no straightforward answer as to whom first to help because, says Aquinas, "[. . .]kinship and need have many levels no general rule can decide the matter, and the prudent man must make his own judgment" (Aquinas 1989:361).

Now, if the distribution of care prioritizes the related other, care must be different from charity and general love of one's neighbor. If established relationships are the main arena for thick care, it seems as if neighbors are only taken into account if they already are part of that structure. The contrast to the ethics of proximity's focus, as represented for instance by Emmanuel Levinas, on who is to be regarded as my neighbor is noticeable:

> The Other becomes my neighbor precisely through the way the face summons me, calls for me, begs for me, and in so doing recalls my responsibility, and calls me into question. (Levinas 1996:131)

Hence, there are differences also in the area of moral responsibility between Gilliganian ethics and an ethics of proximity. When Gilligan talks about two different meanings of the word responsibility, she distinguishes between them as follows: Responsibility, in the justice framework, means commitment to obligations; responsibility in the framework of care means responsiveness in relationships (Gilligan et al. 1988:4). For Levinas, however, moral responsibility means none of these things:

> Responsibility for the Other, for the naked face of the first individual to come along. A responsibility that goes beyond what I may or may not have done to the Other or whatever acts I may or may not have committed, as if I were devoted to the other man before devoting to myself. (Levinas 1996:131)

We may now be able to identify the place of Gilligan's ethical focus within the ethical landscape by imagining a continuum of potential recipients of our moral concern. If the particular unknown person met by chance is located at one end, and the distant, generalized other at the other, the focus of Gilligan's theory lies somewhere in between, where persons are involved with one another. Her main focus is not the particular anonymous other, nor the generalized anonymous other. This emphasizing demarks Gilligan's ethics of care from theories concerned with charity, love and responsibility towards one's neighbors (as well as those concerned with the generalized anonymous other).

In addition to the particular anonymous other and the generalized anonymous other there is another group of potential recipients of care I wish to consider; the suffering individuals made known to us through the media.

These potential addressees of care clearly do not belong in any of the categories referred to. They are not related others as the carer has no established relationship with them, nor are they strangers in the sense that the carer lacks knowledge of their history and circumstances since such information is provided by media coverage. But they are potential beneficiaries of care.

Salience

When the media expose the heartbreaking condition of a sick child, the tragic fate of a refugee or the dreadful poverty of a family, it can be felt as a direct and strong appeal to our moral sentiments, i.e. our compassion, sympathy and empathy. The contextual sensitivity inherent in the definition of thick care might tempt us to see the ethics of care as a spontaneous ethics of the heart—by which I mean a moral approach where the right thing to do is considered to be to immediately follow one's spontaneous emotions of sympathy, compassion and the like. This is how moral response originates, according to David Hume, but it is also rejected by Kant as being based on unstable inclinations. However, if "care" is comprehended as "mature care" the response to need is not based on sentiments alone, nor solely on reason, but on the interplay of cognitive and affective factors as discussed in Chapter 4. Hence, the immediate benevolent response toward the needy other—regardless of their status as unknown stranger on the street or media figure—does not necessarily follow from a Gilliganian ethics of care, as it would from, say, the moral perspectives of Martinsen, Levinas and Løgstrup. Now, while there is a component in mature care that states that immediate deliberation must be carried out concerning outstanding needs, this is not the same as a requirement on fulfilling them. There are several reasons for not doing so: A direct response may not be regarded as being in the best interests of the other; responding would entail too much self–sacrifice; the needy person is not a related other; or other needs are more urgent. And since no reciprocal relationship obtains between the caregiver and person in need, what care is meted out will be of the thin kind, not thick care. Some might say that there is something unsatisfying about this position since the ethics of care is concerned with the particular other and thereby taken to differ from traditional theories where the agent is expected to be prepared to allow their mother to burn for the sake of the overall good, or leave their sick mother behind in order to join the resistance. However, emphasizing that an ethics of care does not call for an immediate response to significant needs is not to say that a carer cannot respond in such cases. The claim is only that the mature carer's response should be based on deliberation and weighting. Within the ethics of care there are reasons for requiring deliberation before performing thin– as well as thick care—reasons that will be made clearer when discussing supererogation in the next section.

Supererogation

"Supererogation" is often understood as "going beyond duty" (Heyd 1982:115; O'Neill 1996:143).[3] This characterization constitutes a problem here since the ethics of care is not an ethics of duty. There is no exact definition of what is required in order to rise above a certain minimum limit of caring. Apportioning of care is left to the agent's judgment. It is therefore hard to determine whether an act is "going beyond one's duty" or not.[4] It may therefore be more appropriate in this context to conceive of supererogatory acts as "going beyond justice", i.e., doing more than required by norms of strict equality or what is expected from a perspective of justice (Kohlberg 1981:251; Heyd 1982:53). To transcend the requirement of justice, which may be necessary in the context of friendship for instance, might therefore be said to be supererogatory. However, even this understanding is problematic, as "supererogatory" is linked to what is permissible and not obligatory. To ask whether it is permissible or obligatory for a friend to go beyond just requirement is to approach the ethics of care with an unfamiliar terminology. How to understand the ethics of care from the point of view of this vocabulary needs to be worked out, but one could say as a first step that a carer is recommended to go beyond justice in order to prevent harm and do good—if it can be done without violating the ideal of care. If going the second mile requires such a quantity of self–sacrifice that it violates the requirement of not harming oneself, and/or at the expense of one's dependents, it is not recommended. This means that there is a limit for how far beyond justice a carer should go. For this reason heroic and saintly acts are not necessarily considered as morally good or meritorious. But a second problem related to supererogatory acts remains: What is perceived as meritorious seems to be comprehended from a perspective of an individualistic ontology—not the relational ontology that forms the backbone of the ethics of care. Paradigmatic examples are often given as single–handed heroic or saintly acts (Urmson 1958). Such acts may jeopardize the person's responsibility for their related others. For instance, from the perspective of care it is not praiseworthy to abandoning one's children to become a saintly nurse elsewhere. What is admirable from a relational perspective might rather be sought in our everyday life, such as the many who take upon themselves unwanted burdens of responsibility for dependents, a responsibility that goes far beyond the limits of what can be considered as fair. This is precisely why there should be a limit on the number of miles a person may go beyond the call of duty or justice for the sake of care. Not only may overextending oneself violate the ideal of care, doing so creates opportunities for cultural, social and political exploitation and suppression. Caring without limits is far from meritorious. Why then, are we sometimes inclined to admire those who do? The mother who sacrifices her own interests for the sake of her children, the nurse who gives up everything to take care of others are often praised and revered rather than warned or given a helping hand. What is praised, however, is altruism. Altruism is indeed important for moral motivation, and a value care ethicists such as Gilligan, Noddings and Martinsen encourage us to cultivate. However, as Beauvoir, Gilligan and others note, our culture has a deep and problematic identification of womanhood with pure altruism. Admiration of altruism in certain situations may outshine the extreme sacrifice and harm the people involved in its application.

If the glorification of a certain value corresponds with ideological, religious or political ideals, the danger of manipulation and exploitation is at hand. Heroic or saintly acts can be idolized in the name of benevolence, true love, the right God, the best nation and so forth.[5] Or they may be comprehended as evil or pathological. As to care and the meritorious aspect of supererogation, there is every reason to be on the alert, and such alertness is one reason why self–sacrifice and self–denying altruism are kept within bounds when comprehending care as mature care. In every situation, the mature caring response is restricted by the requirement neither to sacrifice oneself utterly nor act completely selfishly. Balancing between the interests of others and the interests of self is what determines the level of caring that can be given. This might lead one to believe that caring is an unpredictable and arbitrary activity. To avoid this risk, I shall examine in more detail what it means to judge each case on its own merits.

Judging Each Case on Its Own Merits

Differential treatment is not the same as acting randomly or without awareness of what one is doing. In *Omsorg, sykepleie og medisin* (1989) Kari Martinsen compares the learning of caring (understood as a professional competence in certain types of jobs such as care–work) with the theory of the development of skills in Dreyfus and Dreyfus's book *Mind over Machine: The Power of Human Intuition and Expertise in the Era of the Computer* (1986). She also discusses the learning process in relation to Michael Polanyi's theory of "tacit knowledge" in *Personal Knowledge* (1958). Martinsen's point is that if a nurse has become an expert on caring, she will have developed the ability to intuitively grasp the situation, and provide care adjusted to the particular patient. In professional nursing, caring consists in the individual treatment of a patient. Such treatment does not simply mean to follow rules and instructions, nor does it mean to act randomly. An expert nurse has theoretical knowledge in addition to her experience of caring. Deciding how to act in a particular situation will not require detailed, time–consuming analytic deliberation, it will be based on what Dreyfus and Dreyfus term "intuition" and Polanyi "tacit knowledge" (Martinsen 1989:21–28).

Gilligan discusses individual treatment along the same lines as Martinsen's, not in nursing, however, but in relation to moral development. Gilligan's position is that the ability to provide individual treatment indicates moral maturity. A closer look at her article "Moral Development" from 1988 casts further lights on this view. Here she debates why 20 percent of those who participated in Kohlberg's research on moral development *regressed* in moral maturity scores. In Gilligan's judgment, these participators were among the most advanced in terms of moral judgment. What they had done was to switch over from principled moral thinking and formal reasoning (at the age of 16 they were at Kohlberg's stage 4 and 5) to unprincipled, relativistic judgments (Kohlberg's stage 2) (Gilligan 1988:144). Gilligan's explanation conjures up the participants' experience. Formal thinking clashed with the actuality of their moral experience. Following strict rules is as inadequate in moral life as it is in nursing, and Gilligan says that one must expect this realization to affect moral development. "How can a formal construction of principled morality", Gilligan asks, "with its claims to universalizability and reversibility, be accommodated to the particular and irreversible reality of social experience without undergoing the structural transformation of cognitive stage change?" (Gilligan 1988:149). The transformation resulting from this experience represents a regression in Kohlberg's view; interpreted by Gilligan however, it shows moral progress and epistemological development from the belief of objective truth and justification through moral relativism to the discovery of ethical responsibility (Gilligan 1988:152).

The approach to rules and principles, to their functions and possibilities, is related to the way in which rationality is conceived. Aristotle's depiction of how a virtuous person deliberates how to act is one point of departure here, another is the view on rationality developed by Polanyi (as Gilligan herself mentions in Gilligan et al. 1988; Gilligan 1988), or the Dreyfus brothers on which Martinsen (1989) relies, or to the concept of the rationality characteristic to care as developed by Norwegian sociologists (Ve 1998; 1999: Wærness: 2004). There is no opportunity to discuss rationality here, the important thing being to demonstrate that differential treatment of related others can be perceived as evidence of the competent, morally mature person's ability to judge each case on its own merits rather than proceeding to act without principle and randomly. The selection of recipients is based on (among other things) the caregiver's reading of the situation. Their response must conform with the particular individual's need. Even if we assume that the skillful, competent and virtuous carer is able to perceive the visible needs in an appropriate manner, it is nevertheless difficult to determine whether the visible needs correspond with the actual needs.[6] Correspondence between needs and perceptions presuppose honesty on the part of the potential beneficiaries and the ability to articulate and show their needs. Since selective and individual treatment relies on a correct reading of needs, as well as the carer's situation, possible interpretative pitfalls require a consideration.[7]

Care, Class and Culture

Whether because of natural endowment or socio–economic background, it is a fact that the expression of needs differs. Some people are reserved and taciturn, others complain about their troubles on every occasion. If the potential beneficiaries want to influence the distribution of thick care, the carer must expect to confront a wide range of strategies ranging from innocent smiles and polite flattery, to bribes, manipulation, lies, threats and violence. Such attempts to influence the caregiver can occur in practically any situation; for instance when brothers and sisters want their mother's attention, when the students need advice, and when patients need the attention of a nurse. If the information on the needs is incorrect, the selection of recipient will be based on erroneous assumptions. Making a qualified choice on whose needs deserve attention, and to what degree, correct information is obviously required. On the other hand, how objective and unbiased can we expect related others to be when reporting their subjective needs? Two people might experience the same incident or report the lack of something differently. Operating with an objective estimate over pleasure and pain, as Jeremy Bentham suggested, would fail, and so would any attempt, like Mill's, to give different needs a lexical ordering. And is it not legitimate to try and influence the caregiver in many situations? Lying and menacing behavior and the like are usually considered unacceptable, but what about flattering as a means to get attention? There are also cultural differences concerning what is regarded as admissible behavior. When children fight among themselves for attention it can be considered both a natural part of the developmental process as well as an expression of culturally determined behavior; self–assertion.

When discussing the distribution of care it seems appropriate to consider if external resources influence caring. Aristotle says that "we cannot, or cannot easily, do fine actions if we lack the resources" (Aristotle NE 1099b). Such resources can be almost everything—from upbringing, beauty, health to temperament and fortune.[8] I want to contemplate "fortune" further, since Gilligan has been criticized for ignoring class distinctions in much the same way as Gilligan herself criticizes Kohlberg for ignoring gender differences (Nicholson 1993:98).[9] It is said that a theory like Gilligan's singles out the domestic life "typical of white, middle–class, heterosexual women" while it "fails to capture the experience of the lesbians, black women, and working–class women" (Pierce 1991:62). In the following I consider whether it is thinkable that the caregivers' social position impacts on the choices made prior to the delivery of care.

In *A Naturalistic Study of Abortion Decisions*, Gilligan and Field Belenky (1980:76) claim that the participants in her abortion study came from different social classes and racial and cultural groups. This could be interpreted as if indicating that such factors were taken into account. On the other hand, as Gilligan says in *In a Different Voice* (1982)—a book that in many respects is founded on her previous abortion study—that she does not claim anything about the distribution of sex differences in the wider population, across cultures, or through time. The reason for such modesty, is that "differences between the sexes arise in a social context where factors of social status and power combine with reproductive biology to shape the experience" (Gilligan 1982:2).

Now, rather than deliberating Gilligan's empirical research and methodology, we shall turn to what she actually does—or does not—attend to in her works. An instance of what she does not offer much attention is, in my opinion, the carer's socio–economic position. The factor she does consider concerns primarily her informants' actual and potential relationships. For instance, when asked to consider whether to perform an abortion or continue a pregnancy, they do reflect on how they might cope as a mother. Their reflections focus primarily on their relationships with others, i.e. boyfriend, friends and relatives (parents in particular) (Gilligan 1982), and also on their connections with school and other authorities (Gilligan and Field Belenky 1980:107). Close relations are what the informants state as the most important factors in the process of decision–making on whether they would be able to care for a child. In Gilligan's abortion study it is remarkable that the question of how the girls view their chances to provide economically and materially for a child is not emphasized more strongly in the process of deliberating about the prospects of raising a child.[10] Now, one could say that having a web of relationships to some extent secures and perhaps accommodates these external requirements, and that the responsibility for raising a child does not lie with the mother alone. Even if this holds true, it is an empirical fact that sharing responsibility for raising a child is not always possible, and it is also true that these situations are not given much attention. This is a consequence of the relational ontology of the ethics of care: Solitary individuals do not get much attention. For decision–making, the essential thing is the character of the network one is embedded in. This consideration cuts across class and social position—as much as race and sexual orientation.

The idea of thick care does not correspond completely with ideas such as group identification, class–consciousness or solidarity. To be sure, these phenomena are related to and interleave with thick care, perhaps because they mostly occur, and are maintained more easily within heterogeneous groups, and because solidarity and thick care in practice can be difficult to separate. Nevertheless, a characteristic feature of solidarity is the sharing of, or identification with, a particular attribute such as gender, race or profession. Thick care, on the other hand, is primarily directed towards the uniqueness of the related other. Another difference between thick care and solidarity is that the recipients of solidarity are not necessarily concrete related, but can occupy large spatial and social distances. Solidarity has been said to be an action rendered "to help and support *distance strangers*, especially to those who are destitute and oppressed" (O'Neill 1996:197, italics added). The focus of thick care is the related other; thin care on the other hand corresponds to solidarity.

However, even if thick care is constrained by the nature of the relationship between the needy and the potential carer, class and social position might still have an effect. How caring can we be if we, in Aristotle's words, "lack the resources"? Does not caring require resources like spare time, the opportunity to rest and recuperate to enable one to meet, say, a depressed friend's need for company? Prior to any consideration of a possible link between external resources and care, how the results of caring are to be "measured" needs clarification. There are several approaches: one can evaluate i) from an objective standard; ii) from the perspective of the recipient; or iii) in relation to the caregiver's possessions and attributes. Consequentialism would probably require exact measurement, though hardly if caring is considered a virtue. When care is regarded as a virtue, the three elements cannot be separated, or, one could say that they are all aspects of caring. I mean that even though a complete objective standard for care does not exist, certain "objective" elements remain because they are constant across situations (such as the recognition of the uniqueness of the other, the attempt to comprehend how it is to be the other as opposed to putting oneself in their place, not hurting them and promoting their flourishment etc.). There is also an element of relativity in caring, as it requires a judgment concerning how the interests of other and self should be balanced, a judgment that implies contextual sensitivity and consideration of the needs of the recipient and that of the caregiver. Caring can be regarded as "hitting the mean". It involves an element of objectivity and of subjectivity. Once again, we see the ethics of care's anti–dichotomous approach at work. When caring is considered a virtue it is relatively independent of class and external resources; in some situations, a simple, sympathetic comment might be a sufficient response.[11] Not so, however, when it comes to care–work.

Class, culture and social status play a prominent role in the distribution of care–work, according to Kari Wærness. Wærness has traced in several publications the removal by the Scandinavian welfare states of traditional care–work from the family to the public sphere. It improved women's chances of achieving equality in the home, and of accessing education and paid work. Until recently, Scandinavian women were in the majority in the public care sector. Lately immigrants, still mostly women, have entered these occupations whose status is declining, wages remain low and conditions hard. In other countries, where caring is more frequently parceled out to private companies than in Scandinavia, many families hire women from developing countries as housekeepers and nurses. By attending to the care–needs of the family, people in the household can spend more time on their careers and on enjoying themselves. The historical distribution of care–work in the bourgeois family gave work to maids and governesses from the lower classes. It seems to be reappearing as a global phenomenon, and care ethicists need to discuss and analyze the globalization of the labor market and care–work with regard to class, culture and power (Wærness 2001). For the moment, I want to end this chapter with some reflection on how trust might play a part in caring.

Care and Trust

In the article "Trust and Antitrust" Annette Baier (1986:249) remarks that trust must be present in the moral perspective revealed through Gilligan's research. Baier's depiction of trust as innate to thick care is befitting. Trust, according to Baier, in a first approximation is "accepted vulnerability to another's possible but not expected ill will (or lack of goodwill toward one)" (Baier 1986:235). Goodwill towards the other is a constitutive element in care, and if the relationship is symmetric, the good will is reciprocal. Prior to the reciprocal good will, is trust.

A tacit, but necessary, precondition for care to flourish is that the persons trust each other. Morality itself requires trust in order to thrive, says Baier (1986:232).[12] Trust is obviously important for moral practice, and in another article, "What Do Women Want in a Moral Theory?" (Baier 1993:28). Baier makes an even stronger claim by suggesting that trust is a common presumption for the "ethics of love" as well as for the "ethics of obligations". There are, in my opinion, important differences between the conditions required for carrying out an ethics of love and an ethics of obligation. Baier holds that acknowledging obligations is to believe that some group of persons will meet them, or demand that they be met, and possibly levy sanctions if they are not. It means to trust persons with considerable coercive power over others. Less coercive power is possessed by people who shape our conception of the virtues and expecting us to display them, approving when we do, disapproving and perhaps shunning us when we do not, says Baier (1993:28). Now, some sort of trust must clearly be in place for the practice of an ethics of obligation, but it does not appear to be the same trust as required by an ethic of love or care. Using the concept of "trust" in both cases, as Baier does, hides an important factor: An ethics of obligation can apply under circumstances where there is no room to practice an ethics of care. If two people are mutually distrustful they cannot have a caring relationship, but they can nevertheless carry out their obligation towards each other. Fear of sanctions can make an agent keep their promise. In groups of people where the atmosphere is one of suspicion and fear, however, care has poor prospects. Trust in the other's genuine goodwill, cannot be achieved through threats and sanctions.[13] The motivation for caring cannot be coercion, or fear of coercion. Therefore, Baier's claim that morality itself requires trust in order to thrive needs to be refined as "trust" refers to differing preconditions underlying the morality of care and contractarian theories respectively. When Hobbes's people abandoned the state of nature and created a stable society, did they "trust" each other? It depends on whether or not one can term their reliance on the sovereign as "trust", and that again raises a question of semantics: How many fears and threats can the term absorb without disintegrating?[14] Important here is the presumption that practicing an ethics of care in a Hobbesian state would be close to impossible since the necessary component, i.e., mutual good will, would be absent. Hence, Baier's claim that trust is a common presumption of the ethics of love and of the ethics of obligation seems to fall short. Trust might be preferable in an ethics of obligation, but obligations can be kept as a result of a fear of sanctions—from a sovereign, God or spouse. Individual misbehavior and character flaws can, from the point of view of an ethics of obligation, be dealt with by substituting coercive power for the lack of goodwill and virtue. This is not the case for an ethics of care.

A caring relationship cannot be maintained if one part deliberately destroys the necessary mutual goodwill, and trust seems therefore to be a precondition of thick care. "Trust" can be understood in the way Baier characterizes it, but since her characterization rests on good will, it captures the necessary conditions for an ethics of care—not for an ethics of obligation. This is so because an ethics of obligation can, contrary to a care based moral approach, be applied without any good will between the implicated persons. A caring relationship might be terminated, or transformed into another sort of relationship if the trust disappears—as in the relationships based on the practice of type of care found at Gilligan's level one (selfish care), or level two (selfless care).[15] Relationships based on mature care depend on mutual confidence. A restoration of a broken caring relationship is possible, but not by pressure or force. Only renewed confidence in the goodwill of both parties might suffice to put it back on a working footing.

Notes

1. By "ground story", Martinsen means a narrative that serves as a model for the good life (Martinsen 2000:44, fn.8).

2. On charity, see for instance, Thomas Aquinas, *Summa Theologiæ* (ed. McDermott 1989), p. 349–370, and Den Uyl (1993), "The Right to Welfare and the Virtue of Charity" p. 166–224.

3. David Heyd (1982:115) defines acts as supererogatory if and only if (1) they are neither obligatory nor forbidden; (2) their omission is not wrong, and does not deserve sanction or criticism—either formal or informal; (3) they are morally good, both by virtue of their (intended) consequences and by virtue of their intrinsic value (being beyond duty); and (4) they are done voluntarily for the sake of someone else's good, and are thus meritorious.

4. For an act to be supererogatory, it has to be permitted, in the sense that it is optional. The odd thing with supererogation is that only theories of this kind, i.e. emphasizing judgment, seem to be able to accommodate for "going beyond the call of duty". From a Kantian perspective, the characteristics of a moral act do not leave any room for supererogation. According to Kant, for an act to be moral it must first be performed in conformity with the *commandment* to always act in obedience to the moral law; secondly the maxim has to be *universalizable*. Supererogatory acts fulfill neither criterion, nor do they always satisfy the third condition, that an act is moral only if the *motive is duty*. Supererogatory acts are not *moral* acts in the Kantian framework. For the utilitarian, who seeks to maximize the good, there are no optional acts.

If an act maximizes the good, it can be said to be obligatory, if cannot, it is forbidden. In an ethics of virtue, such as Aristotle's, the question of supererogatory acts is not systematically worked out, but as Heyd points out, supererogation may be understood as what goes beyond justice (*justice* in the legal sense) (Heyd 1982: 42–44,53).

5. Whether a soldier is honored as a hero or punished and characterized as a terrorist does not always depend on his conduct but on whether one endorses the values/ motives propelling the person's conduct.

6. It is of course also difficult to determine what is to be regarded as "actual needs".

7. The awareness of contextual knowledge is claimed to be an alternative moral epistemology, or at least can function as a basis of one (Walker 1992:168). An epistemology based on concrete knowledge might constrain the application of thick care to the sphere of related others, but contextual knowledge is no guarantee against misjudging a situation. Detailed information will obviously affect the decision, and it is probably easier for a mother to make a good decision for her children than for a stranger, or for the teacher who knows a student or a nurse who knows the patients. However, such decisions might also be biased, prejudiced and ill–considered.

8. On this Aristotle says: "[. . .] deprivation of certain externals—e.g. good birth, good children, beauty—mars our blessedness; for we do not altogether have the character of happiness if we look utterly repulsive or are ill–born, solitary or childless, and have it even less, presumably, if our children or friends are totally bad, or were good but have died" (Aristotle NE 1099a–1099b5).

9. Nicholson also claims that Gilligan ignores other factors such as race and historical variables.

10. It should be added that Gilligan in her later works pays more attention to classes and social conditions than in previous work. In *Mapping the Moral Domain*, for example, she says it is reasonable to believe that these factors color moral thinking, and she takes them into consideration in her studies. The conclusion, after correcting for class bias, is nevertheless not significantly different from her previous studies; the types of moral conflicts experienced are more or less the same, the gender differences similar to those observed earlier, and the same applies to the two "moral orientations" Gilligan et al. 1988:159–173.

11. Caring is not to be compared with the ancient virtue of generosity, a virtue connected to fortune and social position.

12. In "Truthfulness and Deceit in Public Life", Sissela Bok (2000:13–24) discusses how lying in public damages trust by cutting the roots of democracy and disempowering the citizens. It is consonant on another level with what might happen in personal relationship when trust is violated.

13. It could to some extent be necessary in the process of habituation of the virtue of care, but once the virtue is integrated, threatening becomes an alien element.

14. In "On the Attitude of Trust", Lars Hertzberg (1988:307–322) discusses the difference between the words "trust" and "reliance". Hertzberg's aim is to illuminate the context of some of the remarks in *On Certainty* by Wittgenstein, and his point of

departure is that the nature of trust is a primitive reaction. He seems to give the story of Abraham and Isaac paradigmatic status when it comes to trust. Hertzberg uses children as examples and sums up the contrast between reliance and trust like this: "In relying on someone I as it were look down at him from above. I exercise my command of the world. I remain the judge of his actions. In trusting someone I look up from below. I learn from the other what the world is about. I let him be the judge of my actions" (Hertzberg 1988:315). Hertzberg's concept of trust is not at all what I have in mind. While it is necessary to make a distinction between trust and reliance, his concept of trust contains many difficulties. Most striking is the fact that it slides towards fanaticism. Further, it lacks the aspects of reciprocity, voluntaries and confidence in one's own judgments, that are central in caring.

15. Friendship of character can also change into one based on pleasure or utility, as Aristotle points out.

~

CHAPTER NINE

Why Care?

Ethical Justification of Thick Care

In its focus on related others the ethics of care differs from most other eth-ical theories. But is a theory that emphasizes moral responsibility towards a particular group, ethically daring with regard to the interests of non–participants in the carer's network of connections? I contend that it is eth-ically justifiable and required, and not necessarily contrary to a broader moral concern. Therefore, I aim in this chapter at providing a philosophi-cal basis for the focus on related others. I proceed first by way of what I call an internal justification (i.e. based on propositions from the ethic of care itself), before suggesting an external ethical justification (i.e. based on mat-ter from other ethical theories).

Harm in Relationships

Making explicit why thick care—caring in relationships—is considered eth-ically relevant is the first step towards an internal ethical justification of the project. Gilligan point to the harm caused by lack of thick care in order to explain its ethical relevance. Problems in relationships appear differently, she holds, depending on whether one applies the perspective of justice or that of care. From the perspective of justice, relationships are organized in terms of equality, and the moral concern is directed "towards problems of oppression, problems stemming from inequality". From the perspective of care, "rela-tionship connotes responsiveness or engagement, a resiliency of connection that is symbolized by a network or web". The moral concern focuses then "on problems of detachment, on disconnection or abandonment or indifference" (Gilligan et al. 1988:xvii–xviii). Furthermore, the moral ideal is one of attention and response, therefore "[. . .] being there, listening, the willingness to help, and the ability to understand—take on a moral dimension, reflecting the injunction to pay attention and nor turn away from need" (Gilligan et al. 1988:16). Gilligan addresses a problem in relationships that carries ethical relevance. The problem is absence and withdrawal of care, which carries ethical relevance because it may inflict harm. The nature of the harm is precisely what Gilligan in her research focuses on. Depicting the nature of the harm would take us too far into the field of psychology. I must only mention in passing that Gilligan (2002:6,15) points to traumas, depression, eating disorders, problems in learning and destructive behavior as partly resulting from disconnections and the absence of care. I will, without question the validity of the assumed causal relations, take for granted that the failure of care causes injury.

Positive and Negative Duties

As Gilligan's notion of relationships can be understood as a variant of special relationships, which give rise to special duties—both positive and negative— we could try to explicate the moral problem to which Gilligan draws attention by applying traditional classifications of duties although they strictly speaking are inadequate to the task before us. Before setting out why, it would be illuminating to clarify the basic terminology.

"Positive duties" are duties to help and "negative duties" are duties not to harm. "General duties" are duties that are held by all, while "special duties" are only held by some since they arise from particular relationships between particular individuals (Goodin 1985:18). Relationships giving rise to special duties are sometimes thought of as voluntary associations, but this is not a necessary condition. The relationship Gilligan is concerned about is not only "contractual". What Gilligan focuses on can also be understood in terms of Scheffler's "associative duties", that is the "responsibility that the members of significant groups and the particular participants in close personal relationships have to each other" (Scheffler 1994:1).[1] These four types of duties cut across one another and constitute four categories of moral duties. There are "general negative duties" (like refraining from giving false promises, coercion and violence); "general positive duties" (for instance, you may have a duty to assist a drowning person). There are also "special negative duties" (for example refraining from abusing your child or beating your spouse); and "special positive duties" (for instance to support and give attention to your child). There is consensus on the status of the negative duties; everyone can claim them. But to whom, how and when the positive duties are incurred are more controversial issues. O'Neill, who holds a Kantian position, claims that the positive (or imperfect) duties are owed to no one in particular (O'Neill 1991:178; 1996:152).

> Some obligations without corresponding rights could be embedded in special relationships: special obligations without rights (if there are any) would constitute elements of certain roles, relationships and ways of life. Examples might be the characteristic requirements of certain roles: the attentiveness of a parent, the patience of someone working with handicapped adults, the trustworthiness of an accountant. (O'Neill 1996:137)

This does not mean that positive duties are not to be fulfilled, only that it is not specified how and when the beneficent actions are to be carried out, the reason being that the need for positive duties is so widespread that we cannot possibly fulfill it. The Kantian view leaves it open for the agent to determine the occasions on which the positive duties are to be enacted. It is also held that Kant implies that the positive duties allow for the interests of inclinations (Blum 1994:40, fn.14).

Two features of these duties are important for my present analysis of the ethical relevance of thick care: The hierarchy of these duties and the characteristics used to distinguish between positive and negative duties. Gilligan's theory can be read as an objection to the view that special negative duties take precedence over special positive duties, and her challenge gives reason to doubt the distinction between positive and negative duties. These two points, the hierarchy of and distinctions between positive and negative duties, are entangled. The following discussion will therefore touch on both points simultaneously.

In special relationships, harm can also be caused by a violation of the obligation to positive duties. The latter is precisely what Gilligan draws our attention to. Not to perform the special positive duties inflicts severe damage. Injuries of both a short– and long–term nature may arise from a lack of involvement, from the absence of active, helpful participation, encouragement and so on. In other words, not performing care may cause harm. Gilligan would, I believe, support Robert Goodin's point that not fulfilling or neglecting negative duties in special relationships is not necessarily worse than neglecting positive duties (Goodin 1988:107–111). Gilligan accentuates the point that, in relationships, it is no less important to help than to avoid doing harm, which is why I previously stressed the point that care is related both to the principle of benevolence and the principle of not hurting (as explained in Chapter 3).

In relationships then, it is not the physical harm, such as parental abuse or wife–beating, that Gilligan highlights. These problems are ethically taken care of and classified as morally wrong according to the negative duties pertaining to special relationships—which in turn are drawn from the general negative duty not to harm.[2] Her theory draws attention to the *psychological and emotional harm* caused by the absence of care, by failing to be caring in relationships. It concerns the issue of nonviolence in a psychological context (Gilligan 1982:102–104). Harm resulting from the absence of care is a phenomenon difficult to capture with the traditional distinction of duties into positive and negative. Negative duties are characterized as non–interference aiming at preventing harm; positive duties as active conduct aiming at beneficent results. Gilligan accentuates situations where passivity is causing harm rather than preventing it, and thereby draws attention to a deficiency related to the traditional distinction between negative and positive duties.[3] Whether harm is inflicted actively or passively is often insignificant, the major concern is that it is inflicted. But perceiving Gilligan's relationships as a variant of special relationships, ethically accommodated for by negative and positive duties, falls short of highlighting the particular injury to which Gilligan draws attention. The distinction also fails to adequately discern the ethical relevance of thick care, because harm is inflicted also when failing to fulfill positive duties.

It should be mentioned that activities aiming at doing good may have unpredictable harmful consequences, and that what appears to be "beneficial" conducts may prove evil and the result of manipulation. Philosophers outside the care tradition such as Scheffler (1994:4), O'Neill (1996:149–150), and Kuhse (1997:153) together with sponsors of care such as Noddings (1989) engage with this problem.[4] Gilligan does not pay attention to this particular phenomenon, instead she draws attention to *harm on another level*: It does not take an exceptionally evil or malicious person to inflict psychological and emotional hurt. More commonplace neglect and disregard of human relations, and a lack of awareness of how attitudes and conduct affect others can also cause harm.

> Care–focused thinkers [. . .] recognize detachment as morally problematic and underscore the tendency in this highly technological age for people to lose sight of human connection, to overlook the way in which people enter and affect one another's lives. (Gilligan et al. 1988:290)

One way of justifying thick care, then, is to show how it relates to a particular moral problem in a particular context: The harm inflicted by failing to care in relationships (Gilligan et al. 1988:135,136). To put it clearly, it is not the ethical relevance of relationships *as such* that is being defended here, as many aspects of relationships do not concern the ethics of care. What matters is a certain aspect of human interaction; thick care—the attitudes and conduct towards those whom we associate with. Gilligan stresses the moral significance of *caring* in our relationships. Failing to care in relationships can cause serious injury, which is precisely why thick care carries moral relevance in Gilligan's theory. Thick care is a buffer against this particular harm—as justice is what redeems harm. As few theories deal with the moral challenges related to our interpersonal lives, Gilligan's ethics of care appears to be a legitimate and required supplement in the traditional ethical landscape.

However, even if we agree on the ethical relevance of thick care, we can indeed question the relationship between our concern for our related others and a broader moral commitment. Does the restricted object of Gilligan's theory entail a narrow moral concern without regard for more general issues? This discussion on the justification of thick care needs to tackle current objections to and justifications for restricting our focus to related others. I start by considering some objections.

Parochialism

Certainly, there are those who worry about the strong emphasis on caring in relationships. The selection of related others as objects of our moral concerns proposed by Gilligan can be seen as conflicting with two fundamental requirements put forward in many modern ethical theories, namely universalizability and impartiality. Onora O'Neill portrays the "contemporary friends of care" in the following way:

> They adopted a vantage point of view from which the importance of certain virtues in certain contexts could be displayed, but to do so they often accepted particularistic approaches which disabled their accounts of justice and severely limited their accounts of virtue. These disabilities are stridently displayed by writers who manifest simple hostility to human rights, who dismiss justice as an ethically inadequate "male" concern, or who ignore the import and importance of the institutions of the public domain (state, economy, society) in favor of celebrating the caring virtues of domesticity and intimacy. These are disastrous limitations in any ethical vision that aspires to relevance to the contemporary world. (O'Neill 1996:141)

One of O'Neill's concerns seems to be that selective care is a threat against a broader moral commitment. Others, such as Helga Kuhse (1997), share her concern. Indeed, Kuhse focuses her discussion on some of Nel Noddings's (1984) examples of conduct where thick care is given precedence over impartial rules or principles. Nevertheless, I believe her point illustrates a relatively widespread impression of the ethics of care:

> [. . .] it is frighteningly narrow and parochial. One–caring cares about the–cared–for, but not, apparently, about the fate of other children who are likely to suffer under the continued existence of what Nodding calls a 'foolish and unfair' rule. (Kuhse 1997:155)

Concern for those outside the caring circle is considered, among others, by Scheffler. He calls his argument "the distributive objection", an objection he levels on behalf of those individuals who are not members of the group or participants in relationships that are thought to give rise to associative duties, duties which can be regarded as unjustifiable whenever the provision of associative duties works to the detriment of people who, for different reasons, are needier (Scheffler 1994:9,11).

I have no disagreement with those who maintain that Gilligan's main ethical scope appears to be specialized. Nor do I disagree with Scheffler that people outside a particular group can be disadvantaged. At a practical level, I recognize at least two ways in which thick care could jeopardize a broader moral commitment. First, if the interests of our related others constantly and consciously are given priority over the interests of strangers our moral behavior will become parochial. Second, there is a possibility that caring for our related others will absorb our entire moral capacity; even if we are aware of our broader moral commitments, we may have no resources left to fulfill them. Our ethical principles would not necessarily be narrow in scope, but our moral conduct might become so. What I do object to, however, is the assumption that a focus of the related others as such should jeopardize a broader moral commitment. This focus is not identical with denying other moral obligations. Nor does it imply that the carer should consume their entire moral energy on tending to their related others. The provision of thick care is not claimed to exhaust the agent's moral obligations. The ethics of care's focus on related others are not asserted to constitute the complete moral realm; it aims only to put emphasis on a specific aspect of the moral domain. This focus needs to be further discussed.

The Different Domain Argument

It is crucial to remember that Gilligan does *not* claim that care in relationships should replace or overshadow impartialist concerns. Her theory is not parochial in this sense. Gilligan holds that there is a *complementarity* between the moral concern stemming from justice and fairness and the caring responsibilities for the related others (Gilligan 1982:165–166). Certainly, conflicts between the two may arise. How conflicts might be handled within a Gilliganian ethics of care was elaborated in Chapter 5. My point here is to emphasize that even if thick care *can* overshadow impartial moral responsibilities, most of the time the two types of duty will not compete, and when they do occasionally clash, it is not obvious that care should prevail.

In *Friendship, Altruism and Morality* (1980), Lawrence Blum presents arguments against the view that an ethical focus on personal relationships entails parochialism. One of his points is that impartiality is required only in some parts of the moral domain. Impartiality is demanded in some circumstances, it is an official capacity necessary within certain public institutions and practices, Blum continues, but our friends have claims that strangers do not have. By taking care of related others, we do not necessarily go against the ideal of impartiality. Therefore, Blum argues for more than one moral point of view (Blum 1980:46–47). His argument, which could be termed the "different domain argument" is compatible with the view I submit here; morality consists both in thick care for particular related others, and in concern for those outside the carer's web of relationship—i.e. thin care. The ability to acknowledge both concerns is a sign of a morally mature person (Gilligan 1982:74,98,164–165; 1987:9,30; Gilligan et al. 1988:117). Rejecting thick care on the ground that caring, in some situations, *may* conflict with other ethical concerns is a facile conclusion.

The Moral Agent Argument

The different domain argument is sometimes pressed further than simply indicating that antagonism between thick care and impartiality does not always arise, but also to support the view that the two moral concerns can coexist. Caring in personal relationships is said to have broader moral implications, implications beyond the individual prevention of harm. It is held to provide the individuals involved with some of the skills and competence required of a moral agent. This line of reasoning is what I call "the moral agent argument". By stressing the beneficial and morally relevant consequences beyond the particular association, the moral agent argument goes against what Scheffler calls the "distributive objections". The reason is that the ability to consider the interests of those outside the group of related others can be understood as requiring a moral mature agent. Such maturity is a precondition for an extended moral concern, and its development requires thick care. Let us inspect this line of reasoning closer.

According to Blum, Gilligan means that the web of relationships in which everyone is embedded encompasses all human beings, not only one's circle of acquaintances (Blum 1993:50). I agree that such indications can be found in her writings, and have named it thin care. But Gilligan does not develop her theory as far as to accommodate this idea. Her theory centers on those with whom we are connected, and the question of how caring is to be extended to all others is not made clear. Hence, Blum's observations of Gilligan's notion of thin care are of no help when it comes to answering *how* care can be extended from close relationships to people *outside* the one's web of established connections. Gilligan is silent here, I therefore look at attempts made by other philosophers to morally justify the prioritizing between thin and thick care. Annette Baier presents one approach.

Annette Baier (1993), who, like Gilligan, raises objections against traditional moral theories, believes that many moral theorists have turned their back on the question of how we deal with our related others. She holds that "in most liberal theories there are only hand waves concerning our proper attitude to our children, to the ill, our relatives, friends and lovers" (Baier 1993:21). If the just society is to last beyond the first generation Baier remarks, addressing Rawls's theory of justice, the obligations of justice must be supplemented by the virtue of being a loving parent. She continues:

> Since there is no coherent guideline liberal morality can give on these issues, which clearly are *not* matters of moral indifference, liberal morality tells each of us "the choice is yours" hoping that enough will choose to be self–sacrificial life–providers and self sacrificial death–dealers to suit the purpose of the rest. (Baier 1993:25)

Why are these matters neglected, and for what reasons ought they not to be? Baier asks,

> Why waste moral resources recognizing as obligatory or as virtuous what one can count on getting without moral pressure? If one can get enough good mothers and good warriors "for free" in the moral economy, why not gladly exploit what nature and cultural history offer? I cannot answer this question fully here, but my argument does depend upon the assumption that a decent morality will *not* depend for its stability on forces to which is given no moral recognition. Its account books should be open to scrutiny, and there should be no unpaid debts, no loans with no prospects of repayment. (Baier 1993:24–25)

Now, why exactly should moral theories pay attention to how we deal with our related others? Besides that failing to care within relationships can be subsumed under the expanded principle of not hurting, there is the view, here presented by Baier, that intimate caring has beneficial moral implications far beyond the inner circle—implications taken for granted in many ethical theories. Moral agents, as understood within the justice perspective, utilitarian and liberal theories, are presupposed to be capable of, for instance, acting and reasoning according to moral principles. How, then, does one become a moral agent? If one accepts the view that a moral agent is a person who has developed the ability to act morally through a process of interactive learning, moral theorists should not turn their back on the question of how we deal with our related others. Referring to the acquirement of vital moral competence is a strategy also adopted by others as a way of justifying the moral relevance of nurturing relationships. Lafollette (1991), for instance, claims that most of us learn to recognize the interests and needs of others through our experience within personal relationships. This learning has moral implications, because it is difficult to imagine how one could promote the needs and interests of others, if one is not able to identify them (Lafollette 1991:331; Vetlesen 1994:28:7–9).

The question is to what extent Baier and Lafollete's "moral agent argument" can be used to justify the ethics of care's focus on thick care. Gilligan is concerned about moral development. In particular, she focuses on the development of care and on the conditions within which such cultivation can take place—i.e., in caring relationships.[5] Also Gilligan holds the view that moral agents are not born with fully developed moral skills—they have to be cultivated. Thick care contributes to the creation of moral agents—understood as persons with ethically praiseworthy skills such as sense of justice, empathy, honesty and the like. These skills are required by liberal and deontological ethical theories alike.

However, unlike Baier and Lafollette, to justify why personal relationships are morally relevant, Gilligan does not need to rely completely on such anticipated beneficial consequences. Instead, her theory can hang on the expanded principle of not hurting, which covers the emotional, psychological and physical harm inflicted by failure to care in relationships. For two reasons I hold this to be a firmer strategy than "the moral agent argument". First, the moral agent argument can be disputed from a meta–ethical point of view, and second, the claimed beneficial repercussions can be questioned from an empirical point of view. Let us start by considering the first point.

The moral agent argument can be questioned from a liberal and a deontological point of view in so far as the argument entails a problem of demarcation between moral and non–moral issues. Since the argument relies on the anticipated beneficial consequences, it may be difficult to delimit these consequences from other aspects of human life which *may* affect the development of moral agents—such as education, natural endowments, culture and socio–economic structures and the like. In an ethics of care, one can anchor the normativeness of thick care in the expanded principle of not hurting since failure to care may cause harm. As this argument neither implies a "disastrous limitation" or problematic expansion of the moral domain, this strategy is not as vulnerable to the meta–ethical critique of distinguishing the moral from the non–moral, as is the moral agent argument advocated by Baier and Lafollette. Giving prominence to thick care simply means that the theory argues in favor of giving special positive duties higher priority than do most ethical theories for two reasons. First, because not fulfilling them is more harmful than is commonly recognized, and second, because refining them is necessary as the traditional way of characterizing them does not adequately accommodate for the harm the ethics of care draws attention to.

The anticipated beneficial consequences, on which the moral agent argument relies, can also be questioned from an empirical point of view. It is not quite clear what kind of data the moral agent argument is founded on. It could be intuition, experience or statistics, but probably it entails psychological reasoning along the line of object–relation theory. Object–relations theories argue that a person's psychological growth, personality formation and the ability to enter and maintain relationships are based on relational experiences in early childhood (Chodorow 1978:7). Gilligan has shown an interest in this area (Gilligan et al. 1988; Gilligan 2002:28–31,168). The validity of the psychological premises in these theories, or of their empirical testing, is not an issue here. The linkage to morality, however, somewhat hastily made by Lafollette (1991) and others, and the anticipated *moral* implications nevertheless are. The point of the moral agent argument is to highlight the morally beneficial implications of thick care. But a normative justification of thick care cannot rely on the moral agent argument, which says that the development of the required moral competence depends on a providential infancy. Acting morally is related to the agent's free and deliberate choice, hence, justifying thick care by reference to the expanded principle of not hurting seems more sound than relying on the moral agent argument. This nevertheless raises another important question: Are the related others those we feel related and devoted to, or are they people we choose to take responsibility for? Are they people we are given responsibility for, people perhaps in need, or who are dependent upon us? Other ethical traditions handle the possible discrepancy between an agent's moral obligation and their emotions and relationships by the claim to impartiality. Kant is an outstanding example:

For love as an inclination cannot be commanded; but beneficence from duty, when no inclination impels us, and even when a neutral and unconquerable aversion oppose such beneficence, is practical, and not pathological, love. Such loves resides in the will and not in the propensities of feeling, in principles of action and not in tender sympathy; and only this practical love can be commanded. (Kant 1992:997–998)

Kant's position secures a broad moral concern. Moral commitment is not confined to the agents loved and/or related others, but also extends to those the agent dislikes, and even to strangers. This is not, however, the moral tradition behind Gilligan's theory, on the contrary, it is a moral framework she criticizes. Still, a carer may experience a certain tension in that those who are near are not necessarily dear. To understand why a carer should care despite a possible sense of aversion we need to find support in ethical theories that conform more closely with a Gilliganian framework than does a Kantian ethics. Robert Goodin's model on protecting the vulnerable can be read as such an attempt. In the following section, I present his thesis as it aspires to bridge a gap, if there is one, between those to whom we feel connected, and those with whom we associate. Goodin's theory represents what I termed the external justification of thick care.

Robert Goodin's Vulnerability Model

In *Protecting the Vulnerable* (1985), Robert Goodin suggests that the vulnerability of others constitutes the moral basis of special responsibilities towards families, friends, clients and so forth. This model opposes the way these duties traditionally are analyzed in terms of self–assumed obligations, and the central argument in the book is that we bear a special responsibility to protect those who are particularly vulnerable in relation to our attitudes and conduct. By "vulnerability", Goodin means psychological as well as physical sensitivity. The duty to protect the vulnerable then, is the duty to prevent harm from occurring, and it is equally compelling whether it requires acting or refraining from acting. In short, the model is an argument for aiding people who are in need and dependent on us for having their needs fulfilled. The more dependent they are, the stronger our duties become (Goodin 1985:109–111).

Dilemmas arise when we cannot accommodate all the needs those dependent on us have. The person facing the dilemma will thus have to balance different responsibilities. While some philosophers (for instance Sartre) deny that balancing responsibilities in this manner can ever be done rationally,

Goodin insists that his notion of vulnerability can help us to resolve such dilemmas. Whom we should favor depends upon the relative vulnerability of each party to us. What needs to be determined is how strongly a party's interests would be affected by our alternative actions and choices, and whether or not she would be able to find other sources of assistance/protection if we failed her (Goodin 1985:119). Vulnerability and responsibility are not only relational in Goodin's model, but also relative. The model therefore implies that we, to a certain extent, may favor those close to us and the reason why differential treatment is legitimate is that persons relatively near to us in space and time probably will be more vulnerable to *us* than remote others are. The interests of related others are likely to be affected more heavily by our actions and choices than those of the more distant. Our nearest neighbors in space and time, says Goodin, are more likely to depend upon us, sometimes even exclusively, for assistance and protection, and continues,

> This fact saves my argument from the traditional *reductio* of requiring that we give everything we have to starving Asians or that we forever save everything for infinitely receding future generations or that we have our own lives and projects constantly interrupted to serve others. My analysis would seem to allow (indeed, to require) us, in effect if not in intention, to show *some* bias towards our own "kind", however defined. Still, that bias must not be absolute. The vulnerability of distant others (including a great many of those starving Asians) to our own actions and choices is surely sufficiently clear, to require us to give their interests some substantial weight in reckoning our own responsibilities. Charity may indeed begin at home, but morally it must not stop there. (Goodin 1985:121)

Now, for several reasons Goodin's model provides reinforcement for the ethics of care's focus on thick care. First, it gives a more precise account of what "relatedness" actually covers. Relatedness is not embedded in the carer's warm feelings, or in the people chosen to be the object of the carer's sense of responsibility. It includes all those in our network who depend on us. And it is not up to the carer alone to decide who is a part of their network. A new neighbor, a new colleague, if dependent on the agent, becomes one of the carer's related others, and is as such entitled to care. In fact, Goodin's vulnerability makes it clear that the network of relatedness should be understood as is, in an ethics of care, an open rather than closed circle. The vulnerability argument underpins the point that "relationship" should be understood in a broad sense, as it refers not only to personal or "voluntary" relationships, but to a variety of connections. It allows us to say that the particular moral concern emphasized by this ethics of care is our mutual vulnerability and responsibility in the multiplicity of human interactions in which the agent engages—and reminds us that our moral concern must not stop at home.

Second, Goodin improves with his model the conflict solving method presented in Chapter 6. Mature care is seen as aiming at balancing the interests of the carer and those cared for, but little advice is forthcoming on how to go about differentiating primary from secondary needs. Goodin suggests vulnerability as a benchmark. This is compatible with what I take to be the idea of mature care. Goodin's standard pays attention to the asymmetry and inequality in strength, resources and power, and may neutralize potential bias in the decision–making process resulting from the agent's likes and dislikes. His model sets out an important aspect the carer should look for when obeying the injunction not to hurt in cases of conflicting interests; and that is vulnerability. From a mature care point of view, one could add that the carer's vulnerability must be given the same weight as the vulnerability of those cared for. Goodin does not pursue this point, but mature care's awareness of both the interests of the carer and the cared–for constitutes another point where the ethics of care and Goodin's thesis enrich each other.

Third, paying attention to the vulnerability of all those affected may illuminate the previous point, that this ethics of care is different from other theories of care such as those of Martinsen, Noddings, Levinas and Løgstrup. More precisely, it demands less of the agent, and the relative aspect of Goodin's thesis tells why. According to Goodin our responsibility towards the related others is not unlimited, unchangeable and everlasting, since our special responsibility derives from the fact that other people are dependent on us and are particularly vulnerable to our actions (Goodin 1986:33). The source of our obligations is the others' vulnerability, not our will to enter into contracts with them. Ethics is about protecting the vulnerable. Professional responsibility for instance, arises from the patient's vulnerability, not from contracts (Goodin 1986:67). So also with parental and filial responsibility; it is dependency and vulnerability rather than voluntary acts of will that constitute the origin of the moral duties involved. As Goodin says,

> Where there is no collective provision for the care of the aged, a special duty falls upon their children to do so; to the extent that communities now make adequate collective provision to meet the needs of the aged (through pensions, etc.), these special duties fall away. (Goodin 1986:35)

Vulnerability is an essential feature of relationships. The degree of vulnerability, however, will depend on the type of relationship. Vulnerability is most "equally distributed" in symmetric relationships, but also here variable.

Among friends for example, susceptibility will vary. For instance, due to changes in circumstances one friend may be more in need than another for a certain period of time. In asymmetric relationships, such as those between a mother and her child, the child obviously is in a weaker position than the mother and has a stronger need for protection. Nevertheless, the mother's interests must also be taken into account. Vulnerability in relationships does not only arise from inequality in knowledge, physical appearance, it should be noticed, but also from inequality in emotions. Goodin draws attention to the circumstance that "the one who cares less can, and often does exploit the one who cares more". In a love relationship, for example, the individual who is less deeply involved has an advantage over the other since the latter's greater concern to prolong the relationship increases their dependency, thus allowing the less involved party an opening that can be used to exploit the other (Goodin 1985:36–37). Both the ethics of care, in particular the concept of mature care, and Goodin's vulnerability model are geared to protect the less advantageous in an asymmetric relationship—as opposed to the aim of traditional contract models that presuppose equal and independent agents.

Fourth, Goodin's model coincides with Gilligan's concern to take account of the context in situations of moral conflict. It steers clear of a relativistic position, and thus avoids capriciousness and parochialism, by establishing a principled point of departure. At the same time, it allows particularistic considerations to be taken into account. In Goodin's model, as in the current version of an ethics of care, both our moral intuitions and the need for principled reflections are well accommodated.

Fifth, the principled point of departure in this ethics of care—the expanded principle of not hurting—and Goodin's principle of protecting the vulnerable are rather akin. Both principles aim first and foremost at protecting the "worst off" from injury. Both theories emphasize that this protection is against psychological and emotional harm, not only physical harm. In fact, as Goodin remarks in a footnote, what Gilligan's informants are concerned about is vulnerability:

> Gilligan's (1977) psychological surveys show that it [i.e. vulnerability] is, in fact, one of the heaviest considerations bearing on the minds of women presented with abortion decisions. (Goodin 1985:120, fn.18)[6]

Sixth, both theories in question can be said to address the traditional dichotomy of positive and negative duties. They are conscious of what may be regarded as an inadequacy related to this dichotomy; it is equally compelling irrespective of the protection of those dependent on us requires positive action or no action.

Finally, and of particular relevance to this chapter's discussion, Goodin's model leaves room for a certain privileging of the related others—without disregarding a broader moral concern. His argument is that our nearest neighbors in space and time are more dependent on our assistance and protection. Goodin thus lends support to the ethics of care's focus on thick care. In order to fulfill the requirement of not hurting, the agent needs to take account of the fact that the related others might be particularly disposed to and/or affected by the agent's distribution of care and concern. Additionally, Goodin's thesis provides an explanation lacking in Gilligan's theory about how we are supposed to proceed towards strangers, i.e. people who are not part of our established network. As the network is open, the carer must regard themselves as part of a broader web of human interactions. Therefore, the stray teenager at the front door (Noddings 1984:47), or the beggar at the street enters the agent's network and is entitled to moral concern to the extent that she is reliant on the carer, and to the extent that the carer is able to alleviate her misery. This approach may mitigate the possible tension between a duty to help those to whom we feel warm and caring, and those who are dependent on us. It also clarifies a basis of the caring responsibility: It derives from the degree of dependency on the carer, and is also determined by the carer's ability to prevent harm to those with which she interacts. Goodin's thesis concerning the protection of the vulnerable alleviates the possible tension between duties to one's nearest and dearest and to others outside the inner circle, and also helps to show that people near to us are not only people towards whom we have warm feelings and with whom we voluntarily establish connections.

Thick Care and Professional Ethics

To further elucidate the focus of Gilligan's ethics, I address both affinities with and differences from professional ethics. Drawing attention to the similarities is meant to illuminate the validity and requirement of a specialized area of concern, while the differences are spelled out in order to highlight some of the distinctive features of the ethics of care.

Different occupations establish norms on how to behave in professional relationships. When, say, doctors, lawyers and teachers elaborate norms of professional ethics, for instance by setting up regulations between therapist and client, teacher and student, nurse and patients, they do so mainly in order to protect their wards' (patients, clients, students) interests. Their wards need to be assured that their particular interests are being tended to in a competent way, that they are being given fair, equal and predictable treatment, that their vulnerability will not be exploited, and so forth. It is commonly held, also by Goodin, that professional ethical norms are required because the relationship is asymmetric in that one part (the professional) is in a more advantageous position relative to the other (their ward). Other characteristics of professional ethics are the free entry into the relationship with the patient, pupil or client,[7] and the obligation to redeem what is specified in the professional code once one has accepted the relationship (Goodin 1985:66–70).

Goodin distinguishes between private relationships—such as family and friendships—and professional relationships. Goodin also says that family relationships are not successfully dealt with from the perspective of a voluntaristic model. Professional and private relationships differ here. "No one chooses his own siblings or parents: we merely tumble into these relationships", he says (Goodin 1985:71). What is more, he differentiates between types or subcategories of private relationships: Between husband and wife; parents and children; father and son, etc. And he does so because the degree of voluntariness in these subcategories varies. As Scheffler says, "some of those relationships are ordinarily entered into voluntarily, but others of them cannot be" (Scheffler 1994:2).

The decisive aspect for Gilligan's concern about relationships is not what Goodin and others seem to focus on, i.e. the *entry* into these relationships (Goodin 1985:71–72). Being in a web of relationship is part of the ethics of care's ontology. Her theory is an attempt to clarify certain aspects of the conduct found *within* these relationships and of the *dissolution* of connections. These features bear resemblance to professional ethics, and are more significant than how the relationships came into being. Gilligan's ethics of care can be seen as an attempt to explicate the specific problems that may arise when people interact, be it in private or professional relationships. It is an effort to reflect on norms concerning how to act in this domain—a concern with strong affinity to professional ethics. Care is to be considered an essential norm required in human interaction, since caring in relationships can protect and promote the interests of the involved. In other words, this ethics of care can be regarded as relationship "code" based on a guiding principle that protects against harm and promotes well–being and human flourishing, and as theory encouraging the development of a particular attitude. Certainly, the prominence of care will vary. It will be more to the fore in relationships between nurse and the patient, mother and child than between lawyer and client.

The moral responsibility for clients is more ethically pronounced, than is the moral responsibility in private relationships, for instance towards children. As an illustration, Goodin points out that "professionals cannot withdraw from a case without giving the client sufficient opportunity to obtain other assistance as that would leave the client dreadfully exposed" (Goodin 1985:67). In some versions of professional ethics it is prohibited to leave one's client without making sure that the ending of the relationship does not harm their interests, that they are attended to elsewhere. Few corresponding ethical codes, however, exist to guide a family through a process of dissolution. Such situations are contexts where the problem of abandonment and detachment in private relationship can easily arise. If these problems are excluded from the moral domain, by reference to "free" and "private" choices, moral theories will be unable to accommodate conduct that injures sensitive interests of particularly vulnerable individuals, such as children. The ethics of care sheds light on this vulnerability, this psychological and emotional susceptibility in particular, which exists in interpersonal relationships. In order to avoid misunderstandings, this ethics does not aim at formalizing our interaction with others, neither by establishing legal codes or fixed conventions. It would not be possible to formalize, say, parenting in the same way as can be done with a professional relationship as we, in our private relationships, participate as complete persons, not merely in terms of a circumscribed role accompanied by a particular role–related manner of behaving. The interests of others must be protected, not necessarily through formalized regulations, but through an increased (ethical) awareness of how vulnerable and often dependent our related others are on our manner or conduct. In turn, this understanding might influence attitudes and induce the development of relational virtues such as care. Gilligan clarifies some of the vital interests and problems that need to be attended to in human interaction. Putting Gilligan's theory alongside professional ethics is meant to illuminate their similarities of purpose, that is to protect vulnerability and to promote flourishing—and to suggest that treating personal relationships as a diffuse and peculiar variant of a special relationship as Goodin tends to do (Goodin 1985:71–92) might obscure the fact that people are as vulnerable in private as in professional relationships. As Gilligan's theory also emphasizes the need to consider both parties to a relationship, her theory also accommodates the carer more explicitly. In my opinion, there is a tendency in Goodin's discussion of professional ethics to focus too one–sidedly on the interests of the clients. We have seen this tendency in Martinsen, Noddings and other care ethicists' theories. True, one half of a professional relationship is more dependent on the other and their interests are more exposed than their therapist's, teacher's or nurse's. Nevertheless, also the professional's integrity needs to be protected.

Gilligan's theory elevates the importance of a specific aspect of the ethical landscape. It does so by showing the compelling significance of caring in relationships in two complementary ways. The first is by showing how injurious detachment, disconnection, abandonment and indifference can be.

The other is by showing the benefits arising from thick care—though I consider this strategy as less firm. There are no weighty arguments why conduct and responsibilities within private relationships should not be considered as ethically relevant as those between teacher and student, therapist and client, and the like. In particular, mature care is significant for arriving at decisions concerning the interests of children (Sandberg 1990:146). Therefore, I consider Gilligan's ethics of care to be an exploration of a certain part of the moral domain—a domain not examined throughout by many other purveyors of ethical theories.

Whether one's ethical project is defined as caring in relationships, protecting vulnerability, promoting welfare or achieving happiness, in order to be exhaustive, both external and internal conditions need to be attended too.[9] Even if both internal (such as developing virtues) and external conditions (such as a minimum of welfare) are ethical issues, this is not to say that every single ethical theory must spell out a response to every problem in moral life. On the contrary, in this chapter I argue that it is quite legitimate to concentrate a deeper analysis on a specific aspect of the moral domain—as long as it is made clear that it is intended as a partial contribution to ethics and moral philosophy. Gilligan for instance, emphasizes that the focus on relationships is not intended to exhaust our moral commitments. Her goal is, she says, "to expand the understanding of human development by using the group left out in the construction of the theory to call attention to what is missing in its account". Seen in this light, her theory and research is a basis upon which to generate new theories (Gilligan 1982:3–4). Her theory has implications for more people than the inner circle of related others:

> As the contemporary reality of global interdependence impels the search for new maps of development, the exploration of attachment may provide the psychological grounding for new visions of progress and growth. (Gilligan et al. 1988:157)

In the next chapter we shall turn our attention from thick care towards thin care. In doing so we shall also chart some aspects of the history of the ethics of care over the past 25 years, starting with Gilligan, and expanding outwards in ever widening cirles.

Notes

1. I cannot see that Scheffler's notion has any particular advantages over the notion of special duties in this context, and I continue to use special duties.

2. It is commonly held that special duties are derived from general duties and attain their moral force from those general duties. However, some aspects of special duties cannot be deduced from general duties, for instance, who in particular should take such duties upon themselves (Goodin 1988:680), and how and when to implement them.

3. Other care–thinkers are also concerned with this. In *Women and Evil*, Nel Noddings (1989:221–222) terms it "inducing the pain of separation", which, among other things, consists in neglecting relations so that the pain of separation follows. Another type of "evil" is to deliberately or carelessly cause helplessness by non–interference.

4. As an example, I quote Noddings: "[The psychiatrist M. Scott] Peck describes parents who totally control their children in the name of preparing them for autonomous futures, wives who dominate their husbands and despise them for their weakness, parents who gives their children destructive 'gifts'—gifts the children do not want and that effectively pass along messages of hate rather than love. In many of these accounts, Peck shows great insight into the ways people inflict pain in the name of good. [. . .] In many of the cases Peck describes, the best solution for a victim of destructive control would be physical separation".

5. I have previously mentioned that harm can be done in the name of care and that personal relationships provide opportunities for abuse and mistreatment as well as growth. Proponents of care and the "moral agent argument" can, of course, agree on its occurrence and wrongness, but claim that it is not caused by *care*. Caring, understood as a virtue for instance, will not per definition have such consequences.

6. In fact, many ethical theories are concerned with protecting the needs of the vulnerable—as pointed out by Robert Goodin (1985). Onora O'Neill (1991:175–85) points out how the recognition of mutual vulnerability plays a part in Kantian ethics. John Rawls (1971) can be said to aim at protecting the worst off, the most vulnerable group, while Thomas Pogge (1998) is concerned with the worst off in a global perspective, and would extend our moral obligation to the outermost concentric circle.

7. The entry is "free" in the sense that the professional has entered into the professional role by her/his own choice of occupation, is able to quit practicing, and (within some limits) selects clients. Family members, brothers and sisters for instance, do not have these choices.

8. This is also one of Aristotle's points in the *Nicomachean Ethics*. The predominant focus since Aristotle has been on the external conditions, and there are similarities between Gilligan and Aristotle in her psychological approach and keen attention to internal conditions. They both present a theory of how to behave in relationships so that excellence, moral skills and the like are developed.

~

CHAPTER TEN

The Circles of Care

When describing the development of the ethics of care, 'extraordinary' is an appropriate term. What twenty–five years ago was considered a rendering of women's moral reasoning in the decision–making required in personal relationships, "the perspective of care" has become an ethical theory whose ramifications affect professional conduct, public policy and global issues. In this last chapter, I want to highlight and discuss certain features in the development of the ethics of care. In particular, I shall focus on its expansion from the private domain to the public and global level. These three domains, one could see them as ever–widening concentric circles, correspond to the three phases in the development of the ethics of care, to which we now shall turn our attention.

The First Phase: Personal and Local Care

Although we can trace the origin of the ethics of care to several sources, publication of Gilligan's *In a Different Voice* was obviously the groundbreaking event. From it proceeded a dedicated ethical theory, a challenge to mainstream theorizing. It was controversial from the start, to feminist ethics and other disciplines.

Most commentators in the first phase were probably concerned about the posited correlation between ethics and gender. Was the mainstream ethic predominantly male? What part did gender play in the ethics of care? Gilligan's practical research and thought were hotly debated. Some believed it lacked validity and philosophical relevance; others wanted to know what a statistical correlation between gender and moral orientation signified. Gilligan's alleged essentialism was discussed, as was how feminism articulated with the ethics of care. Did the ethics of care, with its emphasis on traditional female values and behavior, promote the feminist cause?

Gilligan identified "the different voice" by listening to women trying to decide whether to take an abortion, and to adolescent girls when personal preferences antagonized friends and family. A care–based approach was commonly understood as expressing women's way of tackling personal issues, an approach based on idiosyncratic preferences and spontaneous emotion. Viewed in this light, women's care based approach lay outside the realm of ethics and moral philosophy—the branch of normative thinking representing the "view from nowhere". Kohlberg, for instance, saw care derived ethics as a private, i.e. not ethical, concern. Justice, instead, belongs to the public sphere (Kohlberg 1984: 231, fn.2). The ethical status and relevance of the private domain were also questioned in the first phase. What exactly describes the relationship between care and justice? Are they irreconcilable? Can justice be reduced to care and vice versa? Which of the two is the most fundamental? Do they pertain to different domains? The perspective of care and justice identified by Gilligan also evokes questions on moral reasoning—both descriptive and normative. How do we, how ought we to reason about morality? Should we take an abstract ethical principle as our guide, or actual experience? Should we emphasize the particular over the universal? What is the role of reason and the emotions, and how does the one impinge on the other?

Care ethicists, we should note, invented none of these questions; they are classical issues in moral philosophy. But due to the way mainstream ethics and moral philosophy developed between the late seventeenth century (especially after Kant) and early 1980s, one side of this debate has more or less prevailed and gained authority. Abstract moral principle have been preferred on behalf of concrete experiences, the universal not the particular, rationality not emotions. In a Different Voice shows how women typically apply what mainstream ethics (such as deontology, utilitarianism and liberal theories) discounts. Hence these ethical traditions not only neutralize women's typical way of doing moral reasoning, they also overlook and devaluate values and accomplishments commonly associated with women. Gilligan displays additionally how the perspective of care has been regarded as a sign of moral immatureness. For feminist philosophers, Gilligan's empirical research necessitates a re–examining of traditional moral questions. As Gilligan's empirical findings reveal a statistically significant correlation between sex and moral issues and approaches, it would have been almost impossible to ignore. Silence could be interpreted as a tacit admission that women on average are less morally mature than men, and that their traditional values and challenges are morally marginal.

The classical moral questions, given a renaissance in the early 1980s, are certainly not completely disentangled. But the *approach* to many of the challenges that exercised people during the first phase are now settled. Put differently, care and feminist ethicists tend to agree nowadays that the classical moral questions must be rephrased. The question is not whether the moral agent is to be understood as independent and sovereign, or as connected and dependent. Our comprehension of the moral agent needs to take both these aspects into account; people are dependent and connected, sovereign and dependent. This requires a philosophical effort not only to improve several theories, but to advance new concepts in moral philosophy. Developing a new concept of autonomy and moral agency, for instance, is an important and ongoing task for carers ethicists. The same goes for reason and emotions, and the question is not about founding an ethics solely on emotion or "pure reason". A moral agent has feelings, as well as intelligence, and an adequate ethical theory needs to take both into account. Reason and emotions are interwoven, the resulting fabric important to examine in a moral reasoning sense. We are on the verge of a new understanding of the emotions; no more are they relegated to subjective, egoistic or altruistic impulses, they are considered to be stable dispositions and character traits developed over time. Emotions are not simply subjective (as in relativistic). Compassion, for instance, is as intersubjectively accessible as an abstract formulation—be it the categorical imperative or the minimax approach.

A metaperspective on the ethics of care reveals how this approach is both a characteristic methodological feature of the theory, a source of innovation and provocation. Indeed, it bears the stamp of human ambiguity. We are free and dependent, we have feelings as well as reason, our world consists of personal as well as public challenges. Seeing things in this way gives us space to test new ways of understanding moral issues and moral concepts. Now, attempts have been made before to base ethics on an acknowledgement of human situation as equivocal. Simone de Beauvoir's *The Ethics of Ambiguity* is a case in point. In this book, however, I have examined the ethics of care with Gilligan's articulation as a point of departure, what I conceive to be its potentials and problems. Outstanding is its general approach towards ethics; its strong resistance to dichotomous thinking, and the prevalence of binary moral categories. It challenges therefore a tendency in traditional moral theory to depict and define its subject matter by way of binary classification.

One example is how traditional moral theory conceptualizes moral agents, and also their motives and deeds: Agents are either independent or dependent; their motivation is either egoistic or altruistic; and their actions are seen as being based on reason or emotions. An act is either right or wrong, good or bad. One objection to the ethics of care could be that it relativizes categories such as right and wrong and good and bad. This objection is wrong, however. Lying at the heart of the concept of care and, consequently, of this particular ethical approach, is the ethical injunction not to harm and to promote the well–being and flourishing of others. There is thus an attempt to reconcile what are often regarded as two conflicting principles, one of noninterference and one of active participation. What is more, the agent is required to adjust the injunction to the particular context.

The ethics of care's anti–dichotomous approach inspires critical reflection on the very construction of normative theories. Moral conceptions are constitutive instruments for moral reflections. Moral reflection requires a moral vocabulary, but this vocabulary contains ideals, assumptions and standards that influence our way of asking as well as answering questions. Questioning a particular moral vocabulary implies to the ability to discern which of an agent's particulars are given relevance and which are consequently ignored. Together with bringing to light both neglected and unarticulated ethical issues, and the analysis of the profound moral significance of care in relationships, I take the anti–dichotomous approach to ethics and moral philosophy as one of the ethics of cares most significant contributions to moral theory. It is one of the meta–ethical insights that can be drawn from Gilligan's empirical research. Gilligan also demonstrates the important relationship between moral psychology and moral philosophy: Not only do they share a common history, moral development psychology explores conditions relevant to moral theory such as cognitive abilities, development of concern for self and others, experiences of vulnerability and injuries, and conditions for growth and flourishing. As moral theory is concerned with justifying what morally ought to be done, it needs, as I see it, to pay attention to research on human capacities—if the recommendations of normative theories are to be taken as credible.

It also opens the way for philosophical advances. As moral reflections cannot take place without a moral vocabulary, the rejected concepts must somehow be replaced. By overcoming traditional dichotomies the ethics of care contributes to alter alternative analytical categories. Take, for instance, Gilligan's concept of a connected self. From the perspective of what I have termed the relational ontology of the ethics of care, a moral agent is not, and ought not to try to become, totally independent. But although the connected self is obviously interdependent, it upholds a border between itself and others. It is a related self, but not a subordinated self. The concept of the connected self conceptualizes anthropological assumptions and establishes a central idea—that interpersonal relationships are an indispensable part of moral life. Also, the concept of the connected self links the moral significance of relationships with considerations of, for instance, moral choices. Moral dilemmas are conceptualized as first and foremost concerning an agent's relationships with others. The agent's moral challenge does not primarily consist in finding an abstract way of justifying her actions, but obtaining the best possible solutions for all concerned. Such solutions must nevertheless not be self–destructive for the carer, as the anti–dichotomous approach is at play also when solving moral problems: Concern for self as for others needs to be part of the equation. One way of overcoming the antagonism of concern for self and for others then, is to introduce an alternative concept of self, i.e., the connected self, a concept able to supplant the dichotomous view of the moral agent as either autonomous or heteronomous and pursuing either egotistic or altruistic goals. It is also able to supplant the view that the only way of finding the morally right action in a particular context is by deducing it from a set of pre–established premises. Harmonizing opposites is also a constitutive feature of the concept of mature care. Mature care entails the ability to balance between selfishness and selflessness. This comprehension of care is confronting the dual categories of egoism and altruism, of care and justice. Furthermore, the concept of co–feeling challenges the traditional division between reason and emotion, and the understandings of the nature of relationships also question the traditional way of demarking a public from a private sphere. Comprehending the ethics of care in this way demarks it from other ethical traditions, including those based on benevolence and charity. By addressing our proclivity for binary classification in moral philosophy, we are able to rethink traditional opposites such as those of self and other, care and justice, egoism and altruism, private and public.

In the first phase of the development of the ethics of care, its main focus was on relationships in the private sphere. Hence there was the concern that the agent's broader moral commitments may go by the board. But, as argued, the elaborating of care and relationship is not identical with denying that our commitment ought not to be extended beyond the inner sanctum of moral life. Caring for our related others is what I have termed thick care, but there is also thin care. Thin care is what is performed in the outer circles; towards those we do not know personally or have an established relationship with. Gilligan does not elaborate on thin care, but her theories and findings are, as she herself has suggested, a basis upon which to generate new theories. Indeed, this has happened.

The ethics of care is not only an ethical perspective on personal relationships and certain professions; it is valid for politicians, groups and organizations. In order to understand how the care perspective can be extended this way, we once more have to address how we envisage the moral agent. A carer is not simply a provider working single handedly. Nor are individuals the only recipients of care. Care can be given and received collectively. Altering how we think of carer and cared–for is one step towards expanding the scope of the ethics of care. It widens the area of application. In what follows, I address (a few) aspects of what is termed the socializing and globalizing of care. In doing so I highlight what I take to be some of the social and political implications of the ethics of care.

The Second Phase—Socializing Care

In 1993 Joan Tronto published *Moral Boundaries: A Political Argument for an Ethics of Care*. Tronto argues with others that the ethics of care has significant political implications in addition to moral ones. What would happen, Tronto asks, if the core values of the ethics of care such as compassion, collaboration, responsibility and attention towards needs became the main values for political thinking and practice. It would, she says, defy the traditional borders between ethics and politics, between the private and the public. These demarcations have concealed the ethical and political implications of private caring as defining care as a private concern upholds the privilege position of certain groups (Tronto 1993:61–63). For many caregivers, private caring is a heavy emotional, physical, social and economical burden. A burden which renders political activity, a career and participation in the community difficult, and sometimes impossible. A heavy workload will restrict the carer's autonomy and opportunities. This is one reason why domestic care is a political matter.

Expanding the scope of the ethics of care beyond the domestic sphere has implications for the philosophical treatment of care. By moving from the domestic to public domain, the ethics of care also challenges the essentialist–naturalist debate concerned to determine whether care is based on a pure and uncorrupted female voice, or conveys instead the voice of subordinated women in a patriarchal society. If responsibility for care can be shared, caring is not determined by biological or psychological disposition, but by situation. Defenders of the socializing theory encourage care ethicists to stop talking about "women's voice", and promote the uptake of values traditionally associated with women, by the public sphere as gender–neutral, common values (Hamington and Miller 2006).

Socializing care represents an ethical perspective on public politics and an application of this ethical theory. Socializing can manifest itself through values upheld by the public as a guide to behavior. One consequence of re–siting care, the ideal as well as the work, in the public sphere is the un–gendering of this value and work. Another implication is that care no longer remains a private and marginalized concern, either in political or moral thinking and action. The need for care becomes visible, and, hopefully, care–work distributed more justly (Hamington and Miller 2006:xiii–xiv).

How does the socializing of care take place? We can answer this by revisiting the theory's relational ontology. Comprehending society as relational, as dependent on interdependence, cooperation and dialogue, plays down a theory of society made up of individual right holders, constantly competing to maximize self–interest. What is needed in order to interact in the public domain cannot be expressed through or defined by individual rights. People are embedded in relationship networks where reciprocal care, mutual trust, attention and response are as crucial to public life as to government policy (Held 2006:158). Lack of care is as harmful in public as in private relationships. Socializing care, then, means to protect and promote values and behavior based on the ethics of care, and argue that they are as indispensable as values and actions prescribed by justice. The need for justice is neither discounted nor dismissed, nor is competition or self–assertion. If care, however, is made a central common value, it will have implications for the way political decisions are made. Care is different to freedom and equality, because it must be adjusted to the individual's needs (Robinson 2006). Those affected by it must therefore be consulted by decision–makers. Asking what one can do for others is a core value, and in order to accommodate social needs and make reasonable priorities, participation, dialogue and engagement are required. If the ethics of care can inform political thinking and policy implementation, it will enhance public debate. The ethics of care does not favor paternalism. On the contrary, it is democratic, discursive and inclusive, also In a Different Voice: It is dialogue and cooperation Amy asks for while discussing Heinz's dilemma. Amy wants the people concerned—the druggist, the wife and Heinz—to speak with each other and agree on a course of action. It might be better than what Heinz manages to figure out on his own, relying on abstract ethical principles.

A worry concerning socializing care is that it might be (to use Zygmunt Bauman's expressions) a sign of "liquid modernity" or even "liquid love", by which he means modern individuals' shirking responsibility. Also, it might convey a demanding attitude. A response here is that the request for socializing care is a demand for consistency. A society cannot without reason assume some responsibilities and not others. Advocates of socializing care can argue that care is important for fairness and justice: It is a joint responsibility to make sure that no citizen has to provide more care than they can reasonably manage, and that getting support is not reserved to those who can pay for it.

Another objection to the socializing of care is that it seems to encourage an interference with the private sphere. Obviously, there is a connection between making the personal political—a famous slogan of the 1970s—and making care a public and political concern. A yearning to extend public control into the home is not the motivation behind socializing care. It's intention is the prevention of harm and the promotion of welfare and flourishing. In the political landscape, the political implications of adopting an ethics of care may not seem conducive to liberalism. It has more in common with a social democratic mindset. By taking care as a central value of public policy, the ethics of care suggests there is more to policy making and implementation than cost and benefit analysis. In education and health, for instance, care ethicists would not let targets and performance dictate, but care. Nel Noddings's philosophy is a pertinent example of how the ethics of care can inform education policy and professional thinking.

Another area where care obviously has a contribution to make is family politics. One must not however, mistake the values promoted through the socializing of care with conservative or traditional thinking on the family. Actually, traditional thinking on the family goes against the grain of care socialization. Traditional family ideologies tend to tie women and care together, leaving childcare to women and the domestic sphere (Brandsen 2006). The un-gendering of care that takes place when we take care to center stage serves to destabilize traditional family values which, for instance, create an expectation that the (biological) mother will be the carer. Care comprehended as a value for both women and men has radical implications for how families are organized and child custody worked out (Sevenhuijsen 1998, Pettersen 2000). It affects the image and practice of same-sex marriage (Tronto 2004; Miller 2006; Pettersen 2006). The ethics of care can, as we have seen, be applied to many areas, and it is not limited to the public sphere. The current discussion is pushing the ethics of care to the global level.

Third Phase—Globalizing Care

During the 1990s, feminists drew attention to the negative consequences of globalization on women in the global south. Many women were forced into the sex industry by economic restructuring and eradication of local markets and traditional industries. This, and other global issues, are often addressed by relativist theories such as communitarianism, postmodern, or from a liberal or cosmopolitical standpoint where just distribution and universal rights are in focus (Jagger 2005:185–200). What Gilligan identified as a moral orientation at the individual level, the justice perspective, also appears in a theory with global scope. Theories of justice have been developed both for micro and macro phenomena. Thomas Pogge has made significant contributions by enabling Rawls's theory of the just society to speak to the international community (Pogge 1989; 2002; Follesdal and Pogge 2005).

Several care philosophers, among them Fiona Robinson (2006) and Virginia Held (1995:3, 2006:154), believe in care's global potential. The ethics of care constitutes a novel and promising perspective on international relations and globalization by revealing issues that remain hidden by theories of global justice.[1] Actually, the way Gilligan described moral psychology and moral philosophy twenty-five years ago could be said of the theories of global justice with equal justification today. Agents (nation–states for instance), are typically understood as autonomous and independent. They are to be respected on the basis of rights. Rights are defined and allocated on the basis of self–interest, justice is pre–eminent in social and political arrangements, and the overall goal of which is fair distribution (Held 2006:155).

Efforts towards a just global distribution of burdens and benefits are indeed important, but also towards global issues the ethics of care shows another possible approach. The international agents are portrayed as connected and dependent, not as independent and sovereign. The ethics of care, as we should recall, springs from people's experience of concrete, and often non–voluntary asymmetrical relationships (such as between the child and parent). Also, in this theory, contextual sensitivity is considered crucial in order to make viable moral decisions. This origin makes the ethics of care particularly capable, rather than the opposite, to address international relations (Held 2006:156). A global ethics of care would take it as given that agents are embedded in a global network of relationships, that they are mutually dependent, and that they will not always have entered into such dependencies voluntarily. Environmental issues is an example. The ethics of care, with its awareness of relational dependency and asymmetry, is particularly sensitive to the global interconnectedness and inequality of international agents. As a matter of fact, the international parties are diverse in power and vulnerability: The poor countries in the global south are often more exposed, dependent, have fewer resources and powers than the affluent countries of the global north. The ethics of care has a distinct capacity to accommodate these essential features of international agents and relations, which could easily be disregarded if one insists on applying theories based on individualist and contractual ethical traditions. Its ability to see the relational, the asymmetrical and the contextual, allows it to accommodate historical and cultural differences between the agents on the global arena. This is one of its global level advantages. Furthermore, the ethics of care sees responsibility as the outcome of interaction, but also as something to be shared. It is a perfectly sensible perspective also in the global context. Let us inspect it at closer range.

Perhaps the most visible expression of globalization are the transnational corporate partnerships which pursue business opportunities across national borders and under various regulatory conditions. Together with the nation state, international monetary institutions are a major force in economic globalization, motivated by a wish for profit to expand markets. According to Fiona Robinson, some companies are becoming increasingly aware of their responsibility for the social and natural environment, and their economic and political impact. It is called *corporate social responsibility* (CSR). The question is how this responsibility should be understood. Is it a charity, an expression of altruism, or an investment in goodwill management? (Robinson 2006:173–176).

Robinson maintains that the ethics of care offers a promising view of understanding CSR. Responsibility, in this ethical theory, is understood as embedded in a network of relationships. It is not necessarily a particular individual's, nor something contained within regulated limits. It helps us approach global responsibility from a relational perspective, not one based on rights and rules. It shows that responsibility is more than protecting human rights, upholding laws and regulations. It posits our moral responsibility for each other. The more vulnerable and dependent the others are towards your actions, the greater your responsibility is. For instance, if children are deprived of care because their mothers, as a result of economic globalization, spend too much time working for a transnational cooperation, according to the ethics of care the greatest share of the responsibility would be on the company. Care of the child is not only the mother's or her family's responsibility. A care ethicist would argue that the company ought to compensate the child for the lack of a mother's care by providing, say, day-care or schools and reasonable working condition etc. (Robinson 2006:176). If not, the innocent will continue to suffer, unable to claim their interests and rights, unable to disentangle themselves from the web of relationships affected by globalization.

Seeing global activities from the relational perspective of the ethics of care alerts us to a certain type of relational consequence resulting from economic globalization, and to the most vulnerable, those whose care needs are critical, and those who carry the heaviest burdens of care–work. Care ethicists suggest that CSR should be regarded as a matter of course, not a charitable exception (Robinson 2006:177).

Visions

Both Virginia Held and Fiona Robinson are care ethicists with great visions and aspirations on behalf of the ethics of care. If the ethics of care becomes a central value in our judgments and decisions, as justice, freedom and equality often are, then decision–makers at all levels must recognize their responsibility for the vulnerable and dependent, says Robinson. Held adds that with a basis in the ethics of care, one of the most urgent policy goals will appear to be to provide children with the best possible life chances and education. The ethics of care, she says, could also affect our attitudes to international security and stability. Military power, national sovereignty and economic superiority are not the main road to security and stability. For a care ethicist the main strategy is to secure basic needs, not only among her nearest and dearest, but in all the concentric circles. This, Held emphasizes, together with cultivating good international relations (instead of hostility), recognizing interdependency (not only independency), and furthering dialogue and collaboration (rather than self–concern and sovereignty), are approaches care ethicists would support (Held 2006:159–162). Furthermore, if the ethics of care, with its focus on relations and dialogue gained greater influence, there would be fewer conflicts to solve by way of treaties or coercion, locally and globally.[2]

Another implication of viewing social and global ethical challenges through the lens of the ethics of care, is the possibility to rephrase ethical questions. Again we should recall Gilligan's Amy who refused to reduce the ethical predicament of Heinz's dilemma to a question of whether it is forbidden or permissible to steal the drug. For Amy, the ethical challenge was how to address the situation and accommodate the person's needs in the best possible way. This way of thinking could be used on social and global issues, and we shall close this book with an example of how the ethics of care can be used to rethink global issues.

Virginia Held (1993) suggests that the traditional model of the moral agent—which she terms the "autonomous–man–model"—could be replaced by a "mother–child metaphor". If we prefer more gender–neutral terminology we could borrow Nel Noddings (1984) concept of "the one-caring" and the "the cared–for". The point is that Held wishes to form a concept of the moral agent which avoids a necessary corollary of independence, which posits equality in regard to power and influence, and freedom to enter into and dissolve contracts. Held invites us to join her in a thought experiment. How would the global ethical and political questions appear if we made the mother–child dyad the paradigmatic relation for our ethical assessments? The image of the moral and political agent would appear very different from the symmetric and sovereign contract–partners often depicted in traditional thinking. The mother–child model is based on relationship, not on isolated individuals. This relationship is asymmetric, in–voluntary, and expected to persist for a long time. It is stable, cannot be (easily) exchanged, and its core value is care. Envisaging the moral agent in this way, the ethics of care presents a meta–ethical challenge to a constitutive analytical category of traditional normative thinking not only when it comes to moral theory, but also to global issues. This can be seen as a further development of the model of the relational self, identified by Gilligan in her study of girls' and women's ethical perspective. Held takes the idea of the relational self further, and asks how global issues would be comprehended if our conceptual apparatus was based on the relational ontology of the ethics of care. How to act to protect future generations, the environment and eradicate poverty would appear differently.

Poverty is an urgent global issue and a concern to liberal, contractualist ethical theory. It is also a good illustration of how the ethics of care empowers new ways of thinking. A central question is whether people in affluent countries are morally obliged to help the worst off in the global south. If we have such responsibility, how do we quantify it, how do we justify it to ourselves and to them? If we had adopted the ethics of care as our guide, we would see ourselves as caregivers, and those in poverty as the recipients of care. Whether or not we have a responsibility would not be the question. By definition, a carer has responsibility for the cared–for. And a carer would do what she could in order to make sure that those under her care are not starving (Meyers 2002: 63–64). A carer would try to eliminate the suffering of the cared–for. She would not regard caring as charity, but as issuing from her sense of moral responsibility. As in Held's mother–child metaphor, the agent would aspire to promote the independence of her wards, not make them indebted to her—either in gratitude or money. Held does not dismiss justice, autonomy etc. Her point is to demonstrate how the ethics of care can contribute to a new understanding of ethical issues. The restructuring of global problems by anchoring the ethical outlook in a relational ontology bears indeed parallels to the women in Gilligan's empirical studies who tried to redefine the dilemmas they were given.

The swift growth of the ethics of care in the last twenty–five years, from the private to the global level, is remarkable. One of the reasons for its applicability and rapid development is, I believe, the relational ontology this ethical theory rests on. Traditional ontology fails to adequately accommodate for the fact that dependency and connectedness are dominant features of human life. As to traditional epistemology, its understanding of what counts as relevant knowledge for acting morally seems to narrow. Perceiving differences between self and others, possessing contextual sensitivity are as pertinent to moral understanding as the faculty of abstraction and deduction. This applies whether we consider acting in personal relationship, or are concerned about international relations. The ethics of care provides us with conceptual alternatives when doing moral philosophy. Gilligan's research and ethical ideas probably need to be understood as challenging a traditional research paradigm—to use Thomas Kuhn's terminology—of both moral psychology and moral philosophy. As Kohlberg's research assistant in the 1970s, she became interested in what then was considered to be an anomaly, i.e., the care perspective, and started her own empirical research and theorizing. The extraordinary response to her work also fits a Kuhnian description—the critique, ignorance and even hostility have been interpreted as a defense mounted by adherents of the old research paradigm, while praise and advocacy typically come from those on the fringes of the academic world. It should not come as a surprise that such a challenge to moral philosophy comes from outside this field. According to Foucault, epistemological shifts originate at the periphery, not at the center. Looking at the recent development of the ethics of care, however, it is seems clear that it has moved from the fringes, and heads toward the center of moral attention. The fact is that the ethics of care, as voiced by the girls and women in Gilligan's research has galvanized philosophical progress as it demonstrated the necessity for moral philosophers to listen to findings from other fields, to scrutinize established analytical categories, assumptions and priorities and to investigate their own prejudices in order to arrive more perfectly, at what we morally ought to do—for our nearest and dearest as well as the distant stranger.

Notes

1. Within the discipline of international relations, interaction between agents in the international community is analyzed. The agents are states, governmental—and non–governmental organization and transnational corporations. There are many angels of incidence toward this area of interaction, for instance liberalism, Marxism critical theory, constructivism and poststructuralist. The ability of the international community to cooperate—or lack of such—is significant for important issues concerning environmental questions, wars, sex–industry, poverty, terrorism to mention a few.

2. This does not mean, Held points out that, the need for international law and forces would completely evaporate. Sometimes coercion is necessary, but hopefully it could be reduced.

Bibliography

Agontio, R. (1977). (ed.). *History of Ideas on Women*. New York, Perigee.

Annas, J. (1988). "Self-love in Aristotle". *The Southern Journal of Philosophy* 27, Supplement: 1–18.

Annas, J. (1993). *The Morality of Happiness*. Oxford: Oxford University Press.

Aquinas, T. (1989). *Summa Theologiæ*. Translated and edited by T. McDermott, Westminster, Maryland, Christian Classics.

Ariansen, P. (2000). "Dyr, omsorg og rettferdighet". In *Dyreetikk*, F. Føllesdal (ed.), Bergen: Fagbokforlaget.

Aristotle. (1995). *Nicomachean Ethics*. Translated by T. Irwin. Indianapolis/Cambridge: Hackett Publishing Company.

Baron, M. W., Pettit, P. & Slote, M. (1987). *Three Methods of Ethics: A Debate*. Oxford: Blackwell.

Bartky, S. L. (1997). "Sympathy and Solidarity. On a Tightrope with Scheler". In *Feministis Rethink the Self*, D. T. Meyers (ed.). Colorado and Oxford: Westview Press, 177–196.

Bartlett, E. A. (1992). "Beyond Either/Or: Justice and Care in the Ethics of Albert Camus". In *Explorations in Feminist Ethics. Theory and Practice*, E. B. Cole (ed.). Indianapolis: Indiana University Press, 82–88.

Baier, A. (1986). "Trust and Antitrust". In *Ethics* no. 96:231–260.

Baier, A. (1987). "Hume's Account of Social Artifice—Its Origin and Originality". In *Ethics*, vol. 98, no. 4:757–778.

Baier, A. (1993a). "Trust and Distrust of Moral Theorists". In Winkler E. R. og Coombs J. R. (eds.) *Applied Ethics: A Reader*. Oxford Blackwell, 131–142.

Baier, A. C. (1993). "What Do Women Want in a Moral Theory?" In *An Ethics of Care. Feminist and Interdisciplinary Perspectives*, M. J. Larrabee (ed.). New York: Routledge, 19–32.

Baumann, Z. (1993). *Postmodern Ethics*. Oxford: Blackwell.

Baune, Ø. (1998). "Hvorfor er kasuistisk moral ikke til å komme forbi? Hva er kasuistikk? Om moralsk læring og refleksjon i tilknytning til forbilder og eksempler". In *Skriftserie for HF's etikkseminar*, J. Wetlesen (ed.). Oslo, Universitetet i Oslo. Bind 3, 40–79.

Beauchamp, T. L. (1991) *Philosophical Ethics: An Introduction to Moral Philosophy*. New York: McGraw-Hill.

Beauvoir de, S. (1987). "Women and Creativity". In Moi, T (ed.) *French Feminist Thought*. Oxford: Basil Blackwell, 17–32.

Beauvoir de, S. (2000). *Det annet kjønn*. Oslo: Pax Forlag.

Benhabib, S. (1987). "The Generalized and the Concrete Other. The Kohlberg-Gilligan Controversy and Moral Theory". In *Women and Moral Theory*, E. F. Kittay, & D. T. Meyers (eds.). Totowa: Rowman & Littlefield, 154–177.

Benhabib, S. (1994). *Autonomi och gemenskap. Kommunikativ etik, feminism och postmodernism*. Göteborg. Daidalos.

Bennett, J. (1974). "The Conscience of Huckleberry Finn". In *Philosophy*, vol. 49:123–134.

Bernstein, E. & Gilligan, C. (1990). "Unfairness and Not Listening". In *Making Connections. The Relational Worlds of Adolescent Girls at Emma Willard School*, C. Gilligan, N. P. Lyons & T. J. Hanmer. Cambridge: Harvard University Press, 147–161.

Blum, L., Homiak, M., Housman, J. & Scheman, N. (1976). "Altruism and Women's Oppression". In *Women and Philosophy*, C. C. W. Gould & W. Marx (eds.). New York, 222–243.

Blum, L. (1980). *Friendship, Altruism and Morality*. London: Routledge & Kegan Paul.

Blum, L. (1993). "Gilligan and Kohlberg: Implications for Moral Theory". In *An Ethic of Care: Feminist and Interdisciplinary Perspectives*, M. J. Larrabee (ed.). New York: Routledge, 49–68.

Blum, L. (1994). *Moral Perception and Particularity*. Cambridge: Cambridge University Press.

Bok, S. (2000): "Truthfulness and Deceit". A Grace Tanner Lecture. Center for Human Values, Utha: Southern Utha University Press.

Boyd, D. R. (1990). "The Study of Moral Development: A Bridge over 'Is-Ought' Gap". In *The Moral Domain. Essays in the Ongoing Discussion between Philosophy and the Social Science*, T. E. Wren (ed.). Cambridge, Mass.: The MIT Press, 129–150.

Brabeck, M. (1993). "Moral Judgement: Theory and Research on Differences between Males and Females". In *An Ethic of Care: Feminist and Interdisciplinary Perspectives*, M. J. Larrabbe (ed.). New York: Routledge, 33–48.

Brandsen, C. 2006. "A Public Ethics of Care: Implications for Long-Term Care". In Hamington, Maurice & Miller, Doroty C. (eds.) *Socializing Care. Feminist Ethics and Public Issues*. Lanham: Rowman &Littlefield Publishers, Inc.

Brison, Susan. 2000. "Outliving Oneself". In *Feminist Theory. A Philosophical Anthology*. Oxford: Blackwell Publishing, p. 365–376.

Broadie, S. (1991). *Ethics with Aristotle*. New York: Oxford University Press.

Brown, L. M & Gilligan, C. (1992). *Meeting at the Crossroads: Women's Psychology and Girls' Development*. London: Harvard University Press.

Butler, Judith. 1990. *Gender Trouble: Feminism and the Subversion of Identity*. New York: Routledge.

Chodorow, N. (1978). *The Reproduction of Mothering. Psychoanalysis and the Sociology of Gender*. Berkeley: University of California Press.

Coates, J. (1986). *Women, Men and Language: A Sociolinguistic Account of Sex Differences in Language*. London: Longman.

Colby, A. & Kohlberg, L. (1987). *The Measurement of Moral Judgment*. Cambridge: Cambridge University Press.

Cooper, J. M. (1980) "Aristotle on Friendship". In *Essays on Aristotle's Ethics*, O. A. Rorty (ed.). Berkley: University of California Press, 301–340.

Dalmiya, V. (2002). "Why Should a Knower Care?" In *Hypatia*, vol. 17, no.1:34–51.

Dancy, J. (1992). "Caring about Justice". In *Philosophy* 67, no.262:447–466.

Davis, N. A. 1993. "Contemporary Deontology". In Singer, P. (red.), *Blackwell Companion to Philosophy: A Companion to Ethics*, Oxford: Blackwell Publishers, 205–218.

Den Uyl, D. J. (1993). "The Right to Welfare and the Virtue of Charity". In *Altruism*, E. F. Paul, F. D. Miller Jr. & P. Jeffert (eds.). Cambridge: Cambridge University Press, 166–224.

Dillon, R. S. (1992). "Care and Respect". In *Explorations in Feminist Ethics: Theory and Practice*, B. Cole & Coultrap-McQuin (eds.). Indianapolis: Indiana University Press, 69–81.

Dreyfus, Hubert L. & Dreyfus, Stuart E., with Athanasiou, Tom. 1988. *Mind over machine*. New York: Free Press.

Engelstad, F., Grenness, C. E., Kalleberg, R. & Malnes, R. (1998). *Samfunn og vitenskap: samfunnsfagenes fremvekst, oppvekst og arbeidsmåter*. Oslo: adNotam Gyldendal.

Ericsson, K. (1998). "Sexual Harassment and the Genderization of Work". In *Is there a Nordic Feminism?*, D. Fehr, A. G. Jónasdottir & B. Rosenbeck (eds.). London: UCL Press, 176–197.

Fehr, D. (1997). "Likhet og relevant forskjell i et feministisk og pragmatisk perspektiv". In *Likeverd og forskjell - en etisk intuisjon og dens grenser*, J. Wetlesen, (ed.). Oslo, Universitetet i Oslo.

Flanagan, O. & Jackson, K. (1993). "Justice, Care and Gender". In *An Ethics of Care. Feminist and Interdisciplinary Perspectives*, M. J. Larrabee (ed.). New York: Routledge, 69–84.

Follesdal, Andreas & Pogge, Thomas. 2005. *Real World Justice: Grounds, Principles, Human Rights and Social Institutions*. Dordrecht: Springer.

Freud, S. (1977). *Nytt i psykoanalysen*. Oslo, Gyldendal Norsk forlag.

Friedman, M. (1993). "Beyond Caring: The De-Moralization of Gender". In *An Ethics of Care. Feminist and Interdisciplinary Perspectives*, M. J. Larrabee (ed.). New York: Routledge, 258–271.

Friedman, M. (2004). "Autonomy, Social Disruption, and Women". In *Feminist Theory. A Philosophical Anthology* A. E. Cudd and R. O. Andreasen (eds.), Oxford: Blackwell Publishing, 339–351.

Gadamer, H. G. (1975). Truth and Method. London: Sheed & Ward.

Gilligan, C. & Field Belenky, M. (1980). "A Naturalistic Study of Abortion Decisions". In *New Directions for Child Development*, vol. 7: 69–90.

Gilligan, C. (1982) *In a Different Voice. Psychological Theory and Women's Development*. Cambridge, Mass.: Harvard University Press, 33rd. edition.

Gilligan, C. (1984) "The Conquistador and the Dark Continent: Reflections on the Psychology of Love". In *Dædalus*, vol. 113:75–95.

Gilligan, C. (1987). "Moral Orientation and Moral Development". In *Women and Moral Theory*, E. F. Kittay. & D. T. Meyers (eds.). Totowa: Rowman & Littlefield, 19–33.

Gilligan, C., Ward, J. V., McLean, J., Taylor, & Bardige, W. B. (eds.) (1988). *Mapping the Moral Domain*. Cambridge, Mass.: Harvard University Press.

Gilligan, C. (1988). "Moral Development". In *The Modern American College: Responding to the New Realities of Diverse Students and a Changing Society*, A. W. Chickering & Associates. San Francisco: Jossey-Bass Publishers, 139–157.

Gilligan, C., Lyons, N. P. & Hanmer, T. J. (1990). *Making Connections: The Relational Worlds of Adolescent Girls at Emma Willard School*. Cambridge, Mass.: Harvard University Press.

Gilligan, C. (1990). "Teaching Shakespeare's Sisters: Notes from the Underground of Female Adolescence". In *Making Connections: The Relational Worlds of Adolescent Girls at Emma Willard School*, C. Gilligan, N. P. Lyons & T. Hanmer. Cambridge, Mass.: Harvard University Press, 6–29.

Gilligan, C. (1991). "Women's Psychological Development: Implications for Psychotherapy". In *Women, Girls & Psychotherapy: Reframing Resistance*, C. Gilligan, A. G. Rogers. & D. L.Tolman. New York: Haworth Press, 5–31.

Gilligan, C. (1993). "Reply to Critcs". In *An Ethic of Care. Feminist and Interdisciplinary Perspectives*, M. J. Larrabee, (ed.). New York: Routledge, 207–214.

Gilligan, C., Sullivan, A. M. & Taylor, J. (1995). *Between Voice and Silence. Women and Girls, Race and Relationship*. Cambridge, Mass.: Harvard University Press.

Gilligan, C. (1996). "The Centrality of Relationship in Human Development: A Puzzle, Some Evidence, and a Theory". In *Development and Vulnerability in Close Relationships*, N. J. Mahwah & L. Erlbaum (eds.), 237–261.

Gilligan, C. (2000) "The War against Boys: Carol Gilligan et al. versus Christina Hoff Sommers". In *The Atlantic Monthly*. Digital Version. 286, No. 2, August. [Cited 08.01.02]. Available from: http://www.theatlantic.com/issues/2000/08/letters.htm.

Gilligan, C. (2002). *The Birth of Pleasure. A New Map of Love*. London: Chatto & Windus.

Goodin, R. E. (1985). *Protecting the Vulnerable. A Reanalysis of Our Social Responsibilities*. Chicago: The University of Chicago Press.

Goodin, R. E. (1988). "What is so Special About Our Fellow Countrymen?". In *Ethics*, vol. 98: 663–686.

Greer, Germaine. 1979. *The Obstacle Race: The Fortunes of Women Painters and their Work*. London: Secker & Warburg.

Grimshaw, Jean. 1991. "The Idea of a Female Ethics". In Singer P. (ed.): *Blackwell Companion to Ethics*. Oxford: Blackwell, p. 491–499.

Grimshaw, Jean. 2005. "autonomy and Identity in Feminist Thinking". In *Feminist Theory: A Philosophical Anthology* (ed.) Cudd, Ann E. and Andreasen, Robin O., Malden, Mass.: Blackwell.

Habermas, J. (1990). "Justice and Solidarity: On the Discussion Concerning Stage 6". In *The Moral Domain. Essays in the Ongoing Discussion between Philosophy and the Social Science*, T. E. Wren (ed.), Cambridge, Mass.: The MIT Press, 224–251.

Hamington, Maurice & Miller, Doroty C. (eds.) 2006. *Socializing Care. Feminist Ethics and Public Issues*. Landham: Roman & Littlefield Publishers, Inc.

Harding, S. (1986). *The Science Question in Feminism*. Ithaca, N.Y: Cornell University Press.

Hare, R. M. (1991). "Universal Prescriptivism". In *A Companion to Ethics*, ed. P. Singer. Oxford: Blackwell, 451–463.

Heinämaa, S. (2003). "The body as instrument and as expression". In Claudia Card (ed.). *The Cambridge Companion to Simone de Beauvoir*. Cambridge: Cambridge University Press, 66–86.

Hekman, S. (1995). *Moral Voices, Moral Selves: Carol Gilligan and feminist moral theory*. Cambridge: Polity; University Park: Penn State Press.

Held, V. (1993). *Feminist Morality: Transforming Culture, Society, and Politics*. Chicago: University of Chicago Press.

Held, V. (ed.) (1995). *Justice and Care. Essential Readings in Feminist Ethics*. Colorado: Westview Press.

Held, V. (1998): "Feminist Transformations of Moral Theory". In *Ethics: The Big Question*. Oxford: Blackwell, 331–345.

Held, V. 2006. *The Ethics of Care. Personal, Political, and Global*. New York: Oxford University Press.

Hem, M. H., Heggen. K. & Ruyter, K. (2007). "Questionable Requirement for Consent in Observational Research in Psychiatry" in *Nursing Ethics*. 2007 (14).

Henriksen, J. O. & Vetlesen, A. J. (1997). *Nærhet og distanse*. Oslo: adNotam Gyldendal.

Hertzberg, L. (1988). "On the Attitude of Trust". In *Inquiry* nr. 31:307–322.

Heyd, D. (1982): *Supererogation: Its Status in Ethical Theory*. Cambridge: Cambridge University Press.

Hinman, L. M. (1997). *Ethics: A Pluralistic Appraoch to Moral Theory*, Webpage. [Cited 08.01.02]. Available at: http://ethics.acusd.edu/e2/ChapterTen.html#_Toc404470500.

Hoagland, S. L. (1991). "Some Thoughts about Caring". In *Feminist Ethics*, ed. C. Card. Kansas: University Press of Kansas, 246–263.

Hornsby, J., Frazer, E. & Lovibond, S. (eds.), (1992). *Ethics: A Feminist Reader*. Oxford: Blackwell.

Huff, C. (2002). *Introduction to Psychology*. Webpage. [Cited 08.01.02]. Available at: http://www.stolaf.edu/people/huff/classes/handbook/Gilligan.html.

Hume, D. A (1911). *Treatise of Human Nature*. Reprinted in "Past Masters", British Philosophy Database: "The text was drawn from the 1911 Everyman's Library Edition. The text was carefully checked against the 1886 Green and Grose edition. Page numbers which identify each folio of the Treatise refer to page numbers of the correlative passage in the Second Edition of Nidditch".

Hume, D. (1898). *An Enquiry Concerning the Principles of Morals*. Reprinted in "Past Masters", British Philosophy Database: "The text was drawn from the 1898 Green and Grose, but proofread against 1854 Works, with word discrepancies checked against the 1758 Hume. Two page numbers identify each folio: the first, labeled p., refers to the page number of the correlative passage in the Third Edition of the Nidditch Enquiries; the second, labeled gp., refers to the page number in Green and Grose".

Irigaray, Luce. 1984. *Etique de la difference sexuelle*, Minuit, Paris.

Iser, W. (1978). *The Act of Reading: A Theory of Aesthetic Response*. Baltimore: Johns Hopkins University Press.

Jagger, A. (1998). "Toward a Feminist Conception of Moral Reasoning". In *Ethics: The Big Questions*, ed. J .P. Sterba. Oxford. Blackwell, 356–374.

Jagger, A. (2004). "Globalizing Femininst Ethics". In C. Calhoun (ed.), *Setting the Moral Compass*. New York: Oxford University Press, 233–255.

Jagger, A. (2005). "Global Responsibility and Western Feminism". In Barbara S. Andrew, B. S., Keller, J & Schwartzman, L. H. (eds.) *Feminist Interventions in Ethics and Politics*. Lanham: Rowman & Littlefield, s. 185–200.

Jamieson, D. (1991). "Method and Moral Theory". In *A Companion to Ethics*, ed. P. Singer. Oxford: Blackwell Reference, 476–487.

Jodalen, H. V. & Vetlesen, A. J. (1997). *Closeness. An Ethics*. Oslo: Scandinavian University Press.

Jonas, H. (1984). *The Imperative of Responsibility in Search of an Ethics for the Technological Age*. Chicago: University of Chicago Press.

Juritzen, T. I. & Heggen, K. (2006). "Omsorgsmakt". In *Sosiologi i dag*. Årgang 36, nr. 3/2006, s. 61–80.

Kant, I. (1977) "Observation on the Feelings of the Beautiful and the Sumblime". In *History of the Ideas on Women*, R. Agonito (ed.). New York: Perigee, 129–146.

Kant, I. (1992). *Grounding for the Metaphysics of Morals*. In *Classics of Moral and Political Theory*, ed. M. L. Indianapolis: Hackett Publishing Company, 991–1041.

Kant, I. (1996). *The Metaphysics of Morals.* Cambridge: Cambridge University Press.

Kittay, E. F. & Meyers, D. T. (1989). *Women and Moral Theory.* Totowa, Rowman & Littlefield.

Kittay, E. F. (1997). "Human Dependency and Rawlisan Equality". In *Feminists Rethink the Self*, ed. D. T. Meyers. Colorado and Oxford: Westview Press, 219–266.

Kohlberg, L. (1981). *Essays on Moral Development. The Philosophy of Moral Development.* San Francisco: Harper & Row.

Kohlberg L., Levine, C. & Hewer, A. (1983). *Moral Stages: A Current Formulation and a Response to Critics.* Basel: Karger.

Kohlberg, L. (1984). *Essays on Moral Development. The Psychology of Moral Development.* San Francisco: Harper & Row.

Kohlberg, L., Boyd. D. R. & Levine, C. (1990). "The Return of Stage 6. Its Principle and Moral Point of View". In *The Moral Domain. Essays in the Ongoing Discussion Between Philosophy and the Social Science*, ed. T. E. Wren. Cambridge, Mass.: The MIT Press, 151–182.

Kollontay, Alexandra. 1981. *A Great Love.* London: Virago Press.

Kourany, J. A., Sterba, J. P., Tong, R. (eds.) 1993. *Feminist Philosophy. Problems, Theories and Applications.* New Jersey, Harvester Wheatsheaf.

Kraut, R. (1988). "Comments on Julia Annas' "Self-love in Aristotle". In *The Southern Journal of Philosophy* 27, Supplement, 19–23.

Kuhse, H. (1997). *Caring: Nurses, Women and Ethics.* Cornwall: Blackwell.

Lafollette, H. (1991). "Personal Relationships". In *A Companion to Ethics*, ed. P. Singer. Oxford: Blackwell.

Larrabee, M. J. (1993). "Gender and Moral Development: A Challenge for Feminist Theory". In *An Ethic of Care: Feminist and Interdisciplinary Perspective*, M. J. Larrabee (ed.). New York: Routledge, 3–16.

Levinas, E. (1996). "Ethics as First Philosophy". In *The Continental Philosophy Reader*, ed. R. Kearney & M. Rainwater. London & New York: Routledge, 124–135.

Li, C. (1994). "The Confucian Concept of Jen and the Feminist Ethics of Care: A Comparative Study" in *Hypatia* vol. 9, no.1:70–89.

Lloyd, G.(1995). *Mannlig og kvinnelig i vestens filosofihistorie.* Oslo. Cappelen Akademiske Forlag.

Lyons, N. P. (1988). "Two Perspectives: On Self, Relationships and Morality". In *Mapping the Moral Domain. A Contribution of Women's Thinking to Psycological Theory and Education*, C. Gilligan, J. V. Ward, J. M. Taylor, & W. B. Bardige (eds.). Cambridge, Mass.: Harvard University Press, 21–48.

Lyons, N. P. (1990). "Listening to Voices We have not Heard. Emma Willard Girl's Ideas about Self, Relationships, and Morality". In *Making Connections: The Relational Worlds of Adolescent Girls at Emma Willard School*, C. Gilligan, N. P. Lyons, & T. J. Hanmer (eds.). Cambridge, Mass.: Harvard University Press, 30–72.

Lyons, N. P., Salonstall, J. F. & Hanmer, T. (1990). "Competencies and Visions. Emma Willard Girls Talk about Being Leaders". In *Making Connections: The Rela-*

tional Worlds of Adolescent Girls at Emma Willard School, C. Gilligan, N.P. Lyons & T. J. Hanmer. Cambridge, Mass.: Harvard University Press, 183–214.

Løgstrup, K.E. (1997). "On Trust". In *Closeness. An Ethics*, H. Jodalen & A. J. Vetlesen (eds.). Oslo: Scandinavian University Press, 71–89.

Løgstrup, K. E. (1999). *Den etiske fordring*. Oslo: Cappelen.

MacKinnon. 1994. Quoted in Benhabib, Seyla "From Identity Politics to Social Feminism: A Plea for the Nineties. [Available at http://www.ed.uiuc.edu/eps/PES-Yearbook/94_docs/BENHABIB.HTM#fn3] [Cited 06.01.08. TP]

Martinsen, K. (1989). *Omsorg, sykepleie og medinsin historisk-filosofiske essays*. Oslo: Tano.

Martinsen, K. (2000). *Øyet og kallet*. Bergen: Fagbokforlaget.

Mayeroff, M. (1972). *On Caring*. New York: Harper & Row.

Meyers, D. T. (1997). "Emotion and Heterodox Moral Perception". In *Feminists Rethink the Self*. D. T. Meyers (ed.). Boulder, Colorado: Westview Press, 197–218.

Michaeli, I. (1995). *Omsorg och rättvisa - ett dilemma*. Gävle, Meyers.

Miller, D. (2006). "The Potential of Same–Sex Marriage for Restructuring Care and Citizenship". I Hamington, Maurice & Miller, Dorothy C. (eds.) *Socializing Care. Feminist Ethics and Public Issues*. Landham: Rowman & Littlefield Publishers, Inc.

Miller, D. C. 2005. "A Kantian Ethic of Care"? In *Feminist interventions in ethics and politics: feminist ethics and social theory* (eds.) Barbara S. Andrew, Jean Clare Keller & Lisa H. Schwartzman. Lanham; Rowman & Littlefield Publishers, Inc., 160–180.

Moi, T. (1998) *Hva er en kvinne?Kjønn og kropp i feministisk teori*. Oslo: Gyldendal.

Moody-Adams, M. M. (1991). "Gender and the Complexity of Moral Voices". In *Feminist Ethic*, C. Card (ed.). Kansas: University Press of Kansas, 195–212.

Moore, G. E. (1993). *Principia Ethica*. Cambridge: Cambridge University Press.

Nagel, T. (1978). *The Possibility of Altruism*. Princeton: Princeton University Press.

Nagel, T. (1986). *The View from Nowhere*. New York: Oxford University Press.

Nagel, T. (1991). "Autonomy and Deontology". In *Consequentialism and its Critics*, S. Scheffler (ed.). Oxford: Oxford University Press.

Nicholson, L. J. (1993). "Women, Morality and History". In *An Ethic of Care. Feminist and Interdisciplinary Perspectives*, M. J. Larrabee (ed.). New York: Routledge, 87–101.

Noddings, N. (1984). *Caring: A Feminine Approach to Ethics and Moral Education*. Berkeley: University of California Press.

Noddings, N. (1989). *Women and Evil*. Berkeley: University of California Press.

Noddings, N. (2006). *Critical Lessons. What Our Schools Should Teach*. New York: Cambridge University Presss.

Nortvedt, P. (1996). *Sensitive Judgment. Nursing, Moral Philosophy and an Ethics of Care*. Otta, Tano Aschehoug.

Nunner-Winkler, G. (1990). "Moral Relativism and Strict Universalism". In *The Moral Domain. Essays in the Ongoing Discussion between Philosophy and the Social Sciences*, T. E. Wren (ed.). Cambridge, Mass.: The MIT Press, 109–126.

Nussbaum, M. C. (1997). "Love and the Moral Point of View". In *Closeness. An Ethics*, H. V. Jodalen & A. J. Vetlesen (eds.) Oslo: Scandinavian University Press, 90–128.

Okin, S. M. (1989). *Justice, Gender, and the Family*. New York: Basic Books.

O'Neill, O. (1991). "Kantian Ethics". In *A Companion to Ethics*, P. Singer (ed.). Oxford: Blackwell, 175–185.

O'Neill, O. (1996). *Towards Justice and Virtue. A Constructive Account of Practical Reasoning*. Cambridge: Cambridge University Press.

Outka, G. (1972). *Agape: An Ethical Analysis*. New Haven: Yale University Press.

Pettersen, T. 1996. "Forskjell og likeverd". In Sæter. Gjertrud (red.) *HUN – en antologi om kunnskap fra kvinners liv*. Spillerom: Oslo 1996. s. 135–150.

Pettersen, T. (2000a, 28. 01) "Barnas beste og likestilling". In *Dagbladet* [Oslo]

Pettersen, T. (2000b, 14. 02) "Delt omsorg - til foreldrenes beste?" In *Dagbladet* [Oslo]

Pettersen, T. (2003). "Mitt eller ditt barn? Om omsorgsetikk og fattigdomsproblemet". In *Arr. Idéhistorisk tidsskrift* nr. ?, 2003, 75–83.

Pettersen, T. (2006a). "Vennskap og kunnskap. Læring i et aristotelisk perspektiv" i Bostad, I. & Pettersen, T. (red.) *Dialog og danning. Det filosofiske grunnlaget for læring*. Oslo: Scandinavian Academic Press. s. 65–86.

Pettersen, T. (2006b). "Moralsk frihet og situasjon: Simone de Beauvoir". In *Norsk filosofisk tidsskrift*, vol. 41, nr. 4, s. 284–298.

Pettersen, T. (2006c). "Omsorg som etisk teori". in *Norsk filosofisk tidsskrift*, nr. 2/2006, vol. 41, Oslo: Universitetsforlaget, s. 151–163.

Pettersen, T. (2006d). "Hva er et ekteskap?" Oslo: Barne- og likestillingsdepartementet.

Pierce, C. (1991). "Postmodernism and Other Skepticisms". In *Feminist Ethics*, C. Card (ed.). Kansas: University Press of Kansas, 60–77.

Pidgen, C. (1991). "Naturalism". In *A Companion to Ethics*. P. Singer (ed.). Oxford: Blackwell, 421–431.

Pogge, T. (1989). *Realizing Rawls*. Ithaca: Cornell University Press.

Pogge, W. T. (1989). "The Categorical Imperative". In *Grundlegung zur Metaphysik der Sitten. Ein kooperativer Kommentar*, H. Otfried (ed.). Frankfurt am Main: Vittorio Klostermann GmbH.

Pogge, W. T. (1998). "The Bounds of Nationalism". In *Rethinking Nationalism, Canadian Journal of Philosophy*, Supplementary Volume 22, J. Couture et al. (eds.). Calgary: University of Calgary Press, 463–504.

Pogge, T. (2002). *World Poverty and Human Rights*. Cambridge: Polity.

Puka, B. (1990). "The Majesty and Mystery of Kohlberg's Stage 6". In *The Moral Domain. Essays in the Ongoing Discussion between Philosophy and the Social Science*, T. E. Wren (ed.). Cambridge, Mass.: The MIT Press, 182–223.

Puka, B. (1993). "The Liberation of Caring: A Different Voice for Gilligan's 'Different' Voice". In *An Ethic of Care. Feminist and Interdisciplinary Perspectives*, M. J. Larrabee (ed.). New York: Routledge, 215–239.

Puka, B. (1994) "Interpretive Experiments: Probing the Care-Justice Dabate in Moral Development". In *Caring Voices and Women's Moral Frames. Gilligan's View*, B. Puka. (ed.). New York & London: Garland Publishing, 421–440.

Rakowski, E. (1993). *Equal Justice*. Oxford: Oxford University Press.

Rawls, J. (1971). *A Theory of Justice*. Oxford: Oxford University Press.

Reich, W. T. (1995). "History of the Notion of Care". In *Encyclopedia of Bioethic*. New York: Macmillan, 319–331.

Robinson, Fiona. 2006. "Ethical Globalization? States, Corporations and the Ethics of Care". In *Socializing Care: Feminist Ethics and Public Issues*. (eds.) Hamington, Maurice & Miller, Dorothy C. Lanham, Md.: Rowman & Littlefield Publishers.

Romain, D. (1992). "Care and Confusion". In *Exploration in Feminist Ethics*, B. E. Cole & S. Coultrap-McQuin. Indianapolis: Indiana University Press.

Ruddick, S. (1995). "Injustice in Families: Assault and Domination". In Held, V. (ed.) *Justice and Care. Essential Readings in Feminist Ethics*. Colorado: Westview Press, 203–223.

Ruyter, K. W. & Vetlesen, A. J. (red). (2004). *Omsorgens tvetydighet:egenart, historie og praksis.*Oslo: Gyldendal akademiske.

Røssaak E. (1998). *Det postmoderne og de intellektuelle. Essays og samtaler*. Oslo: Spartacus Forlag.

Sandberg, K. (1990). *Barnets beste. Om barnefordeling, rettspraksis og rettferdighet.* Oslo: Ad Notam Gyldendal.

Scheffler, S. (1982). *The Rejection of Consequentialism: A Philosophical Investigation of the Considerations Underlying Rival Moral Conceptions*. Oxford: Clarendon Press.

Scheffler, S. (ed.) (1991). *Consequentialism and its Critics*. Oxford: Oxford University Press.

Scheffler, S. (1994). *Families, Nations and Strangers*. The Lindley Lecture, University of Kansas, Department of Philosophy, University of Kansas.

Schneewind, J. B. (1990). "The Misfortunes of Virtue". In *Ethics*, vol. 101:42–63.

Schott, R. M. (2004). *Feministisk filosofi: en introduksjon*. København: Gyldendal.

Searle, J. R. (1998). "How to Derive 'Ought' from 'Is.' In *Ethics: The Big Questions*, J. P. Sterba (ed.). Malden, Mass.:Blackwell, 38–43.

Sedgwick, S. (1990). "Can Kant's Ethics Survive the Feminist Critique?" In *Pacific Philosophical Quarterly* 71:60–79.

Sevenhuijsen, Selma. 1998. *Citizenship and The Ethics of Care: Feminist Considerations on Justice, Morality and Politics*. London: Routledge.

Sherman, N. (1991). *The Fabric of Character. Aristotle's Theory of Virtue*. Oxford: Clarendon Press.

Sinnot-Armstrong, W. (1988). *Moral Dilemmas*. Oxford: Basil Blackwell.

Smith. A. (1790). *The Theory of Moral Sentiments*. In "Past Masters", British Philosophy Database: Reprinted from the 6th edition.

Sommers, C. H. (2000). "The War Against Boys". In *The Atlantic Monthly*, Digital Version. 285, No.5, May. [Cited 08.01.02]. Available from: http://www.theatlantic.com/issues/2000/05/sommers.htm≠bio

Stern, L. (1990). "Conceptions of Separation and Connection in Female Adolescents". In *Making Connections: The Relational Worlds of Adolescent Girls at Emma Willard School*, C. Gilligan, N. P. Lyons & T. J. Hanmer, Mass.: Harvard University Press, 73–87.

Svenneby, E. (1999) "Edith Stein (1891–1942)". In Rustad, L.M og Bondevik, H. (eds.) *Kjønnsperspektiver i filosofihistorien*. Oslo, Pax.

Svenneby, E. (1999a) *Også kvinner, Glaukon! Frihet og likestilling i et filosofihistorisk og kjønnspolitisk perspektiv.* Oslo: Emilia.

Thilly, F. W. (1958). *A History of Philosophy.* New York: Henry Holt and Company.

Thomas, L. (1991). "Morality and Psychological Development". In *A Companion to Ethics*, P. Singer (ed.). Oxford: Blackwell, 464–475.

Tong, R. (1993). *Feminine and Feminist Ethics.* Belmont, California, Wadsworth.

Tronto, J. C. (1993) *Moral boundaries: a political argument for an ethic of care.* New York: Routledge.

Tronto, J. C. 2004. "Marriage: Love or Care?" I Shanley, Mary Lyndon (ed.): *Just Marriage.* Oxford: Oxford University Press.

Urmson, J. O. (1958). "Saints and Heroes". In *Essay in Moral Philosophy*, A. I. Melden. Seattle: University of Washington Press, 198–216.

Ve, H. (1998). "Rationality and Identity in Norwegian Feminism". In *Is There a Nordic Feminism? Nordic Feminist Thought on Culture and Society*, D. Fehr, B. Rosenbeck & A. G. Jónasdóttir (eds.). London: UCL Press, 325–343.

Ve, H. (1999). *Rasjonalitet og identitet.* Oslo: Pax Forlag.

Vetlesen, A. J. (1994). *Perception, Empathy, and Judgment: An Inquiry into the Preconditions of Moral Performance.* Pensylvania: Pennsylvania State University Press.

Vetlesen, A. J. & Nortvedt, P. (1996). *Følelser og moral.* Oslo: AdNotam Gyldendal.

Vetlesen, A. J. (2002). "Etterord". In *Med en annen stemme: psykologisk teori og kvinners utvikling*, C. Gilligan. Oslo: Gyldendal Akademiske, 207–220.

Walker, L. J. (1993). "Sex Differences in the Development of Moral Reasoning: A Critical Review". In *An Ethic of Care. Feminist and Interdisciplinary Perspectives*, M. J. Larrabee (ed.). New York: Routledge, 157–176.

Walker, U. M. (1992). "Moral Understandings: Alternative "Epistemology" for Feminist Ethics". In *Exploration in Feminist Ethics. Theory and Practice*, B. E. Cole & S. Coultrap-McQuin. Indianapolis: Indiana University Press, 165–175.

Walker, U. M. (1998). *Moral Understandings: A Feminist Study in Ethics.* New York: Routledge.

Walker, U. M. (2002). "Morality in Practice: A Response to Claudia Card and Lorraine Code". In *Hypatia*, vol. 17, no.1:174–182.

Wiestad, E. (1995). "Kantian Pleasure and Feminine Theory: Dialogue with an Adrocentric Philosopher". In *Opuscula. Examen philosophicums småskriftserie* (Våren), 25–41.

Wiestad, E. (1999). "Skjønne og gode handlinger: To Kant-perspektiver på moralen". In *Kjønnsperspektiver i filosofihistorien*, L. M. Rustad & H. Bondevik (red.) Oslo: Pax forlag.

Williams, B. (1972). "The Amoralist". In Morality. Cambridge: Cambridge University Press.

Williams, B. (1991). "Consequentialism and Integrity". In Consequentialism and its Critics, S. Scheffler (ed.).Oxford: Oxford University Press, 20–50.

Wong, D. B. (1989). "Three Kinds of Incommensurability". In Relativism: Interpretations and Confrontation, M. Krausz (ed.). Notre Dame: University of Notre Dame Press, 140–158.

Woolf, Virginia. 1976. Et eget rom. Oslo, Gyldendal Norsk Forlag.

Wærness, K. 2001. "Maktens globalisering". I Makt og kjønn i offentlig omsorgsarbeid: Makt- og demokratiutredningen Oslo. Uniped: Rapport nr. 34.

Wærness. K. 2004. "Omsorgsetikk, omsorgsrasjonalitet og forskningens ansvar". I Omsorgens tvetydighte: Egenart, historie og praksis Knut W. Ruyter og Arne Johan Vetlesen (red). Oslo: Gyldendal Akademiske. s. 261–281.

Zimmerman, J. K. (1991) "Crossing the Desert Alone: An Etiological Model of Female Adolescent Suicidality". In Women, Girls & Psychotherapy: Reframing Resistance, C. Gilligan, A. G. Rogers & D. L. Tolman. New York: Haworth Press, 223–240.

~

Index

The Abortion Study, 12, 19, 144
abusive relationships, 34, 36, 129, 169n6
adolescence, 52, 15n3
adolescent, 4, 48n15, 52, 96 Gilligan's study of, 86, 89, 172
altruism, 13, 14, 77, 123–127, 129, 130, 136, 141, 175, 180
altruistic emotion (s), 60, 71, 129, 173–175
altruistic care, 16n15, 58, 99, 114, 123–127, 136, 137
Amy, 6, 90–93, 101, 102, 107, 108, 177, 181. *See also* Jake
Amy and Jake, 6, 7, 20, 68, 86, 90, 92, 93, 101
Annas, Julia, 73
anonymous other, 115, 117–122, 133, 137, 138
Aquinas, Thomas, 24, 137, 138, 148n1
Arendt, Hannah, 75
aristotelian, 49, 71, 127
Aristotle, 5, 24, 36, 39, 66, 76, 82, 112n24, 142, 144, 145, 149n8, 168n9; friendship, 128–132, 150n15

associative duties, 152, 156
asymmetric: care, 131, 132, 134; relationships, 78, 127, 130, 132, 135, 163, 164, 166, 179, 180, 182
attachment, 12, 13, 29, 33, 52, 93, 128, 168
Augustine, St., 24, 39, 48n9
autonomous, 11, 12, 39, 58, 65, 77–79, 102, 104, 111, 169, 175, 179; autonomous-man-model, 182
autonomy, 52, 78, 80, 97–102, 120, 121, 125, 127, 129, 173, 176; moral, 51, 57–59
Ayer, Alfred, 62

Baier, Annette, 22, 32, 53, 146–148, 158–160
balance, 14, 98, 99, 121, 122, 129–132, 146, 161, 175; egoism and altruism, 127, 136 ; care and justice, 104; self and other, 16n15, 36, 58, 60, 85, 120
Bartky, Lee Sandra, 53
Bartlett, Ann Elizabeth, 92, 106
Bauman, Zygmunt, 122n24, 178
Beauchamp, Tom L., 40, 88

Beauvoir, de Simone, 21–23, 25, 29n8, 35, 58, 75, 115, 141, 173
beneficial consequences, 33, 43, 119, 157, 159, 160
benevolence, 70, 88, 89, 126, 141, 175; principle of, 47, 73, 83, 153
beneficience, 41, 73, 74, 119; principle of, 41, 42
Benhabib, Seyla, 15n5, 25, 102, 105, 106, 115–117, 133n6
Bennett, Jonathan, 74, 75, 84n9
binary, 54, 89, 90, 93, 99, 100, 173, 175
biological determinism, 21, 22, 48n10
Blum, Lawrence, 51, 53, 59, 60, 71, 72, 157, 158
both/and, 54, 60, 100
bottom up model, 31, 32, 44
boys, 5,11, 12, 15, 18
Brison, Susan, 59
Butler, Judith, 21, 22

Camus, Albert, 106, 107
Card, Claudia, 22
care and justice, 8, 9, 20, 21, 51, 54, 57, 85, 86–97, 99–111, 172, 175
care perspective. See perspective of care
care-work, 123–126, 134, 141, 146, 177, 181
care-worker, 123–126
categorical imperative, 16, 61, 67, 82, 103, 173
charity, 115, 125, 137, 138, 148n1, 175, 180, 182
Chodorow, Nancy, 11, 12, 16n12, 17, 28n2
class, 11, 22, 32, 33, 102, 111, 143–146, 149n10
co-feeling, 51, 55–57, 59, 62–64, 78, 81, 82, 175
cognition, 51–55, 69
cognitive, 1, 52, 54, 61, 80, 81, 92, 104, 139, 142, 174
The College Student Study, 19

communication, 101, 102, 105, 108
communitarian, 26, 82, 179
compassion, 17, 45, 63, 69, 89, 97, 126, 135, 173, 176
concept of self, 6, 11, 58, 68, 74, 175
concrete other, 105, 107, 115, 117
conflicts, 7, 61, 84–98, 103,117, 126, 163
connected self, 11, 12, 174, 175. See also related self
connectedness, 1, 5, 33–35, 40, 44, 49, 59, 72, 77–79, 100, 101, 106, 180, 183
consequentialism, 96, 118, 120, 122, 132, 133, 137, 145
consequentialist, 115, 117–120
considered judgment, 76
contextual: knowledge, 91, 108, 118, 123, 149; sensitivity, 14, 54, 75, 80, 96, 99, 135, 139, 146, 179, 183
contract, 4, 79, 147, 152, 163, 164, 180, 182

decision-making, 19, 57, 58, 83, 93, 97, 101–103, 115, 116, 123, 144, 145, 163, 171
deontological, 4, 6, 16, 74, 76, 79, 120, 121, 159
deontology, 46, 66, 82, 120, 121, 137, 172
dependency, 11, 34, 35, 40, 45, 49, 52, 58, 59, 72, 77–81, 121, 131, 163–165, 179, 183
Derrida, Jacques, 59
Descartes, Rene, 21
detachment, 9, 12, 52, 93, 152, 154, 167
developmental psychology, 1, 3, 31, 43, 52
dialogue, 82, 101–106, 177
dichotomies, 14, 16n17, 54, 174
dichotomous, 10, 77, 81, 82, 86, 92, 93, 100, 146, 173–125

dichotomy, 45, 69, 99, 114, 164
Dickens, Charles, 118, 133n9
differential treatment, 66, 75, 82, 89,
   117–119, 135, 137, 141, 143, 162
dilemma(s), 3–7, 19, 32, 49, 68, 86–92,
   95–104, 107–109, 111, 161, 162,
   175, 177, 181, 183
discourse ethics, 102, 103, 105, 112
distant other (s), 113, 114, 121, 129, 162

early childhood, 10–12, 48, 52, 115,
   160
egoism, 13, 14, 57, 61, 67, 99, 124, 127,
   129, 130, 175
egoistic, 173, 174
either/or, 54, 60, 63, 100
emotion (s), 6, 51–63, 69–77, 125–127,
   139, 160, 164, 172–174
empathy, 11, 46, 56, 64, 78, 139, 159
epistemological, 47, 68, 77, 81, 82, 96,
   142, 183
epistemology, 55, 63, 80, 81, 183
Erikson, Erik, 11
essentialism, 22, 26, 29, 172
expanded principle of not hurting,
   41–45, 59, 74, 83, 99, 160

fact and value, 37, 39
fairness, 8, 9, 66, 79, 90, 91, 101, 111,
   129, 157, 178
feeling (s), 18, 51–64, 69–71, 73, 76,
   78, 161, 162, 165, 173. See also
   emotion(s); See also co-feeling.
family, 22, 33, 35, 116, 118, 120, 125,
   128, 146, 166, 167, 169, 172, 178
feminine ethic, 24
feminism, 23, 116, 172
feminist: ethicists, 125, 173; ethics,
   23–28, 88, 105, 171; philosophers,
   28,53, 116, 172; philosophy, 27, 45;
   theory, 22, 24, 115. See also
   philosophy
Ferguson, Adam, 53

flourishing, 33–37, 46, 47, 59, 72, 79, 85,
   89, 99, 108, 123, 129, 131, 166, 167,
   174, 178
Foucault, Michel, 59, 183
Freidman, Marilyn, 59
Freud, Sigmund, 5, 11, 18
friends, 71, 89, 114, 118, 128, 130, 137,
   140
friendship, 36, 45, 71, 49, 71, 106, 116,
   123, 127–131, 140, 166

gender differences, 6, 9, 18, 54, 144
generalized other, 195, 117, 122, 135, 138
Gilliganian ethics, 53, 77, 109n1, 138,
   139, 157, 161
girls, 1, 2, 5, 6, 11,12, 18, 23, 52, 84, 86,
   89, 144, 172, 182, 183
global, 26, 33, 46, 106, 114, 122, 146,
   168, 169, 171, 176, 178–183
Godwin, William, 120
Good Samaritan. See samaritan
Goodin, Robert, 49, 133n9, 153,
   161–169
Greer, Germaine, 35
Grimshaw, Jean, 59

Habermas, Jürgen, 4, 67, 105, 111
Hanmer, T.J., 101
Harding, Sandra, 84
Hare, R.M., 39, 40, 65
Hawthorne Effect, 20
health politics, 11
Heinz's dilemma, 6,7, 32,68, 6, 90–92,
   101, 107, 108, 177, 181–184
Held, Virginia, 24, 25, 46, 88, 179
Herman, Barbara, 70
Hobbes, Thomas, 105, 147
Hume, David, 24, 37, 45, 51, 53, 61, 62,
   139
Husserl, Edmund, 21

idiosyncratic: knowledge, 91, 105;
   information, 102, 116, 117, 133

imagination, 56, 57, 63, 64, 81, 104,
    111
impartial, 8, 45, 67–71, 76, 77, 118–120
impartialist, 119, 133, 156
impartiality, 45, 67–71, 76, 155, 157,
    160
incompatible, 58, 82, 103, 104, 110,
    115, 118, 131
independence, 10, 57, 58, 79, 101–102,
    182, 183
independency, 5, 11, 35, 40, 59, 77, 79,
    181
integrity, 78, 98, 100, 103, 127, 167
interactive universalism, 105
interdependence, 10, 33, 58, 168, 177
interdependent, 6, 8, 11, 39, 52, 101,
    102, 175
Irigaray, Luce, 23, 59
is/ought distinction, 38

Jagger, Allison, 102, 105
Jake, 7, 32, 90, 91. See also Amy
Jake and Amy. See Amy and Jake
justice perspective. See perspective of
    justice

Kant, Immanuel, 17, 18, 24, 35, 39, 40,
    45, 51, 67–79, 82, 83, 103, 139, 153,
    160, 161
kantian, 61, 69–71, 73, 76–78, 103, 153
Kierkegaard, Søren, 53
Kittay, Eva Feder, 79
Kohlberg, Lawrence, 1–7, 11, 15,17, 39,
    65, 67–69, 76–78, 82, 102–105, 110,
    111, 115, 116, 140, 142, 144, 172
Kollontay, Alexandria, 35
Korsgaard, Christine, 70
Kristeva, Julia, 59
Kuhse, Helga, 118, 155, 156

Lafollette, Hugh, 159, 160
level (s), 181; in Gilligan's theory, 13,
    14, 16n14, 36, 38, 47, 58, 73, 86,

97–100, 106, 123, 148; in Kohlberg's
    theory, 1–7, 77, 83n3, 104
Levinas, Emmanuel, 122, 138, 139, 163
liberal, 44, 46, 66, 79, 158, 159, 172,
    179
listening, 44, 48, 49, 80, 101–103, 105,
    172
loyalty conflicts, 89
Lyons, N.P., 101
Løgstrup, Knud E, 122, 139, 163

MacKinnon, Catharine, 24, 25
Martinsen, Kari, 14, 122, 123, 127,
    131–136, 139, 141, 142, 163, 167
Marx, Karl, 53
masculine, 6, 17, 19, 22, 26, 66
masculinity, 18, 19, 53
mature agent, 58, 78, 86, 99, 100, 124,
    157
mature care, 14–16, 36, 38, 41–43, 47,
    47–60, 70, 73, 80, 85, 86, 113–115,
    123–127, 129, 131, 132
men, 14, 19, 24, 27, 32, 34, 35, 37, 39,
    41, 44, 45
Merleau-Ponty, Maurice, 21
meta-ethical, 28, 33, 37–39, 159, 160,
    174, 182
Meyers, Diane T, 53, 83n3
Mill, J.S., 39, 105, 143
Moi, Toril, 21, 22
moods, 60, 71, 125. See also emotion(s);
    See also feeling(s)
Moore, G.E., 37
moral autonomy. See autonomy
moral development, 1–7, 12, 14, 15, 33,
    36, 38, 40, 43, 53, 58, 61, 65, 86, 96,
    97, 103, 123, 142, 159, 174
moral domain, 42, 65, 71, 77, 92, 94,
    113, 116, 157, 160, 168
moral maturity, 1, 5, 57, 58, 62, 78, 87,
    89, 98, 100, 142, 15, 76
moral musical chairs, 55, 67, 87. See also
    Kohlberg

moral ontology, 45, 63, 78
moral philosophy, 21, 27, 28, 31, 32,
 37–39, 44, 45, 53, 59, 65, 68, 77, 88,
 113, 168, 172–174, 183. *See also*
 philosophy
moral point of view, 62, 67–72, 83n3,
 103, 105, 157
moral reasoning, 2–9, 19, 43, 54, 65, 97,
 81, 92, 104, 105, 121, 125, 171–173
moral responsibility, 75, 81, 113, 115,
 121, 122, 138,139, 151, 157, 166,
 180, 183. *See also* responsibility
moral sentiment, 62, 74, 76, 139
motivation, 59–61, 67, 72, 115, 119,
 124–127, 129, 141, 147, 174, 178

Nagel, Thomas, 13, 32, 110n6, 120
natural caring, 60, 61, 73, 74
naturalism, 37–39, 44
naturalistic fallacy, 37, 39, 44
near (and dear), 113, 115, 117–121,
 126, 137, 161, 162, 165, 181, 183
negative duties, 41, 42, 122, 152–154,
 164
Nietzsche, Fredrich, 53
Noddings, Nel, 14, 26, 48, 51, 59–62,
 73, 74, 76, 132, 141, 154, 156, 163,
 165, 178, 182
nonviolence, 154
nursing, 119, 122, 125, 133n13, 142
Nussbaum, Martha, 53, 56

object-relation(s), 11, 160
Okin, Susan, 2, 8, 84,
O'Neill, Onora, 70, 155,
ontological, 10, 34, 77, 78
ontology, 34, 43, 45, 63, 78, 106, 114,
 140, 145, 166, 174, 177, 182, 183
oppression, 9, 10, 23, 24, 26, 35, 52, 58,
 106, 107, 135, 151

parochialism, 32, 155–157, 184
partial, 45, 53, 69, 71

paternalism, 129, 130, 177
paternalistic, 125, 129, 130, 132, 177
perspective of care, (care perspective),
 1, 8–13, 16, 20, 21, 25, 28, 31–33,
 40, 41, 43, 46, 47, 53–55, 81, 91,
 92–96, 98, 99, 103, 108, 140, 151,
 171, 172, 176
perspective of justice, (justice
 perspective), 7, 8, 9, 12, 20, 23, 54,
 69, 90, 93–95,108, 140, 151, 159,
 179
philosophy, 21, 27, 38, 44, 45, 53, 89,
 178. *See also* moral philosophy
Piaget, Jean, 3, 5, 11, 52
Plato, 15n4, 48n9, 105
Pogge, Thomas, 122, 169, 179
political, 18, 35, 80, 89, 125, 141,
 176–180, 182
Polyany, Michael, 52
positive duties, 152–154, 160
postmodern, 26, 59, 179
poverty, 114, 122, 128, 139, 182,
 184n1
pre-conventional stage, 3. *See also*
 Kohlberg
pre-oedipal, 11, 12
prescriptivism, 39
principle of beneficence. *See*
 beneficence
principle of benevolence. *See*
 benevolence
principle of equality, 82, 83
principle of non-maleficence, 41–44,
 72
private/public, 44, 45, 114, 116
private domain, 44, 45, 46, 94, 171,
 172
private sphere, 95, 114, 175, 178
problem-solving, 52, 81, 92, 100
professional care, 123–126
professional ethics, 123, 165–167
psychological development, 12, 19, 38,
 39, 87, 100

public domain, 44, 45, 176, 177. *See also* private domain
public sphere, 94, 146, 172, 177, 178. *See also* private sphere
Puka, Bill, 2, 67, 77, 92, 110n16, 111n17

rabbit-duck, 92, 93, 95, 117, 145
race, 11, 22, 102
rationality, 51, 91, 142,
Rawls, John, 44, 66, 67, 76, 79, 82, 105, 119, 120, 158, 179
reason, 2–9, 13, 37, 53, 54, 57, 58, 59, 62, 77, 78, 124, 127, 139, 172, 173–175; pure, 27, 69, 82; practical, 69, 78
reasoning. *See* moral reasoning
reconciliation, 54, 59, 60, 85–87, 92, 96, 103, 105–107, 174
reduction, 39, 103, 105, 107
reflective equilibrium, 76, 112n24
related other, 54, 58, 68, 71, 77, 98, 113–115, 117– 119, 121–124, 135, 137–140, 143, 145, 151, 155–163, 165, 167, 168, 175
relational ontology. *See* ontology
relativism, 26, 82, 95, 96, 142
responsibility, 58, 72, 81, 88, 96, 104, 109, 113, 115, 120–122, 138, 140, 142, 145, 151, 152, 160–166, 176, 178, 180, 182
rights, 4, 6, 44, 67, 77, 81, 83, 91, 98–100, 103, 106, 120, 126, 137, 177, 179–181
The Rights and Responsibility Study, 19
Robinson, Fiona, 46, 179–181
Romain, Diane, 34
Rosenthal Effect, 35, 40
Rousseau, Jean J., 24, 35
Ruddick, Sara, 59,
rules, 3–6, 8, 52, 57, 81, 92, 120, 121, 142, 156, 180

sacrifice, 26, 97, 124, 125, 129, 135, 137, 141. *See also* self-sacrifice
Salonstall, J.F., 101
Scheffler, Samuel, 120, 152, 154, 156, 157, 166
Sedgwick, Sally, 70
self-interest, 13, 67, 97, 99, 120, 134, 177, 179
selfish(ness), 14, 36, 38, 59, 60, 67, 73, 97, 106, 125, 129, 136, 141, 148, 175
selfless(ness), 13, 14, 38, 55, 57–59,73, 97,125, 126, 136, 148, 175
self-sacrifice, 13, 14, 36, 41, 45, 97, 99, 115, 123–126, 129, 132, 137, 139, 140, 141, 158. *See also* sacrifice
separation, 12, 18, 29n5, 52, 110n15, 169n10
sex/gender, 20, 22, 23
sexism, 23, 27
sexual difference, 5, 6, 21, 23
sexual harassment, 83
Shaftesbury, Lord, 53
Sigmund Freud, 5, 11, 18
Sinnot-Armstrong, Walter, 87, 90, 91, 98, 108
Smith, Adam, 53, 63n6
socializing care, 176–178
Sophia, 37, 48n11
special duties, 152, 163, 168, 169
spontaneous, 59, 60, 70, 76, 108, 139, 172; care, 123, 136, 137
stage theory. *See* levels
stages. *See* levels
strangers, 71, 113, 115–118, 134–137, 139, 156, 157, 161, 165
Summers, Christina, 15n1, 18, 19
supererogatory, 140, 148n2
symmetric care, 131,132, 134, 163
sympathy, 53, 61, 69, 75, 104, 108, 111n21, 126

teenagers. *See* adolescence
trust, 135, 146–148, 177
theoretical-juridical model, 32, 36
thick care, 56, 114–122, 128, 138–140,
    143, 145–148, 151, 153–157,
    159–162–165, 168, 175
thin care, 114, 116, 119, 132, 145, 157,
    158, 168, 175, 176
third way, 57, 82, 107–109
Tronto, Joan, 24, 25, 53, 176

universalizability, 6, 40, 45,65, 67, 69,
    72, 73, 104, 105, 111, 142
universalizable, 47, 72
utilitarian, 4, 84, 89
utilitarianism, 46, 66, 71, 74, 120, 121,
    159

veil of ignorance, 67, 82. *See also* Rawls
Vetlesen, Arne Johan, 53, 54, 63n4,
    63n5, 92,
vice, 125, 130
view from nowhere, 45, 114, 172,
virtue, 24, 45, 46, 59, 70, 76, 83, 137,
    147, 148, 158; of care, 125, 145, 146,
    149n13, 167; of friendship, 127–131;
    of justice, 67; intellectual, 80; moral,
    46, 80
vulnerability, 45, 56, 91, 102, 146,
    161–165, 167–168, 169n7, 174, 180
Vygotsky, Lev, 52

Walker, Mary Urban, 66
Williams, Bernard, 62, 66, 133n9
Woolf, Virginia, 35